Microsoft·Press

Microsoft® AGE of EMPIRES® II
The Age of Kings™

Mark H. Walker

PUBLISHED BY
Microsoft Press
A Division of Microsoft Corporation
One Microsoft Way
Redmond, Washington 98052-6399

Library of Congress Cataloging-in-Publication Data
Walker, Mark (Mark H.)
Microsoft Age of Empires II : The Age of Kings : Inside Moves / Mark H. Walker.
p. cm.
Includes index.
ISBN 0-7356-0513-0
1. Microsoft Age of empires. I. Title. II. Title: Microsoft Age of empires 2. III. Title: Microsoft Age of empires two. IV. Title: Age of kings.
GV1469.25.M572W24 1999
793.93'25369--dc21 99-42531
CIP

Printed and bound in the United States of America.

1 2 3 4 5 6 7 8 9 MLML 4 3 2 1 0 9

Distributed in Canada by Penguin Books Canada Limited.

A CIP catalogue record for this book is available from the British Library.

Microsoft Press books are available through booksellers and distributors worldwide. For further information about international editions, contact your local Microsoft Corporation office or contact Microsoft Press International directly at fax (425) 936-7329. Visit our Web site at mspress.microsoft.com.

Acquisitions Editors: Tamara D. Thorne, Christey Bahn
Project Editor: Sandra Haynes
Manuscript Editor: Kristen Weatherby
Technical Editor: Marc Young

Dedication

This book is dedicated to TJ's Grandfather, Grandmother, and the billions of people who wake up every day and smile, love, cherish, laugh, race cars, play baseball, dance, smile, strive, fail, try again, help someone, tell jokes, ride roller coasters (even when they are scared), visit friends (even when they are tired), and love their parents (even when it's hard). People are good. If you don't believe that, you need to wake up, smell the coffee, turn off the news (who needs it?), and go out and play.
It's OK. Really.

Mark H. Walker

Contents

Contents

Contents

Acknowledgments

Thanks to everyone at Microsoft Press, Microsoft, and Ensemble Studios. Special thanks to Christey Bahn for the job, Tamara Thorne for the coordination with the product group, Sandra Haynes for the project management, Marc Young for the technical editing, Kristen Weatherby for the manuscript editing, Dan Latimer for the layout, Rob Nance for the artwork, and Tim Znamenacek and the Age II product team for their technical advice and insight. Extra thanks to Janice, Denver, Jessica, Ayron, Mike, Mark, and Andy for their hard work.

Mark H. Walker

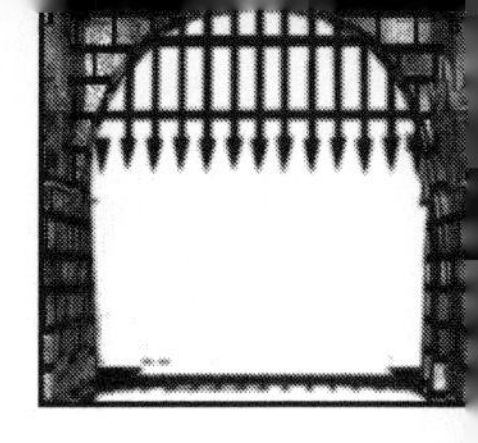

Life in the Age of Kings

A couple of years ago, Microsoft released the critically acclaimed *Age of Empires*. Intelligent, innovative, but most of all, fun, the game went on to sell over two million copies. *Age of Empires* naturally struck a chord with gamers, making it one of the most successful real-time strategy games of all time. Microsoft had uniquely intertwined the saga of ancient world history with a vast array of different units and buildings. Accordingly, each civilization exuded distinct characteristics—from various architectural designs to each empire's own textbook strategic strengths and weaknesses. The result was spectacular.

Empire builders could not get enough. Gamers came out in droves for the *Age of Empires* expansion pack, *The Rise of Rome*. Obviously, the kingdom of Caesar was a suitable addition to other classic empires, such as Egypt, Persia, and Greece. But history doesn't stop there, nor does humankind's love of conquests. Therefore, it's time to brace yourself for yet another momentous historical event, the much-anticipated sequel and heir to the *Age of Empires* throne: *Age of Empires II: The Age of Kings*. This time Rome has been squashed and the world is in the middle of a great and long cultural upheaval. It's up to you to build an empire out of this newly sprung chaos.

Setting the Stage: The Premise of Age of Kings

Microsoft Age of Empires II: The Age of Kings covers the Middle Ages (500-1500 AD). Much has changed since invaders crashed the Romans' toga party. Christianity and Islam have risen into prominence, and barbaric tribes are struggling for control of a fallen empire. The sequel takes us from there through a period of feudalism and chivalry to a world of castles, universities, and other seeds of pre-Renaissance study and technology (shown in Figure I-1). Like its predecessor, *Age of Empires II* covers four ages of cultural, military, and economic development. This time, though, there are no togas.

Figure I-1 *The king's Castle towers over his village.*

Figure I-2 *The Persian War Elephants return for another romp.*

What's New in Age of Kings

Expanding on the epic scope of the original, Microsoft has added a horde of new features to *Age of Empires II*. First, 12 new civilizations make their debut. These include a wide range of both Eastern and Western civilizations, from the Britons and Vikings to the Chinese and Turks. The only empire to return from the series' first installment is the Persian Empire (as shown in Figure I-2). For all 13 civilizations, new and unique forms of architecture and technology evolve from the Dark Age through the Imperial Age.

Microsoft has also added more realism to their sequel. The game now features an improved economic base and female peasants help their male counterparts gather resources. Each civilization also includes unique units, such as the Japanese Samurai and the Saracen Mameluke. Furthermore, gamers can participate in historical events like the Crusades and the Hundred Years' War. You even have the ability to guide Genghis Khan's great Mongolian army or ride with Joan of Arc into the Battle of Orleans (as shown in Figure I-3).

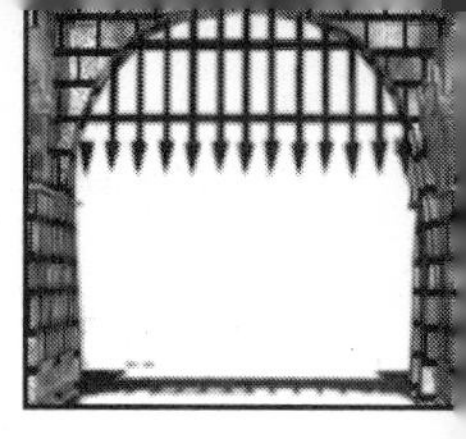

But the fun doesn't stop there. *Age of Kings* brings more insight and technology to the battlefield than the original *Age of Empires*. Among some of the practical improvements are customizable hotkeys and a new interface. For example, an interesting addition to the interface is the Idle Villager button, which readily reveals Villagers who have finished tasks and need reassignment. A Set Gather Point button allows you to direct units in production to a specific spot. Such features help the gamer save time and use resources more efficiently. Other exciting features include new maps and a campaign editor, which allows gamers to design their own missions.

Figure I-3 *Joan of Arc leads a caravan of supplies and troops to Orleans.*

Who This Book Is For

This strategy guide is designed for both hardcore and casual gamers. Novices will learn some new tactical maneuvers, while experienced players can add to their repertoire of advanced economic and military strategies. Learn which civilizations are best suited for each map and the strategies that work best against certain unique units. If you're looking for campaign walkthroughs, every mission is covered in detail. Perhaps you want to impress your long-distance buddies on the MSN Gaming Zone. Well, you've come to the right place. As your official strategy guide, everything you ever wanted to know about *Age of Empires II* is here.

How the Book Is Organized

Before starting, here's a brief summary of how the book is laid out. The first two sections deal with the basic components of the game. Part One is dedicated to the different *Age of Empires II* civilizations. Chapters 1 through 13 cover each civilization, along with their strengths and weaknesses. Included

Figure I-4 *This is one way to thin out a crowd.*

are introductory background information and detailed strategies for all four ages. Part Two (Chapters 14 and 15) discusses specific tactics and tips for all units and technologies, accompanied by several pages discussing general combat strategies. (See Figure I-4.)

The third section takes you through single-player and multiplayer scenarios. In short, Part Three (Chapters 16 through 18) is the "final word" on mounting successful conquests. Chapter 16 details campaign walk-throughs for four medieval heroes: Joan of Arc, Frederick Barbarossa, Genghis Khan, and Saladin. Chapter 17 provides in-depth strategies for Random Map, Regicide, and Death Match scenarios. Chapter 18, a guide for beating flesh-and-blood opponents, covers multiplayer empires.

The Last Word

Now that you understand how the book is organized, it's time to read it. So turn the page, and enter the Age of Kings.

Part I

Civilization-Specific Strategies and Backgrounds for *The Age of Kings*

Microsoft Age of Empires II: The Age of Kings picks up where the first game's expansion pack left off. Rome has fallen, marking the beginning of the Middle Ages. The result is a group of warring tribes and civilizations striving to build an empire of their own. Some of the more notable kingdoms include those of Genghis Khan's Mongols, Justinian's Byzantines, Sultan Osman's Turks, and the Chinese T'ang Dynasty. Overall, 13 different civilizations are featured:

- Britons
- Byzantines
- Celts
- Chinese
- Franks
- Goths
- Japanese
- Mongols
- Persians
- Saracens
- Teutons
- Turks
- Vikings

Each civilization uses similar weaponry; however, available technologies and units depend on each empire's unique history. For example, Persians have a strong cavalry of War Elephants, Vikings sail in Longboats, and the Japanese commission their famed Samurai warriors for battle. Other historical characteristics taken into account include China's large population and the Ottoman Empire's (Turks') heavy use of gunpowder units. To better acquaint you with these diverse features, the following chapters contain strategies and information for all 13 civilizations.

Chapter One

The Britons

Like much of Europe during the early Middle Ages, Britain was besieged with countless invasions and battles. In fact, Attila's Huns were driving through the continental mainland at about the same time that Germanic and Danish tribes migrated to the British Isles. By the ninth century, Britain was composed primarily of Angles, Saxons, Jutes, and Celts. The southern part of Britain, settled by Anglo-Saxons, came to be called "Angle Land" (or England), while the northern part of the island was named after the Scotti, a Celtic tribe inhabiting the area. A distinct culture with its roots in the north soon emerged in southern Britain—the Britons. As missionaries brought Christianity to many of these new inhabitants, others entertained themselves with stories of adventure and valor, primarily in the form of the Arthurian legends and Beowulf tales.

Britain itself offered plenty of sword-wielding adventures in the latter part of the Middle Ages. Vikings began attacking the coast in the ninth century. Nearly 200 years later, William the Conqueror and the Normans captured the crown of England. The Crusades followed some time later, with Britain's own Richard the Lionhearted demonstrating his bravery and strength in the Holy Land. The Hundred Years War then ensued in France. The advent of the English Longbow contributed to major victories in the early stages of the war. Inevitably, though, the Franks (with the inspiration of Joan of Arc) were able to beat back the Britons from France.

Maximizing Strengths and Minimizing Weaknesses

At first glance, it might seem that the Britons should be the offensive powerhouse of *Age of Empires II* (as shown in Figure 1-1). Such a notion is to be expected since England is the "land of kings," known worldwide for its royalty

Figure 1-1 *The Britons harbor a classic hack-and-fling army.*

and castles. No doubt, the Britons are a strong civilization; however, they lack some of the more decisive abilities and heavy hitting units offered to other civilizations. For instance, British Monks do not have the ability to convert buildings or other Monks. The English also lack gunpowder-based units; in fact, they are the only civilization that doesn't use the Cannon Galleon. The unavailability of certain Imperial Age siege weapons, too, can create problems late in a game.

Despite such deficiencies in technology, the Britons, needless to say, still field quite an army and have many other strengths. For starters, the English put lots of emphasis on using archery in combat. When the Britons are engaged in team play, their Archery Ranges train Archers faster than any other in the game. Furthermore, the Blacksmith upgrades and increased range advantages in the Castle and Imperial Ages encourage you to continue creating Crossbowmen and Arbalests. (See Figure 1-2.) Their superiority to rival Archers is obvious.

Tip: *Create more than one Archery Range on a map to use all of your archery advantages to the fullest. Use the foot Archers for defense and offense. Place them on hilltops to attack enemy Villagers parading by.*

Additionally, the Briton's special unit is the Longbowmen, who are foot archers with extended range—think Robin Hood on steroids. These guys were especially influential in battles against the Franks and Celts. Stationed behind a line of melee units, Longbowmen can do serious damage to an opponent's Knights and Cavaliers. I recommend using

them in all of your land attacks. Their range and attack strength are unmatched by any other medieval Archer.

Figure 1-2 *British Arbalests hone their skills at the Archery Range.*

The Infantry and Cavalry are no slouches either. They do not have special skills, but the plentitude of units and technologies available makes them formidable complements to the Longbowmen. They are especially great at injuring an opponent during the Castle Age—before any of your foes have a chance to use gunpowder technology.

How Changes Through the Ages Affect Tactics

The Britons are a strong civilization in any age, whether it's Dark or Imperial. They do, however, change form as they march through time. The following sections will show how to make the best of the metamorphosis and march them to victory.

Dark Age

At the beginning of the Dark Age, your Town Center should produce 10 to 20 Villagers, and the first ones should build Houses. Meanwhile, send your Scout Cavalry over the terrain to search for resources and the enemy's location. Keep an eye out for Sheep. For each herd of Sheep you find, send a Villager to that area to shepherd them back to the Town Center. Have your Villagers collect Wood as well.

Note: *Conserving resources is important, especially in the beginning of the Dark Age. British Shepherds work faster than those from other civilizations, so it's advantageous to keep Sheep for food. Besides, whereas Farms require a Mill and Wood to keep them running, resources such as Sheep and Deer only need a Villager to look after them.*

Send some Militia in to battle enemy Villagers. If you can, destroy their Barracks first. Disrupt the enemy's economic progress, military progress, or both as much as possible. However, don't recklessly send your units into a well-defended village to be massacred. After all, "discretion is the better part of valor," as Shakespeare once wrote. Build a Mill and some Farms to stockpile enough food for progression into the next Age. Upgrade to the next level as soon as possible.

Feudal Age

Build a Blacksmith and then an Archery Range while upgrading your Militia to Men-at-Arms. Send some Archers and Skirmishers to guard Gold and Stone sites near the enemy settlement. While they're protecting the sites, order several Villagers to mine the area. Construct some Watch Towers nearby if you encounter frequent opposition.

Invest in the upgrades provided at the Blacksmith. Next, send some Men-at-Arms and Archers to destroy enemy sites such as Mining Camps. If you are playing on a map with a significant amount of water, send Galleys to attack enemy Fishing Ships (as shown in Figure 1-3). Place Stone Walls around your

Figure 1-3 *Coordinate Galley attacks upon enemy Fishing Ships to cripple the opponent's economy in seafaring missions.*

island or location. These structures will buy you time if enemy Transport Ships try to establish a beachhead near your settlement. If you find enemy excursions a problem, just wait until the next Age when you can direct Heated Shots from your Towers at the ships.

Tip: *Construct a Market if you are playing on a map with limited resources. In those cases, buying and selling goods is the quickest way to advance to the next Age.*

Castle Age

This is the period of the game where things usually get interesting. Not only do you have more resources, but you also have a greater and more diverse number of units at your disposal. In general, these two advantages can require or lead to two things: research and battles. Don't skimp on either; otherwise, you'll be out of the picture by the time you enter the Imperial Age.

Continue with upgrades at the Mill and Blacksmith. Erect a University, Stable, and Siege Workshop. Produce a group of Light Cavalry and Crossbowmen. Next, build a Castle and Town Center near the enemy's settlement, using the Light Cavalry and Crossbowmen to defend the builders. Train some Longbowmen at the Castle. It's time to begin your attack on the enemy's village.

Set up a group of Longbowmen and Knights, place them in Flank Formation, and send them into the opponent's camp. Attacking the same target from different directions "sandwiches" enemy units, enabling you to effectively thin out enemy units. While enemy mobile units are distracted, concentrate Mangonel firepower upon your foe's Castle Age buildings, in particular the University.

Tip: *Build a University. Although Chemistry isn't much help at this point, Ballistics can improve the accuracy of your Archers—another step toward creating the perfect warrior. Unfortunately, many enemies can use Chemistry research to create gunpowder units in the next Age. That's why you need to destroy as many enemy Universities as possible.*

Imperial Age

The Britons are not as well equipped for battle in this Age as in previous ones. They lack the big guns—the Cannon Galleon and Bombard Cannon—that medieval enemies such as the Franks and Saracens have. The key to taking down civilizations with such technology is either to prevent them from building a University or to utilize your strength in numbers by executing lots of attacks with Cavaliers and Longbowmen (as shown in Figure 1-4).

Figure 1-4 *Continue to emphasize your strength in numbers in the final stages of a game.*

Fortunately for the Britons, other enemies—such as the Celts and Vikings—lack Bombard Cannons and Bombard Towers. The Vikings, however, do have a strong navy capable of building Cannon Galleons. When playing against the Vikings in seafaring battles, concentrate in the Feudal and Castle Ages on dominating the water with many War Galleys and Fire Ships. Because of their firing speed and maneuverability, Fire Ships are also the best British naval vessel for battling enemy Cannon Galleons. (See Figure 1-5.)

Figure 1-5 *Fire Ships are best suited for sinking Cannon Galleons.*

Unique Unit Tactics: Longbowman

Note: *The Longbowman's range is longer than that of the typical Archer, while still yielding about the same attack points as the Man-at-Arms.*

British Longbowmen are perhaps one of the best unique units in the game, as they can shoot farther than any archery unit in *Age of Empires II.* With that advantage, they can stand far away from the battle, sparing them from enemy Crossbowmen's fire. Using them in Flank Formation (as shown in Figure 1-6) allows gamers to surround enemy units with a barrage of firepower, improving accuracy and decreasing the damage done to the melee units.

Stationing a horde of Longbowmen on ledges or hills gives them free reign to attack unsuspecting enemies while awarding them the game's height bonus. Just make sure that you place them in Stand Ground mode so that they do not rush into a situation they cannot handle. For protection, use a couple of melee units to guard the Longbowmen. You can also garrison several Longbowmen in one of your Towers to increase the structure's attack points.

Figure 1-6 *Placing Longbowmen in Flank Formation has obvious advantages.*

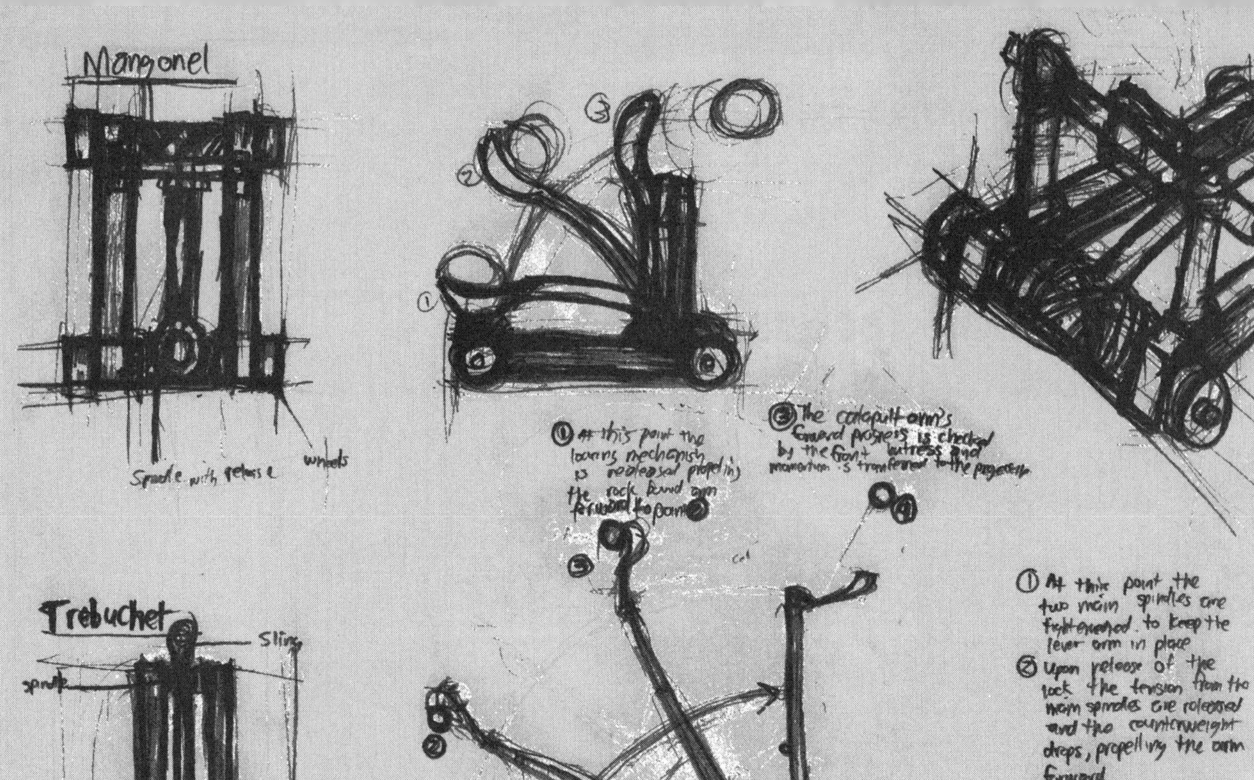
Mangonel
Spindle with release
wheels
① At this point the locking mechanism is released propelling the rock bound arm forward to point ③
③ The catapult arm's forward progress is checked by the front buttress and momentum is transferred to the projectile
Trebuchet
Sling
spindle
main counterweight
① At this point the two main spindles are tightened to keep the lever arm in place
② Upon release of the lock the tension from the main spindles are released and the counterweight drops, propelling the arm forward
③ At this point in the arms arc, the projectile is released from the sling and continues along the trebuchet arm's arc
④ The counterweight completes it's descent and the arm comes to rest as the projectile hurls on

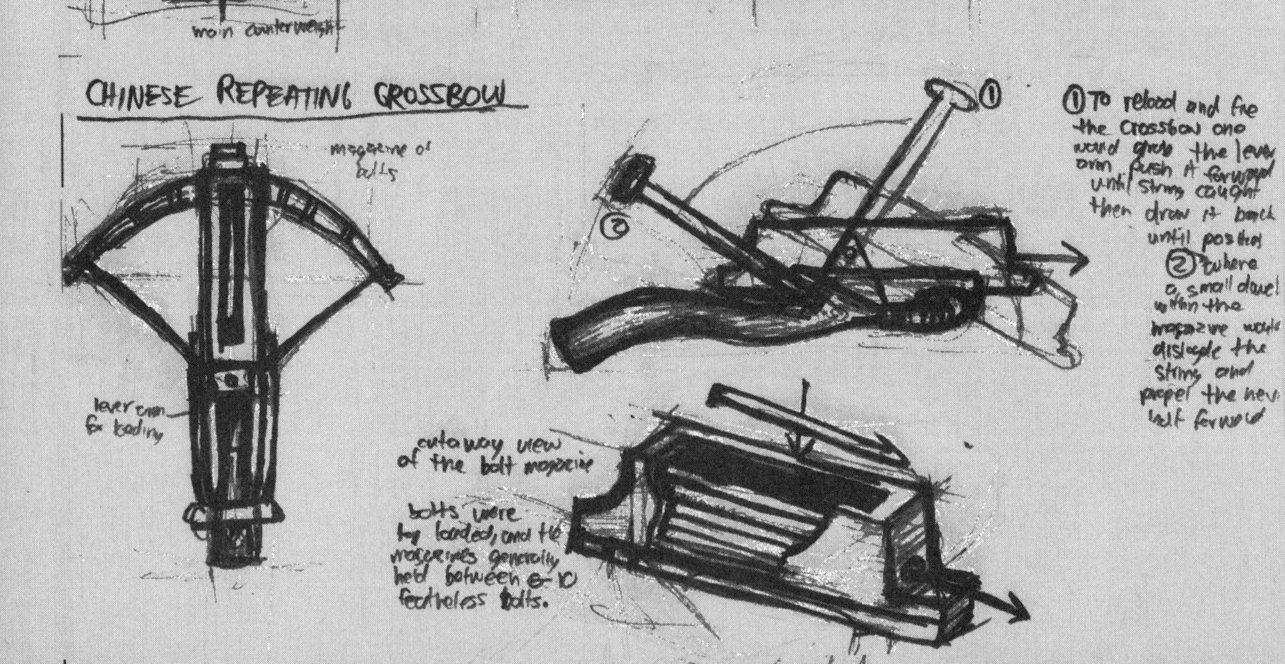
CHINESE REPEATING CROSSBOW
magazine of bolts
lever arm for loading
① To reload and fire the crossbow one would grab the lever arm push it forward until string caught then draw it back until position
② where a small dowel within the magazine would dislodge the string and propel the next bolt forward
cutaway view of the bolt magazine
bolts were top loaded, and the magazines generally held between 8-10 featherless bolts.

Chapter Two

The Byzantines

The Byzantine Empire was one of the richest and longest-standing empires of the Middle Ages. When the Roman Empire fell, the eastern section of that dominion, known as the Byzantine Empire, remained strong for nearly a thousand years. The Byzantine Empire was able to survive due to its strategic location on the Aegean and Black Seas. Maritime trade and accessibility to the East established the Byzantines as an intellectual and economic powerhouse. In addition, along with Ireland, Byzantine civilization played a pivotal role in the propagation and development of Christianity during the first few centuries following Rome's fall. Ample evidence testifies to this fact, including the famous Hagia Sophia, or Church of the Holy Wisdom, in present-day Istanbul.

The heart of the Byzantine Empire included the Balkan Peninsula and parts of Asia Minor. Although the kingdom's location was indeed essential to its success, it also led ultimately to the empire's destruction. In the beginning, enemies consisted primarily of Persians and numerous migrating Gothic tribes. However, with the rise of Islam, Byzantine later became a battlefield for holy wars with the Saracens and Turks. By the twelfth century, the once flourishing empire was experiencing a period of decline that ultimately led to its demise just three centuries later.

Maximizing Strengths and Minimizing Weaknesses

In *Microsoft Age of Empires II*, the Byzantines are a defensive civilization; however, the civilization harbors numerous advantages that are beneficial for offensive tacticians. First, the Byzantines have one of the best navies of all the civilizations offered in *Age of Empires II*. Unlike other maritime powerhouses such as the Vikings, Japanese, and Chinese, the Byzantines have access to all

Tip: *The Byzantine Fire Ship is inferior to enemy vessels like the Galleon and War Galley; however, it can be effective in battle with these ships if it is used properly. Here's how to win with this ship: Group about four Fire Ships together and attack a single War Galley or Galleon. Once the enemy ship is surrounded, it is vulnerable to hits from all sides. Also keep in mind that the Fire Ship has a more rapid rate of fire and moves faster than most Galleons. This combination makes it a dangerous adversary in close combat.*

seafaring technology. Furthermore, their Fire Ships have more attack points than most other civilizations' Fire Ships. (See Figure 2-1.) And the Fire Ships in *Age of Empires II* are historically accurate as well; the Byzantines actually used a fire spray in naval battles against the Arabs.

When you are playing as the Byzantines, you cannot research Masonry and Architecture during the game. This may at first appear to be a weakness, but it's not. The Byzantines already have sturdy walls and structures; their buildings begin with more hit points than equivalent structures in any other civilization. With this advantage, you can concentrate on other technologies such as those involving gathering and production. You'll need these technologies to stay competitive in the early stages of battle, especially when you are fighting against civilizations that have advantages collecting resources, such as the

Figure 2-1 *A group of Fast Fire Ships can easily take down an enemy Galleon.*

Teutons, Franks, and Vikings. Because the Byzantine buildings are stout, they don't need to rely on Watch Towers to the extent that other civilizations do.

Of all 13 civilizations, the Byzantines offer access to the most military units. If the civilization has a weakness, it involves a lack of significant Imperial Age siege technology. For instance, Byzantines cannot build Heavy Scorpions or Siege Onagers. They also cannot research Siege Engineers at the University, something that prevents their siege weaponry from attaining attack point upgrades. With such technological dearth, the Byzantines must rely on the Trebuchet more than any other civilization. A strong navy of Cannon Galleons and Fast Fire Ships is also important for combating this deficiency of long-range, building-busting firepower in seafaring scenarios.

Tip: *The Byzantines, having no early gathering and production advantages, are relatively inefficient when it comes to collecting resources. There are three strategies you can use to counter this disadvantage. First, always build camps near resources; this will cut down on the travel time of your Villagers. Research early economic technologies, such as the Wheelbarrow and Horse Collar, and build a Market for trade. (See Figure 2-2.)*

Figure 2-2 *A Market is often an important structure for obtaining resources in the early stages of Byzantine play.*

How Changes Through the Ages Affect Tactics

As weaponry evolved, tactics changed. Simple bands of Militia and Archers could raze Feudal Age villages, but it took Cannons, Trebuchets, and thousands of warriors to level the Castles of later eras. The following section walks through the Ages and discusses the changing tactics that will aid in your search for victory.

Dark Age

Figure 2-3 *Use the Scout Cavalry to quickly find resources.*

Use your Scout Cavalry not only to scout the map for enemies but also to find resources. (See Figure 2-3.) Once you have located resources, send your Villagers to those sites. Place Mills in areas with high amounts of Sheep, Deer, and Forage Bushes. Don't be afraid to spread yourself out. Remember: Byzantine structures are less prone to destruction due to their higher level of hit points. If you are on a river or sea, build a Dock, and then construct some Fishing Ships to scour the water for food. You must take advantage of all available resources early in the game to get the Byzantines off on the

> **Tip:** *Build a Barracks, and then create several units of Militia. Use these soldiers to protect any known resources. Although you might lack efficient methods of hunting and farming, cutting off your enemies' resources is a great way to even things out.*

right foot. Remember to escort the Villagers with Militia. Wolves generally wait 30 to 40 tiles from most settlements, and they can be pretty aggressive toward unguarded Villagers.

Feudal Age

You still have to focus on resources at this stage of the game—but not entirely. Erect an Archery Range as one of your first Feudal Age buildings. Skirmishers, a product of the Archery Range, cost less than they do in other civilizations. So produce several, and direct them to assault the enemy. Target Villagers and economic sites such as Markets, Mining Camps, and Town Centers. You will not likely defeat the enemy at this time, but you can disrupt their production level. Meanwhile, build a Market if you find yourself running low on resources. Don't forget to research Wheelbarrow, Loom, and Horse Collar technologies at the Mill and Town Center.

Note: *Although Byzantine buildings are sturdy, some of their classic opponents still have ways of destroying them. In Team play, Saracen foot Archers have an additional attack point when they attack buildings. Saracen Cavalry Archers are also more damaging when they battle buildings, regardless of who owns those buildings—allies or enemies.*

Castle Age

Two Byzantine Castle Age units—the Pikeman and the Camel—require fewer resources for production than they do when other civilizations build them. You should direct hordes of Pikeman and Camel units to take out chief enemy structures—in particular, those buildings with unparalleled strengths. For example, Saracen and Briton Archers can be extremely damaging against the Byzantines, so you'll want to besiege their Archery Ranges to prevent production of new Archers. Persian Docks work faster than those in other civilizations, so destroying them will keep the Persian navy from becoming too powerful. But Byzantine

Note: *Camels are slow Cavalry units. When using them in battle, be sure to research Husbandry at the Stable. This increases their speed. In addition, keeping Byzantine Monks—which have excellent healing powers—nearby restores wounded units, allowing them to enter battle again quickly.*

Pikemen and Camels aren't just effective against buildings; they work well together against most enemy Knights.

> **Note:** *Cataphracts provide a hefty advantage in combat. In some scenarios, you can even get by without a Stable!*

In the Castle Age, the Byzantines have access to their special unit, the Cataphract. Think of these cavalry units as an intermediate figure between the Knight and the Cavalier. They are fairly strong, providing more hit and attack points than the Mameluke (as shown in Figure 2-4), the unique figure of the Byzantines' arch-nemesis, the Saracens. Combine Cataphracts with your Pikemen, Camels, and Onagers, and then watch some enemy structures fall. Bring a slew of Monks behind your troops for healing purposes. Just make sure, though, that you place some Guard Towers near your encampments; otherwise, the same fate you are imposing upon your enemies might befall you.

Figure 2-4 *Cataphracts are ideal opponents when you are fighting Mamelukes.*

Imperial Age

If the Byzantines have one military weakness, it's the shortage of siege weapons offered in the Imperial Age. Enemies like the Teutons, who have strong towers, and the Turks, who have fast Bombard Towers, only exacerbate the problem. What can the Byzantines do to thwart such attacks and conquer their foes?

First, destroy key enemy structures such as Universities and Siege Workshops. These are the prime providers of ballistic warfare. Next, create several

Trebuchets. (See Figure 2-5.) These ballistic units have extremely long ranges, making them ideal for crumbling towers and siege weapons. Distracting your opponent with attacking melee units is a great way to buy time for obliterating more of their buildings, such as Archery Ranges and Stables.

Tip: *Trebuchets come in handy for both offensive and defensive strategies. For instance, place them just inside your walls to prevent enemy forces from setting up siege equipment. Also, bombard enemy settlements from afar, leaving Cataphracts and Cavaliers to guard the Trebuchets.*

In seafaring battles, use Fire Ships and Galleons to put a strain on enemy islands. Send Fire Ships to attack enemy ships, while your Cannon Galleons shell the enemy Docks. Next, concentrate your fire on their military buildings and economic structures. To produce ships faster, remember to research the Shipwright technology. This is an absolute necessity when fighting an efficient shipbuilding civilization such as the Vikings.

Figure 2-5 *The Trebuchet is one siege weapon from which the Byzantines are not barred access.*

Unique Unit Tactics: Cataphract

Although weaker than most Imperial Age melee Cavalry units, Cataphracts are still effective armored combat figures. Naturally, they shine in the Castle Age—before the appearance of heavy hitters like the Paladin and Heavy Camel. They are also superior to a lot of other *Age of Empires II* unique units. In conjunction

Tip: *You need to put your Cataphracts to good use during the Castle Age. Just make sure that your enemy is not an Age ahead of you. Otherwise, heavier units may slaughter your troops.*

with Pikemen, Crossbowmen, or both, Cataphracts are successful in taking out Longbowmen (Britons), Throwing Axemen (Franks), and Chu Ko Nus (Chinese). They also have far more hit points than unique enemy units such as the Janissary (Turks) and Mameluke (Saracen)—an advantage in reenactments of the European's crusades against the Muslims.

Use the Cataphract in raids upon enemy structures. While the Pikemen, Skirmishers, and Camels distract your opponent's forces, sneak the Cataphracts in to eradicate Mills, Monasteries, Blacksmiths, and other enemy structures. Cataphracts also come in handy for guarding structures and resources. For example, you can place them near Gold and Stone Mines to restrict enemy Villagers from gathering resources. Whatever you do, though, these units should play a large part in your military strategy. Use them wisely.

Chapter Three

The Celts

Celtic tribes roamed Northern Europe for centuries before they were driven back to what is known today as Ireland, Scotland, and Wales. Numerous megalithic rock structures, most notably Stonehenge, were built by these ancient peoples. One of the earliest accounts we have of the Celts comes from Julius Caesar, who battled these tribes during the Romans' conquest of Gaul (present-day France). Understandably, interest in the Celts has ascended from Roman times into modern-day pop culture. Today, discussions range from Celtic nature worship and Druidic practices to the great heroes of the Celtic Scotti tribe, William "Braveheart" Wallace and Robert the Bruce.

Despite the aura of mystery commonly associated with the Celts, they were in fact one of the most influential cultures in Europe during the early Middle Ages. Much like Constantinople and Rome, Irish settlements—with their numerous monasteries—became popular centers for learning. During the few centuries when most of Europe was embroiled in Gothic invasions and political instability, Ireland and Scotland remained free from turmoil. But this peace was not permanent. Vikings raided their coasts during the ninth century. Two centuries later, the Scotti battled the Britons for control of Scotland—an event immortalized recently in an Oscar-winning film.

Maximizing Strengths and Minimizing Weaknesses

The Celts are best played by *Microsoft Age of Empires II* veterans. The Celts require efficiency and aggressive attacks. Because the Celts lack most of the usual Imperial Age technology, playing with this tribe demands early and con-

Figure 3-1 *Celtic Militia units attack a British settlement.*

stant sieges upon the enemy. The only way to win without an ally is to pound away at your opponent and prevent him from reaching the final Age (as shown in Figure 3-1).

Victories are rare when your opponent has graduated to the Imperial Age, because of the difficulties that can arise in this later stage. Although the Celts have rapid-firing siege equipment, they lack gunpowder-based land units such as the Bombard Tower, Bombard Cannon, and Hand Cannoneer. To compound matters, Blacksmiths cannot research Imperial Age upgrades that affect Celtic archery and cavalry units. Production technology such as the Two-Man Saw and Crop Rotation are absent in this period as well. With so many deficiencies, it's almost impossible to defeat the enemy once they've progressed to the Imperial Age and their level of technology surpasses your own.

> **Note:** *Celtic Monks do not have access to upgrades common in both the Castle and Imperial Ages. For example, Celtic Monks lack—among other things—the ability to research Atonement, used to convert enemy Monks, and Block Printing, used to increase the conversion range.*

The strengths of the Celts are few but can still be adequate, especially in the first two Ages. Celtic infantry units are quicker than those in other civilizations—even after opponents have researched Squires in the Castle Age! Another advantage lies in the Celts' siege equipment; it fires faster than units used by other civilizations. If you are to win, you must use these two advantages as early and often as possible.

Celtic infantry units offer many different strategies for the user. For starters, infantry units are instrumental in baiting enemy figures into combat. Because they are so quick, they can lead enemy Archers and foot soldiers into ambushes without suffering serious injuries themselves. They can also act as bait to lure the enemy out of a fortress while you direct other units to rush in and destroy their buildings. These nimble-footed infantry are useful in their own attacks upon enemy buildings as well. Their speed enables them to pull out of dangerous situations, leaving the enemy far behind. Although it may seem trite, harassing your opponent can disturb them enough to deter their progress.

> **Tip:** *If you reach the Imperial Age and haven't won yet, don't despair. Upgrade your siege weapons. To increase their range and the degree of damage they inflict, research Siege Engineers at the University. This adds +1 (tile) to your siege weapons' range and increases the damage they inflict by 20 percent.*

By the Castle Age, you should bring in the rapid-firing siege weapons for the coup de grace. Set them up on hills (where they receive an attack bonus) near enemy settlements, and then rain destruction upon your opponent's units and buildings. Place Knights around the Mangonels (as shown in Figure 3-2), using the Stand Ground and Guard buttons. Employ Woad Raiders to intercept any Cavalry or foot Archers that approach the siege equipment. The goal is to sack the opponent before they can acquire any gunpowder units—otherwise your tribe might just go up in smoke.

Figure 3-2 *This is an effective formation for your siege weapons.*

How Changes Through the Ages Affect Tactics

The Celts are a powerful civilization, but even the most fearsome warriors require leaders. On the other hand, leadership is based on knowledge; you can't lead what you don't understand. So read on, Celtic leader, and glean the knowledge needed to lead your tribesmen (and women) to victory.

Dark Age

At the beginning of the Dark Age, set up a Barracks while your Villagers gather resources such as Forage Bushes, Sheep, and Deer (shown in Figure 3-3). Create several units of Militia, sending them out to harass the enemy village. Next attack the Town Center and Barracks. Taking down the Town Center severely handicaps the opponent economically, while destroying the Barracks prevents the enemy from counterattacking. It is important that you continue to harass the enemy throughout the Dark Age—never stop.

If you are on a map with large bodies of water (for example the Archipelago, Baltic, or Islands maps), set up a Dock and some Fishing Ships. The Celts have a good navy, lacking only the Fast Fire Ship and Elite Cannon Galleon. Creating a Dock will begin to put the civilization in position to use this advantage. This is especially important when you are fighting against the Britons, the only civilization that lacks the capacity to build the Cannon Galleon.

Figure 3-3 *Send Shepherds to gather Sheep before wasting Wood for planting Farms.*

Feudal Age

The Celts are not one of the most efficient groups offered in the game; they need lots of technology and research to keep up with opponents. The Wheelbarrow and Horse Collar are necessities, and investing in Mining Camp technology such as Gold Mining and Stone Mining are good ideas, too, especially in maps with few resources. Nevertheless, often the Celts have to rely on the Market for economic support. If you haven't used the Market much before now, this civilization will soon make you an expert on trading.

Construct a Blacksmith, investing in Forging and Scale Mail Armor for your infantry. Fletching improves tower range and attack points. Upgrade the Militia into Men-at-Arms and research Tracking for improved line of sight. Meanwhile, order some of your Villagers to erect Watch Towers near the enemy settlement. With towers and infantry invasions, your opponent should have a difficult time erecting structures and collecting resources—which is exactly what you want.

> **Tip:** *Markets are valuable structures and the great* Age of Empires II *economic equalizer. For example, civilizations poor in Stone, but rich in Wood (such as the Celts), might trade their bulging wagons of Wood for Gold and subsequently buy all the Stone they need. In addition, after erecting a Market, you can send the Market's Trade Cart to trade with friendlies, thus pumping up your Gold income.*

Castle Age

In the Castle Age, you should continue your assaults upon enemy settlements and attempt to obliterate them. Upgrade your infantry into Long Swordsmen and Pikemen, shown in Figure 3-4. Build a University and research the Guard Tower and Murder Holes to improve your towers' efficiency. Place a Castle, Stable, and Siege Workshop near the towers, and prepare some Woad Raiders, Knights, and Mangonels for an all-out attack upon the

> **Tip:** *Although Celtic Monks are weak, they are effective healers. To increase the number of times you can attack your foe, pull your wounded infantry out of battle every now and then to be resuscitated by your Monks. This is much quicker and easier than producing new troops after your old troops die. Don't forget, Monks also work well in the center of a Box formation, where they can heal themselves and the soldiers surrounding them at the same time.*

Figure 3-4 *Upgrade your infantry for more assaults against the enemy.*

enemy. If you have the time, create some Archers and Crossbowmen and add them to the battle as well.

Imperial Age

Relatively speaking, the Celts are at their weakest during this time of the game—unless they happen to be in control of the map and an Age or two ahead of their enemy. Continue assaulting the enemy, and use the Castle as a strategic production unit to create Trebuchets and Elite Woad Raiders. Before you do any of this, though, research Conscription; this will increase production speed at the Barracks, Stable, Archery Range, and Castle—making your attacks almost nonstop.

Note: *As in the previous Ages, a constant barrage of force is needed to defeat the enemy.*

In seafaring missions, research Chemistry at the University and build Cannon Galleons for island sieges. Use them to obliterate Castles or other Imperial Age structures. Don't forget to research Dry Dock and Shipwright technology, especially when you are up against naval powerhouses such as the Vikings, Byzantines, and Japanese. Continue to haul infantry in Transport Ships for use in infiltrating enemy settlements. If you employ these strategies, before you know it, the white flag will be waving.

Unique Unit Tactics: Woad Raider

Like other Celtic infantry, the Woad Raider is fast. The Woad Raider is basically a quick melee unit with a sturdy attack force. He combines speed, with a greater number of attack and hit points than typical *Age of Empires II* infantry. In this way, the Woad Raider is very similar to the Japanese Samurai, a powerful melee foot soldier that can pounce on his opponent like a lunging tiger. Consequently, the Woad Raider is most effective when used in combination with Long Swordsmen and Pikemen (see Figure 3-5). Such swarming attacks are essential for Celtic victory.

Figure 3-5 *A horde of Woad Raiders and other Castle Age infantry swarm into enemy territory.*

The Elite Woad Raider is an even more terrifying killing machine. He carries over 60 percent more attack points than are afforded the typical Woad Raider. These are numbers comparable to powerful cavalry units such as the Paladin and Cavalier. Elite Woad Raiders are excellent in attacks against all types of units. Because of their speed, they can

> **Note:** *The Woad Raiders' rapid attack speed doesn't allow enemy Archers many shots at them. Even when backing up, Archers have little time to aim and shoot before being run down by the nimble Woad Raiders.*

handle special units like the Briton Longbowmen and the French Throwing Axemen with ease (see Figure 3-6). Furthermore, because of lower resource requirements, a horde of Woad Raiders is much more expendable in battle against a Saracen Mameluke than a group of cavalry units is—and the Woad Raiders are just as effective. They really are one of the toughest and most valuable of all the special units.

Figure 3-6 *These Elite Woad Raiders would have made "Braveheart" proud.*

Chapter Four

THE CHINESE

Chinese civilization developed along the Yellow River thousands of years ago. During this period, the area quickly blossomed into one of the wealthiest and most influential parts of Asia. China continued to play a dominant role in the Far East for much of the Middle Ages. Despite periods of political disarray, the Chinese remained strong enough to thwart most enemy attacks. The exception came in the thirteenth century when Kubla Khan and the Mongols successfully annexed China to their empire. A century later, though, Chinese rebels were able to overthrow Mongol rule, establishing the Ming Dynasty.

Throughout much of the medieval period, China was a fertile ground for both intellectual and mercantile trade. Inhabitants practiced a variety of religions, such as Buddhism, Taoism, and Confucianism. Some of the most notable Chinese inventions of the Middle Ages included fireworks, the compass, and movable type printing. The Chinese also discovered gunpowder in the eleventh century—but rarely used it for weaponry. Two centuries later, Marco Polo traveled to China. His tales about the Orient fascinated Europeans, opening the portal for a number of trade routes between the East and West.

Maximizing Strengths and Minimizing Weaknesses

In the fourth century BCE, Sun Tzu wrote *The Art of War,* the oldest existing military strategy guide. Fortunately, you won't need to rely on Tzu's manual to command the Chinese in *Microsoft Age of Empires II*. They are one of the strongest and best all-around kingdoms in the game, having more access to technologies and units than most other civilizations do. In fact, if the Chinese have a true weakness, it's their lack of high-powered Imperial Age units such as the

Hand Cannoneer, Bombard Cannon, and Paladin. But such deficiencies are far from being a problem, especially when you consider all of the kingdom's strengths.

The Chinese begin the game with three more Villagers than other civilizations—a game feature representative of China's huge population in the Middle Ages. Use this advantage to find and gather as many resources as possible. If the map you're on offers little food, there's no need to panic. Chinese Farms produce more food than farms in other civilizations. Construct a Mill, and then sow a few fields as shown in Figure 4-1. Your food supply will quickly soar.

Figure 4-1 *Chinese Farms provide more food than the average civilization does.*

When you reach the Feudal Age, direct several attacks on the opponent. Although this is not always necessary, it's not a bad idea to wear down the foe. This also ensures that the enemy civilization doesn't gain the advantage in siege and melee units in the Imperial Age. Of course, cheaper technology costs for the Chinese easily prevent this from happening. Though it is nothing special

> **Tip:** *To increase your Farm's production, research the Horse Collar and Wheelbarrow in the Feudal Age and the Heavy Plow and Hand Cart in the Castle Age.*

in relation to other civilizations, the navy is also an effective means for keeping the enemy—excuse the pun—at bay. Chinese research speeds are quickened because they have lower technology costs than most other civilizations. This feature along with the availability of almost all Infantry, Cavalry, and Archery units—as well as a formidable navy—should create a force great enough for even the most amateur gamer to match "fists" with his or her enemy.

If they are used properly, Chinese forces should be able to defeat most opponents before the opponent can advance very far into the Imperial Age. The Chinese special unit, the Chu Ko Nu, carries rapid-fire crossbows that can pick apart an opponent's infantry in no time. Demolition Ships, shown in Figure 4-2, are also much sturdier than other civilizations' counterparts, so it's highly unlikely that the enemy will destroy them before they hit their target. The Chu Ko Nu and Demolition Ships complement a variety of other Chinese units and strategies. If you add all this to an aggressive attack plan in the Castle Age, the Chinese should be well on their way to victory.

Figure 4-2 *Demolition Ships are sturdier than other civilizations' counterparts, allowing for more hits.*

How Changes Through the Ages Affect Tactics

The Chinese are quite a force to be reckoned with. For instance, Chinese Farms produce more food and their technological upgrades cost less than they do for other civilizations. Furthermore, the Chinese have one of the best all-around armies and navies. Their primary weakness lies in a lack of land-based gunpowder and siege units. Nevertheless, the Chinese usually hold their own against most opponents.

Dark Age

Figure 4-3 *The Chinese begin with three additional Villagers.*

As mentioned earlier, the Chinese begin with three additional Villagers in the Dark Age (as shown in Figure 4-3); however, they have a lower stockpile of food than other civilizations at this time. Luckily, the extra Villagers come in handy for gathering more food. Since the Chinese have Farming enhancements, search the map for non-farm-related food supplies. This is advantageous because gathering "free" food is still quicker

> **Note:** *A Farm battle occurs when both sides use their Farms to try to produce more food resources than their opponent. To win a battle like this, you usually have to play as either the Franks or the Chinese. These two civilizations have the efficiency and technology to excel at such tasks.*

and more cost effective than an efficient Farm. Second, using as many Sheep, Deer, and Boars as you can forces the enemy into a Farm battle—one that you're almost guaranteed to win.

Feudal Age

This Age inaugurates your technology advantages. For the Chinese, technologies cost 10 percent less during this stage of the game. For each Age that follows the Feudal Age, technologies cost 5 percent less than they did in the previous period. Because you have such great technology advantages, you should research as many enhancements as you can at the Blacksmith, Mill, and Town Center. Produce some Men-at-Arms and Archers, and place them near the enemy encampment. Make sure they are in Stand Ground mode, so they can prevent the expansion of the enemy's dominion. You also want to construct some Watch Towers; these are helpful in preventing enemy expansion as well. Continue creating Farms for food. If you haven't done so already, collect some Gold and Stone, and build a Market for trade. These will come in handy if you find that your colony is lacking the resources needed to upgrade to the next Age.

> **Tip:** *Remember that Japanese fishing techniques are quite advanced. If you are playing against that civilization, send Galleys out to destroy their Docks, Fishing Ships, and Fish Traps. In the Castle Age, use your Demolition Ships for this purpose as well.*

Castle Age

During this Age, you get the chance to use some more Chinese strengths—Monk powers and the Chu Ko Nu. Along with the Byzantines, Japanese, Saracens, and Teutons, the Chinese have some of the most able Monks in the business. However, with the low technology costs, researching all of the

Figure 4-4 *With Monks in this formation, healing units or converting enemies is much easier.*

available powers is less of a hassle than it can be in other civilizations. A favorite trick of mine involves using the Monks with the Chu Ko Nu and Cavalry in a Box Formation. (See Figure 4-4.) With the Monks sandwiched in the middle, they are free to convert enemy Monks and heal wounded soldiers, as they aren't within striking distance of enemy Infantry and Cavalry. From a Box Formation, I especially like to use the Monk's Redemption feature to convert enemy buildings into my camp.

Imperial Age

Tip: *Because the Chinese have advantages both in the firepower of the Chu Ko Nu and in strong Monks, the Castle Age is ideal for winning a Standard game by Relics. After all, the additional Monk powers make the clerics' travels safer. In addition, use the Chu Ko Nu in combination with your Cavalry and siege weapons for defense.*

The Chinese lack a number of gunpowder units and siege technologies that other civilizations can gain through research. To keep the enemy in check, do not let them build a University. If they already have, send troops in to destroy it. Consequently, because they can no longer

research Chemistry and Siege Engineers, the opponents are restricted to much of the same ballistic weaponry offered to the Chinese. Meanwhile, research Conscription at the Castle so that the Chinese can produce hordes of Elite Chu Ko Nu and Trebuchets. Combine these units with Cavaliers and Two-Handed Swordsmen. Swarm into the enemy settlement using the Flank Formation. The speed and number of your attacks will devastate the enemy.

Note: *The Chinese, like the Mongols and the Japanese, lack the ability to train Paladins. Therefore, the two prime enemies of the Chinese cannot gain the upper hand with their Cavalry units.*

Unique Unit Tactics: Chu Ko Nu

The Chu Ko Nu is named after the improved crossbow that the Chinese archery units carried in the Middle Ages. Unlike other archers, this unit provides quicker firepower and damage at the expense of a slightly shorter range. Nestled behind a frontline of Cavalry melee units, as shown in Figure 4-5, the Chu Ko Nu is deadly. With protection, they provide a decisive edge in both defensive and offensive operations. If you thought the British Longbowmen were bad news, wait until you get your hands on the Chu Ko Nu.

Figure 4-5 *The Chu Ko Nu flail nonstop at the enemy.*

> **Note:** *The Chu Ko Nu are not ideal for destroying buildings of any type. However, they are useful in some circumstances for demolishing ships, such as a Galley or War Galley. In fact, a group of Chu Ko Nu can sink these ships easily. Of course, they also work well against infantry units like Skirmishers, Pikemen, and Swordsmen.*

In one-on-one combat, the Elite Chu Ko Nu can take down a Cavalry Archer. Keep this in mind when fighting against the Mongols, whose Cavalry Archers fire faster than their counterparts in other civilizations. In fact, the Mongolian Mangudai, a unique Cavalry unit, has only a few more hit points than the Chu Ko Nu. This is quite rare considering that foot Archers are significantly less durable than their Cavalry Archers. What's more, the Chu Ko Nu offer range and attack points like the Mangudai. Overall, taking on the Mongolian Cavalry Archers is easy as long as the Chu Ko Nu are on the battlefield. Without them, though, the Chinese don't have a chance against the Mongols.

Like most ballistic units, the Chu Ko Nu unit works really well when set up on hills. To wreak havoc on enemy infantry and Villagers, sprinkle several Chu Ko Nu on elevated areas. Accordingly, use a group of Knights to guard the unique units from attackers. Open fire on unsuspecting opponents passing by (as shown in Figure 4-6). This is an excellent way to get rid of several enemy Villagers at once. You should also use the Chu Ko Nu for guarding critical buildings within your camp.

Figure 4-6 *Chu Ko Nu battle opponents from a hilltop.*

Enemies that infiltrate the area will not have a chance to destroy your Stables or Monasteries. Whether they are used in defensive or offensive tactics, the Chu Ko Nu's rapid-firing techniques make them essential elements in nearly all land battles.

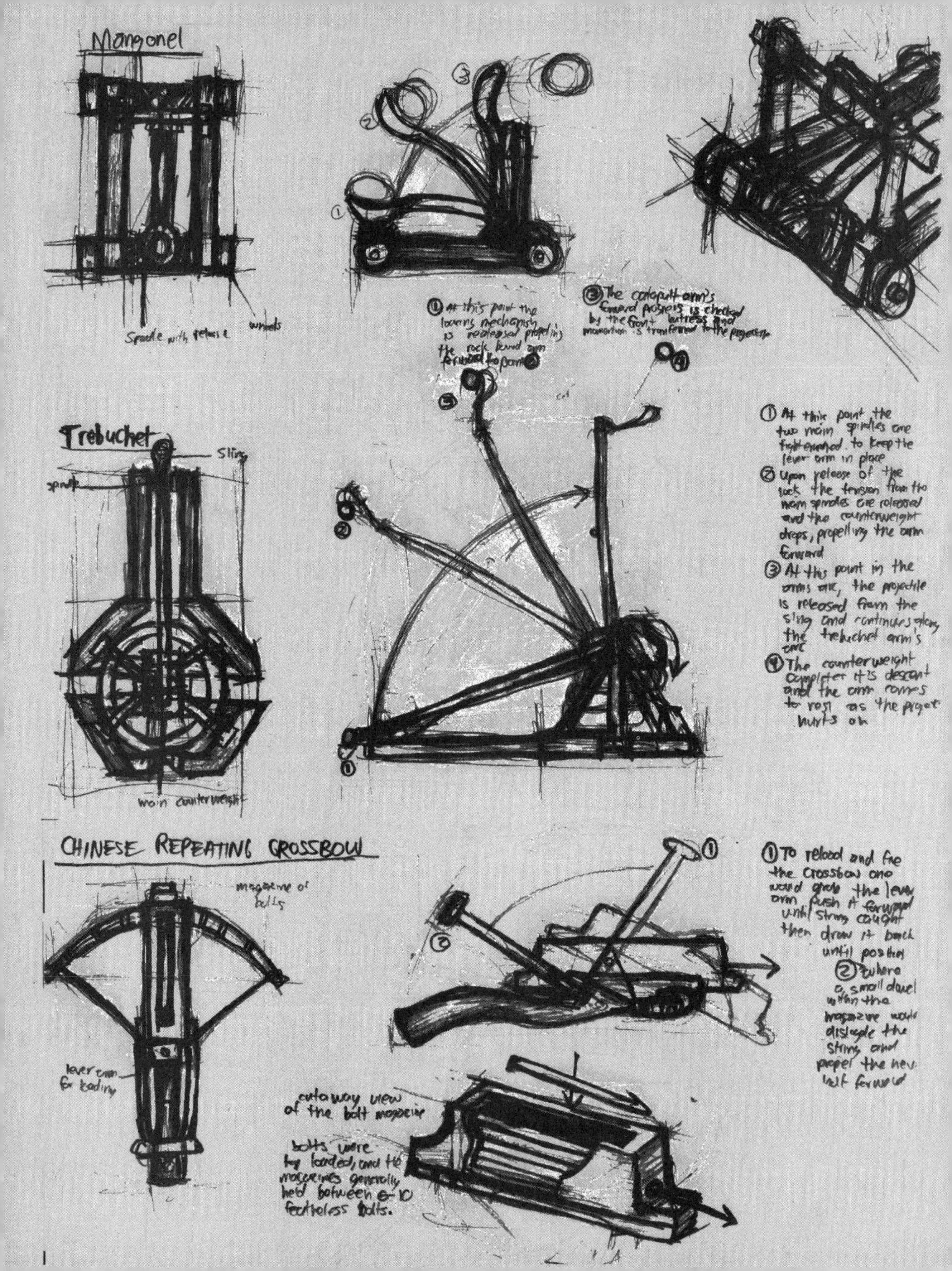

Mangonel
wheels
Trebuchet
sling
main counterweight
① At this point the two main spindles are
lever arm in place
② Upon release of the
the counterweight
drops, propelling the arm
forward
③ At this point in the
the projectile
is released from the
sling and continues along
the trebuchet arm's
④ The counterweight
and the arm comes
to rest as the
CHINESE REPEATING CROSSBOW
magazine of
bolts
lever arm
for loading
① To reload and fire
the crossbow one
the lever
until string caught
then draw it back
② where
a small dowel
within the
string and
cutaway view
of the bolt magazine
bolts were
magazines generally
held between
featherless bolts.

The Franks

The Franks were one of the many Germanic tribes to migrate south during the early half of the first millennium. The invasions that accompanied this migration ultimately led to the fall of the Roman Empire. By the sixth century, under the leadership of the great chieftain Clovis, the Franks had successfully gained control of the Rhine River Valley. Boasting of such heroes as Charles the Hammer, Charlemagne, and Joan of Arc, the Franks continued to play a major role in the development of Western civilization for the next thousand years—including the preservation of Christianity and the establishment of the université.

The Islamic Saracens and Moors, Goths, Vikings, and Britons were France's primary enemies during medieval times. During the late fifth century, the Franks pushed the Visigoths west of the Pyrenees. In 732, the Franks prevented Muslims from progressing any farther into Western Europe than Spain. Later, in the ninth century, the Vikings invaded France several times, contributing to the country's economic and political disarray. From 1337 to 1453, Britain battled France in the Hundred Years' War. With Joan of Arc's help, the French were able to turn the tide of the campaign and ultimately win the war.

Maximizing Strengths and Minimizing Weaknesses

In *Microsoft Age of Empires II*, the Franks have a number of advantages in the early stages of battle. For starters, in scenarios where you have a low number of dietary resources (such as Sheep, Fish, or Forage Bushes), building a Mill can give you a leg up on your enemy in a hurry. (See Figure 5-1.) For example, farming upgrades are free when a Mill is in place. Free farming upgrades are a great advantage, as they allow the speedy growth and collection of garden

Figure 5-1 *The Mill is an early advantage for French Farm production.*

foods to be attained without research. In addition, technologies such as the Horse Collar, the Heavy Plow, and Crop Rotation increase the amount of food that can be harvested from the fields. Such strategies, needless to say, save time and resources—allowing you to concentrate more on building an army of appropriate structures.

Other opponents with early benefits in food resource and gathering technology include the Persians and Vikings. However, only the Franks and Teutons have advantages in farming, which means that they have no problems producing food even in a dry, depleted desert. For this reason, maps with low food resources are almost always to the Franks' advantage.

> **Tip:** *Always erect a Mill and Barracks (in that order) as your first two structures when you're playing as the Franks. The Mill will allow your Villagers to grow and gather food more quickly on the Farms. The Barracks allows you to progress to the Feudal Age. At that stage, you can build the Stable and then the Knights.*

Knights are another French advantage. The French units have more hit points than Knights within the other civilizations. This makes them an effective melee weapon in Castle Age assaults, especially when the enemy civilization is an Age behind. When this is the case, use the Knights to disrupt the enemy village, taking control of the game by forcing your opponents into a defensive state. You don't have to conquer the area; just try to knock off a few Villagers, Farms, and Lumber Camps, as shown in Figure 5-2.

How Changes Through the Ages Affect Tactics

Tip: *If there are numerous dietary resources on the map, your goal is to deny the enemy's access to them. Place Watch Towers or Palisade Walls near Forage Bushes, Sheep, and Deer to keep enemy Villagers away. This forces the enemy to build Farms, placing the advantage in your hands. Farms cost Wood, unlike other food resources, which are free. Why waste resources when you don't have to?*

The Franks fought off numerous attacks from enemy civilizations, including the Moors, Vikings, and Britons. With advantages throughout the first three Ages, the Franks have the ability to strike early and garner more than their share of resources. With such benefits, it's no wonder that this French civilization was able to thwart enemy assaults for over a thousand years.

Figure 5-2 *French Knights wreak havoc upon an enemy settlement.*

Dark Age

As discussed earlier in the chapter, you can build a Mill in this Age to allow the Franks to use free farming upgrades such as the Horse Collar and Heavy Plow. This provides quicker access to food, which, in turn, allows you to more quickly churn out Villagers to take control of the map's other resources. Always build some Farms, but try to keep "free" food such as Forage Bushes and Deer away from the enemy.

To be successful in the early stages of the game, you need to progress to the next Age as soon as possible. Civilizations that advance early always have the upper hand. You need to erect at least two Dark Age buildings to advance to the next Age: one should be the Mill, and the other should be the Barracks. Once you complete the Barracks, you can begin constructing the Stable. The Stable, in turn, produces two important units: the Knight and the Scout Cavalry. Make sure the Knight escorts the Scout Cavalry; this will provide ample protection for your reconnaissance group.

Tip: *Two Scout Cavalry units also combine to make a good reconnaissance group. They are fast, they see well, and the unit duplicity usually ensures that at least one will escape from any trouble encountered.*

Feudal Age

While your Scout Cavalry explores the map, build a Blacksmith shop. Various Blacksmith technologies such as Forging and Scale Barding Armor help improve the Knights' skills. (See Figure 5-3.) More technology is offered in the next two Ages, which provide enhancements for cavalry and infantry troops. Be sure to invest in Blacksmith technologies throughout the game, especially when you're involved with more than one enemy.

Figure 5-3 *To improve your Knights, invest in Blacksmith technologies.*

Castle Age

The building materials used to construct French Castles cost 25 percent less than those used in most other civilizations. If you have a stockpile of Stones, it

is worth your while to build one or two Castles for defensive purposes. A Castle has the same range as a Watch Tower, but it can deliver twice the damage. A Castle also makes taking down a fortress of walls difficult or even impossible for an enemy without ballistic units.

> **Tip:** *Use the Knights to disrupt the enemy, forcing them onto the defensive. If you are playing against the Britons, taking out their Archery Ranges is not a bad idea. These British buildings take 20 percent less time to build than those of the Franks. Archery is also a strength of the Britons, so crippling the enemy in this area is always good practice.*

The Castle is not just for defensive purposes, though. These structures produce the Franks' unique unit, the Throwing Axeman. These troops throw axes at the enemy; think of them as Archers with lots of bite. They have more stamina than the Crossbowman but are still easily taken out by heftier units. They can be upgraded to Elite Throwing Axeman in the Imperial Age. Stationing them on hills is advantageous for taking out enemy Villagers parading about the map.

> **Tip:** *Don't forget to build a Siege Workshop when your objectives involve taking down enemy fortifications. Only units produced there, such as the Mangonel and Battering Ram, are powerful enough to get the job done right.*

Imperial Age

One of the primary goals in *Age of Empires II* involves ascending to the Imperial Age while preventing your enemies from doing so. (Naturally, you always want to keep the upper hand.) Many of the chief upgrades attained via the Stable and Siege Workshop can make a decisive difference in a long, hard battle. Technologies such as Blast Furnace and Plate Barding will help compensate the Franks' Cavalry, which does not have a Paladin in its arsenal. Be sure to use other technologies at your disposal. For instance, you need to research Chemistry at the University before you can produce gunpowder units.

Consider using the Elite Throwing Axeman for long-range attacks on enemy Cavalry and Archery units. This special unit has the same range as the Crossbowman, but it is more stout and provides a little more damage, as shown in Figure 5-4. Use the Elite Throwing Axeman in conjunction with heavy-hitting ballistic units that lack lots of hit points, such as the Bombard Cannon and

Figure 5-4 *Think of the Elite Throwing Axeman as a stout Crossbowman.*

Hand Cannoneer. Place the Axemen in a Box formation around the less durable gunpowder units. The special units can fend off opponents, preventing enemy melee and Archery units from easily attacking your Bombard Cannons and Hand Cannoneers.

Tips for the Conqueror or Heroine: Joan of Arc

Joan of Arc is an excellent warrior, with a stamina and vigor similar to the French Knight. Although she is one hardy lady, and quite an inspiration to the French cause, she's unfortunately not immortal. And because Joan's life is integral to the campaign's success, you don't want to risk it unnecessarily. That's why it's best to keep her out of the fray unless she is assisted by a horde of melee units.

Joan the Defender

Figure 5-5 *Joan of Arc defends a Mangonel.*

One of the most common uses for a unit of Joan's status is as prime defender. Use Joan to guard vulnerable ballistic units such as the Mangonel and the Bombard Cannon, as shown in Figure 5-5. This is safe use for Joan because such units are usually some distance from the trenches. In addition, Joan can compensate for those units' lack of hit points with her own when things get dangerous. Just make sure that some Crossbowmen or Cavalry Archers guard her back in case she gets more than she bargained for.

A Heroine's Grace

Managing Joan of Arc is a balancing act. She is tougher than most French infantry—an aspect that makes her useful in many combat situations. However, because of her importance to the campaign, Joan cannot be thrown recklessly into every battle. Mediating these two positions is the key to effectively winning the missions. It can be difficult, but there is a way to do this.

Figure 5-6 *Place Joan in the Box Formation for extra protection.*

First, place Joan into a formation, as shown in Figure 5-6. I prefer to use the Box Formation. This allows Joan to march into battle with various units surrounding her for protection. She can then mix it up on the battlefield, but once she's "in the red," you must pull her out. The accompanying formation will guard her as she retreats from the fray. Next, have a Monk nearby heal the French heroine. Once she and her troops are ready, send her back in to fight.

Tip: *Pulling Joan out of a skirmish, healing her, and then sending her back into battle is an important element in winning the Hundred Years' War. Such measures protect Joan while still making the most of her strengths.*

Unique Unit Tactics: Throwing Axeman

The Throwing Axeman, as mentioned earlier, is sort of like an Archer on steroids. Place these units in front of or beside ballistic units such as the Crossbowmen or Arbalests. This way, they can protect the weaker figures from melee attacks while obtaining help from them in a skirmish. Just make sure that you place a formation of Knights or Cavaliers in the front line to protect the Axemen and Archers. Because of Axemen's attack bonus against buildings, sending them to flail away at enemy structures is often a good idea.

Throwing Axemen are good for thinning out dangerous areas with few enemies. For instance, a mix of Knights and Throwing Axemen can take out a band of Highwaymen with ease. I especially like to take Wolves down with Throwing Axemen. Before having time to bite, the Wolf is out cold. One Wolf usually takes about four blows with the flying hatchets before succumbing to death. Little Red Riding Hood would be proud!

> **Tip:** *With their range and attack points, the Throwing Axeman is useful for taking out the Samurai. When you're attacking, though, always fire at the enemy while backing up. Keep your distance; you don't want to get too close to this fast-swinging fellow.*

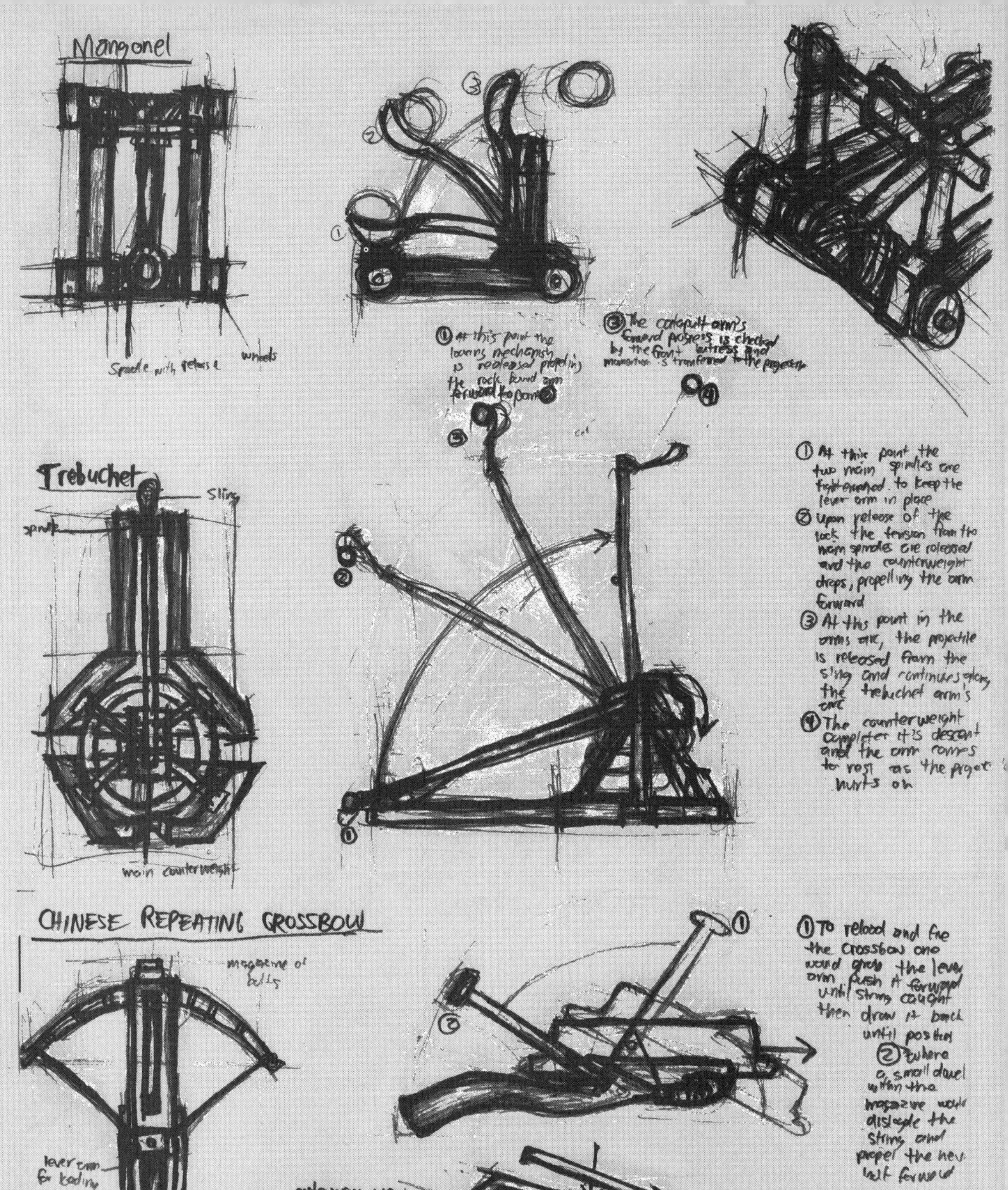

Mangonel
wheels
The catapult arm's
Trebuchet
Sling
main counterweight
At this point the
lever arm in place
Upon release of the
drops, propelling the arm
forward
At this point in the
is released from the
the trebuchet arm's
The counterweight
and the arm comes
CHINESE REPEATING CROSSBOW
lever arm for loading
To reload and fire
the crossbow one
then draw it back
a small dowel
within the
dislodge the
string and
bolt forward
cutaway view
of the bolt
bolts were
feathrless bolts.

Chapter Six

The Goths

The Goths, originally from Scandinavia, migrated to the Black Sea region in the third and fourth centuries. Unable to stop the Huns' march into Eurasia, these Germanic tribes had been slowly driven into Europe. At first, the Goths descended onto the Baltic peninsula. However, continual advances by the Huns forced the tribes to move westward. By 410 CE, the Goths had done what no other civilization had been able to do—they sacked the city of Rome. Eventually, these barbaric conquests resulted in the Roman Empire's total collapse, marking the end of the Classical Age and the beginning of the Medieval Period.

As the Goths migrated through Europe, they splintered into two groups—the Ostrogoths and the Visigoths. After battling the Huns, the Ostrogoths swept into Italy in the sixth century, where they battled the Byzantines. The Visigoths, however, had already pushed into southern Gaul and Spain by 480 CE. There they struggled in numerous battles with the Franks. The Visigoths were able to maintain their station there, though, until the Muslim conquest of Spain in the eighth century. Most eyewitnesses give historical accounts involving the Goths in terms of their courage and physical fortitude. These tribes obviously glorified these attributes in their folklore—all that now remains of this civilization. Consequently, a great deal of Western Medieval mythology derives from the Gothic tradition, most notably tales involving dragon-slaying exploits.

Maximizing Strengths and Minimizing Weaknesses

The Goths are one of the weaker civilizations in *Microsoft Age of Empires II*. Although they have numerous strengths, some significant weaknesses remain a hindrance in the later Ages. For instance, after the Dark Age, Goths cannot build any defensive structures except the Watch Tower. The limitation of Monk powers hampers Castle Age strategy, and the Imperial Age cavalry and available siege technology are nothing to brag about. These flaws put a damper on both defensive and offensive strategies, especially in multiplayer scenarios.

But a civilization that conquered Rome surely has to have some bite to it—and the Goths, indeed, display some key advantages. For example, infantry are a bright spot throughout the game. Not only do they cost less than foot soldiers in other civilizations, but they also inflict more damage upon buildings than other infantry (see Figure 6-1). Furthermore, Gothic Villagers earn attack bonuses when battling against Wild Boars. Finally, with perhaps the most ample economic technology availabilities of any civilization, the Goths generally provide a strong start that invites gamers to explore early offensive tactics.

Figure 6-1 *Goth infantry carry attack point bonuses against buildings.*

> **Note:** *Gothic military strengths include a strong infantry (during the Feudal, Castle, and Imperial Ages) and a diverse fleet of naval weaponry.*

Unfortunately, the infantry do not have the support that other civilizations have. Gothic cavalry units are some of the weakest in the game, similar to those in the Viking and Japanese camps. Monks cannot convert buildings, and second-tier siege weapons in the Imperial Age (for example the Siege Onager and Siege Ram) are absent. The Goths, luckily, have a strong navy capable of producing Fire Ships and Cannon Galleons. In fact, the civilization is usually competitive throughout all seafaring missions, whereas other missions often require the Goths to come out firing almost immediately.

How Changes Through the Ages Affect Tactics

Of all the civilizations in *Microsoft Age of Empires II,* the Goths rarely stayed in one place over a long period of time. Accordingly, they lack a lot of buildings, especially structures such as Stone Walls and Guard Towers. But who needs defenses when you're always on the attack? The Goths have some of the toughest and most brutal sword-wielding infantry in this period.

Dark Age

Although they lack any farming or timber enhancements, the Goths have a major advantage in attack points against Wild Boars. As a result, only one Hunter is required to take a Wild Boar, instead of the usual two, which spares additional Villagers for erecting Houses. Furthermore, gather as many food resources as possible before planting Farms. Remember, nearly all civilizations began as hunting and gathering nations before converting to agriculture.

Note: *Wild Boars, shown in Figure 6-2, provide more food points than any other animal. In fact, one Wild Boar contains over three times the points of a Sheep and nearly twice those of a Deer.*

Figure 6-2 *Gothic Villagers should gather as many Wild Boars as possible since they can inflict extra damage points against the swine.*

Build a Barracks and produce several rounds of Militia. Although you do not need to send them out into battle just yet, try to "stockpile" as many of these soldiers as you can. You want to be thinking ahead to the Feudal Age technologies that will become available. At that time, all infantry units can be upgraded appropriately by simply researching Men-at-War, and they also deliver additional attack points against buildings. The more units you have to upgrade, the stronger your army will be.

Note: *If you are playing on a team, Goth Barracks create units significantly faster than if you're playing alone. You might even want to build more than one. Then you'll be able to create twice as many foot soldiers in half the time.*

Feudal Age

In most scenarios, it's best for the Goths to attack their enemies during this stage of the game. First, place a Watch Tower or two inside your village; the Watch Tower is one of the few static weapons Goths have for defense (as shown in Figure 6-3). Next, invest in infantry weapon or armor technologies, such as Fletching or

Scale Mail Armor, at the Blacksmith. Generate some Archers at the Archery Range. Spend time later on the archery weapon or armor upgrades.

Send the Men-at-Arms to hack away at peripheral enemy buildings, being careful not to attack a well-defended Town Center. Place the Archers in another group, and have them follow the infantry, thus providing backup in tough situations. Attack as many buildings as possible, but pull out when too many enemy soldiers confront you. In some cases, your men will not be able to run from faster units such as the Celtic infantry. That's why additional Scout Cavalry are necessary for keeping Celtic Men-at-Arms busy.

Figure 6-3 *Unfortunately, Watch Towers are the best defensive structures the Goths can muster.*

> **Tip:** *Placing the infantry in Flank Formation allows your soldiers to surround a building. When units are not so close together, they have room to take more shots at the structure.*

Castle Age

As a result of the lack of Gothic defensive structures and tough melee cavalry units in the Imperial Age, you must quickly solidify an offensive front during this period. Of course, if you are playing on a map with a significant amount of water, your navy can sustain the Goths well into the next era. At this point, you

Figure 6-4 *A Goth Fire Ship sends an enemy Fishing Ship up in smoke.*

should construct some War Galleys and Fire Ships to raid enemy ships (see Figure 6-4). Start your building process with the Fishing Ships, and then move up to the fighting ships.

Erect a Stable and University. Train several rounds of Knights, and continue weapon and armor upgrades at the Blacksmith. Research Ballistics at the University to improve the accuracy of your Crossbowmen. Send the Knights and Crossbowmen close to the enemy site to defend a nearby location where you'll build a Castle. Next create some Huskarls. These are representatives of an armored warrior class—the Goths' unique infantry unit. Meanwhile, build a Siege Workshop and several Mangonels and Scorpions.

> **Tip:** *Placing a Castle near the enemy settlement allows the structure to eliminate enemy Villagers searching the area for resources.*

> **Tip:** *If your enemy is stationed inside fortified Walls, you cannot attack the Walls with your infantry. Enemy Towers and Archers can easily make mincemeat of your men. Instead, use Trebuchets to put a gaping hole in enemy defenses.*

Direct three groups against the enemy settlement. The first group should be made up of Knights, Archers, and Scorpions. Order them to take out the opponent's troops. Place the Huskarls and some Long Swordsmen in the second group, using them to battle the buildings. Include the Mangonels and the rest of the Long Swordsmen in the third group to attack any other buildings.

Imperial Age

Figure 6-5 *Construct more Watch Towers around your village to thwart attackers.*

The beginning of this period brings you ten additional Villagers. Have them build military structures, repair damaged buildings, or both. Place more Watch Towers near your Village (as demonstrated in Figure 6-5) if you've been inundated with attackers. Research Heated Shot to provide additional attack points against enemy warships. You'll also need to research Chemistry, which is necessary for building the Cannon Galleon, a ship that provides plenty of defensive and offensive firepower.

> **Tip:** *Research Conscription at the Castle. This helps you quickly generate decisive land-based units such as the Huskarl, Hand Cannoneer, and Cavalier.*

Continue the raids upon the enemy compound. In those seafaring missions, don't hesitate to bombard settlements with your Cannon Galleon. Use Fire Ships to guard the Cannon Galleons. Send a Transport Ship full of infantry to destroy enemy buildings, too. Before you know it, the opponent will be turned into rubble.

Unique Unit Tactics: Huskarl

The Huskarl, shown in Figure 6-6, was a zealous warrior class that helped the Goths plunder and attack settlements within other civilizations. They were instrumental in the Goths' success against the Romans. In *Age of Empires II,* Huskarls carry a large amount of Pierce Armor. This, needless to say, makes

Figure 6-6 *The Huskarl is a human wrecking ball.*

them quite effective in combat. Normally a melee infantry is hit by both enemy melee and archery units. Such situations create a sort of double-whammy effect. The Huskarl doesn't have to worry about this. His Pierce Armor shields against most arrows, enabling him to defeat melee opponents *and* Archers.

Because of the increased number of attack points Gothic infantry have when battling against buildings in the Feudal, Castle, and Imperial Ages, the Huskarl is a potent warrior. Send him in with other melee foot soldiers to eradicate enemy structures. The Huskarl, in conjunction with Mangonels and Trebuchets, leaves little question as to how Rome fell fifteen hundred years ago.

Note: *Huskarls match up well against most infantry, cavalry, and archery units. They are very effective against special archery or ballistic units such as the British Longbowmen, the Chinese Chu Ko Nu, and the Turkish Janissary.*

Chapter Seven

The Japanese

In addition to the Chinese and Mongols, the Japanese were one of the most important Far Eastern civilizations of the Medieval Period. Like much of Western Europe, Japanese history in the Middle Ages was punctuated by warring clans. These clans, called "uji," constantly struggled for a basic, but rare, commodity—suitable farming land. The owners of fertile terrain were the most powerful of the uji. Many of these powerful owners parlayed their control of Japan's rice agriculture and fishing trade into political and economic dominance.

By the latter Middle Ages, ceaseless clan skirmishes had bred a military government and a warrior class called the Samurai. The Samurai dedicated their lives to honing their warrior skills, and they often pledged loyalty to a clan lord or landowner in return for room, board, and instruction. The warriors' self-discipline, courage, and fearlessness were known throughout the land. They were perhaps the best-trained medieval combatants in the world, responsible for spearheading the defeat of two Mongol attacks in the thirteenth century.

Maximizing Strengths and Minimizing Weaknesses

The Japanese are the dominant seagoing civilization in the game; don't fight against them (unless you are commanding another nautical power such as the Vikings) on the Archipelago, Coastal, or Islands maps. This Oriental kingdom has too many maritime advantages, both economic and military, to defeat them

Figure 7-1 *Nothing gets in the way of a Japanese Fishing Ship and its catch.*

on the "water" maps. For example, their Fishing Ships, shown in Figure 7-1, are the most efficient and sturdy of any *Microsoft Age of Empires II* civilization. Furthermore, Japanese Docks can construct all vessels except the Heavy Demolition Ship. Simply put, the nation wields an impressive armada.

> **Note:** *The Japanese Monk (as shown in Figure 7-2) is one of the most powerful clerics in the game. In fact, these Monks belong to one of only four civilizations capable of using all Monastery research. (The other three civilizations are the Byzantines, Saracens, and Teutons.)*

On land maps, the Japanese don't fare quite as well. Although the Japanese field a stout army, it lacks the brawn of the Persians and Byzantines. For instance, the Japanese can't create siege heavies such as the Bombard Cannon, Siege Ram, and Siege Onager. Additionally, Japan's Cavalry is not quite as good as those of their Eastern rivals, China and Mongolia.

Healthy Archers and infantry, however, compensate for the lack of siege and Cavalry muscle. Every Stable and Archery Range unit and technology is available. Japanese Monks are also very powerful, capable of helping out with an assortment of tasks, from standard healing to several conversion options. But the Samurai is Japan's greatest advantage. This figure delivers fast, hard-hitting attacks. If you can employ these warriors adeptly, you will be able to slay even the most brawny of enemies.

Figure 7-2 *This Monk hauls a Relic to his Monastery.*

How Changes Through the Ages Affect Tactics

Make no mistake, the Japanese are dominant in any age. Nevertheless, understanding how best to employ their units can even further strengthen their position. Follow along to see how the Japanese can bring the other civilizations to their knees.

Dark Age

Economic forces dictate the early stages of the game. As usual, your strategy for gathering resources depends on the map and its raw materials. On a map dominated by water, build a Dock or two, and then create 7 to 12 Fishing Ships. On maps with little water, construct a Mill near whatever food source you are gathering, and direct a band of Militia to attack enemy Villagers as they search for food. Remember, hunting and gathering is a zero-sum game—whatever food the enemy wins is your loss.

Note: *Japanese Builders can construct Mills, Lumber Camps, and Mining Camps with fewer materials than most civilizations need for the same task. Accordingly, it's a good idea to scatter two or three of these buildings near the various raw material sources.*

Feudal Age

Now is the time to extend your military boundaries and enhance your economic status. This expansion is especially important on land maps, where the Japanese cannot invoke their maritime dominance and will need all the land they can control in order to harvest enough resources to expand their empire. On these maps, send Miners to as many different Gold and Stone sites as possible. Research economic technology such as the Double-Bit Axe. You will probably have to build a Market and use the buying and selling options to collect the right resources to build units and upgrade to the Castle Age.

If you are playing on a large lake or sea, continue scouring the area for Fish. Build Fish Traps to increase your catch.

Tip: *In some seafaring missions, Wood is scarce. You may, however, trade your surplus of Fish for Gold and then buy Wood with the Gold.*

Note: *Japanese Fishing Ships have twice as many hit points as other civilizations' Fishing Ships. Although Japanese Fishers don't require as much protection as other ships, it's a good idea to patrol your fishing area with a Galley or two. This way if the opponents attack, the Galleys can respond while the Fishing Ships run.*

Construct a few Galleys from your Docks. Have some of the Galleys escort your Fishing Ships while the others destroy enemy ships. Build a Blacksmith and an Archery Range. Next, pack some Men-at-Arms, Scout Cavalry, and Archers into a Transport Ship (as shown in Figure 7-3), and raid any known enemy locations. Kill enemy Villagers and peripheral buildings. Once your raiders begin taking losses, drag them back onto the Transport Ship.

Figure 7-3 *Send some troops by way of Transport Ships to the enemy's island.*

Castle Age

Intensify your attacks on enemy settlements. These attacks are crucial when you are competing on land-based maps. It's important to win before the enemy constructs its hefty Imperial Age melee Cavalry and siege equipment. Here's how to do it: Erect a Castle and Stable near the enemy camp. Build an army of Samurai, Knights, Long Swordsmen, and Crossbowmen, and move them into the opponent's village. Meanwhile, don't forget to erect a Monastery and University.

> **Tip:** *Monks are invaluable combatants. Place them inside a Box Formation of Knights and Samurai. Use them to convert enemy buildings—especially Mining Camps, Lumber Camps, and Town Centers—and at the same time, heal the warriors protecting them.*

If the enemy is stationed across the ocean, establish a beachhead on the island's coast. Erect a Castle and Stable there. Produce Samurai and Knights, while sending other troops via Transport Ship to attack the enemy by land. Meanwhile, order fleets of Fire Ships and War Galleys to assault enemy vessels and Docks. Leave Demolition Ships at your Docks for protection, as shown in Figure 7-4.

Figure 7-4 *A fleet of Demolition Ships is an ideal form of nautical defense.*

Imperial Age

Again, the type of map you're playing on dictates your strategy in this Age. When you're on land, direct Samurai, Cavaliers, Champions, and Hand Cannoneers to attack the enemy village. Don't, however, forget the Trebuchets. They are handy for demolishing enemy Walls and Castles.

> **Note:** *Keep in mind that Japanese infantry attacks more rapidly than other civilizations' infantry can. The Cavalry receives no such bonus, so use infantry whenever possible.*

Use the Monks for converting enemy economic buildings (Mills, Lumber Camps, and so forth) and important units (such as unique units). Researching Block

Printing increases the conversion range. Illumination will also help Monks regain their faith faster.

Sea maps enhance your maritime dominance. Send a flotilla of Elite Cannon Galleons to bombard enemy military and economic structures from afar. Aim for buildings such as Docks, Stables, and Castles first; these provide the greatest threat to your assault. Once they're out of the way, continue pounding. You may have to send in a Transport Ship of troops to finish off those structures unreachable by the Galleon guns.

> **Tip:** *Send a group of Monks into battle, flanked by several Cavaliers. While the melee Cavalry are mixing it up with the enemy, have each Monk convert a key enemy unit (as shown in Figure 7-5). The Monks are excellent for turning Persian War Elephants, Byzantine Cataphracts, and Mongolian Mangudai to your side.*

Figure 7-5 *A group of protected Monks converts a Persian War Elephant.*

Unique Unit Tactics: Samurai

Without a doubt, the Samurai are the best infantry units in *Age of Empires II*. Their quick attack and fast movement make them formidable opponents for enemy melee Cavalry and most other unique units. However, the Chinese Chu Ko Nu, with their fast attack, can be a problem. Overall, though, the Samurai is an awesome killing machine.

> **Tip:** *In hard-fought struggles against other maritime powers, you'll need to research Dry Dock and Shipwright technologies to improve your warship performance. In these close contests, any little advantage can make the difference between victory and defeat.*

Note: *Although he dishes out about the same amount of damage per strike as the Goth Huskarl and the Celtic Woad Raider, the Samurai's attack speed allows him to make more strikes in less time than these enemy units (as shown in Figure 7-6).*

Samurai are particularly devastating against enemy buildings and unique units. Direct your melee Cavalry and infantry to occupy the opponent's troops while your Samurai sneak in to attack their structures. Demolish military buildings such as Stables, Guard Towers, and Castles. The Samurai's speed and high amount of damage points are guaranteed to deliver quite a blow to the enemy.

Figure 7-6 *The Samurai's quick jabs can finish off tough opponents like the Huskarl in seconds.*

Because Samurai are both inexpensive and lethal, they are effective melee Cavalry unit killers. Additionally, researching Conscription enables you to create enough Samurai to waste a few on suicide attacks. Have the Samurai thin out the more brawny enemy units, and then send your melee Cavalry and infantry in to finish off the enemy village.

Chapter Eight

The Mongols

Genghis Khan and his Mongol horde struck fear into the hearts of Europe and Asia during the twelfth through fifteenth centuries. From the vast rich Empire of China to the heart of Eastern Europe, they were unstoppable—conquering all that stood before them. In Eastern Europe, they became known as "the Devil's horsemen."

The Mongols were fierce warriors, living on a vast plateau with few resources. They fought each other for centuries until a man named Temujin (later renamed Genghis Khan, meaning Great King) united them, and together they invaded and pillaged neighboring civilizations to slake their unending bloodthirst and hunger. Despite their renowned cruelty and apparent primitive beginnings, their empire stretched across much of two continents and lasted for 300 years.

Genghis began his conquest with 25,000 warriors. Yet this relatively small "war band" slew over 300,000 Chinese men, women, and children when Khan swept through northern China and sacked the capital city of Beijing in 1215—a mere four years after consolidating his power. The Mongols believed in terror and subjugation, razing buildings, burning crops, and slaying innocent noncombatants and soldiers with equal brutality. The mighty Temujin died in 1227, yet upon his deathbed he made his son Ogedai promise to continue the conquest.

Ogedai completed the conquest of northern China and then invaded Europe. He sacked Kiev in European Russia in 1240 and then invaded

Hungary. He followed his father's tactic of brutally sacking one city so that the others would surrender without a costly fight. When Ogedai died while on campaign in 1241, the entire army withdrew to Mongolia and squabbled over who was to succeed him.

Hulagu was the next Khan, and, to Europe's relief, the Mongols concentrated on Asia Minor and the Middle East. In 1258 they took Baghdad, slaying some 100,000 citizens. But it was only two years later that Egyptian Mamelukes (a warrior-slave caste) defeated the army in what is now Israel. This ended the Mongol threat to the Holy Land and lands east.

Another grandson of Genghis, Kublai Khan, succeeded the throne, and he is best known for hosting Italian explorer Marco Polo. During his reign, he completely conquered China and established the Yuan Dynasty in 1279.

They might have begun their Empire as murderous barbarians, but the Mongols quickly assimilated the ways and science of the cultures they conquered. It is said that at the height of the Empire, a single woman, traveling alone with a bag of gold, could walk the entire Silk Route trade route (between China and the Middle East) safely.

Maximizing Strengths and Minimizing Weaknesses

The Mongols are horsemen, pure and simple. They are extremely powerful in Feudal and Castle Ages, but it is also easy to amass large Cavalry formations and destroy enemies in the early centuries of play. They are best played with an aggressive style and unrelenting attack pattern. Build up small armies and pillage and burn enemy settlements to the ground, all the while gathering and building your next force of attackers. If your enemy survives and makes it to the later ages, you must continue to harass them, with an eye on advancing

and defending yourself. Upgrade Cavalry units first, and use them in hit and run attacks, mainly to slay Villagers, ruin Town Centers, and hamper enemy resource gathering. In the Feudal Age, simple Scout Cavalry can be used to great effect, as shown in Figure 8-1. Just as when you play using the Celts, distracting your enemy as you advance in technology can be a very effective tactic.

Figure 8-1 *A group of Scout Cavalry hack away at an enemy Mill.*

How Changes Through the Ages Affect Tactics

The Mongols are a powerful civilization—a powerful and, due to their Cavalry, fast-moving civilization. Nevertheless, brute force alone does not win many games in *Age of Empires II*. You must employ the brute force intelligently to triumph. Read along and see how to tame the Mongol hordes and use them most effectively through the Ages.

Dark Age

As usual, you want to build a Barracks, a few Houses, and several Villagers. Send the Villagers to gather all the basic resources, herd Sheep if you can, and build a Dock to fish if you're near water. Try to advance to the Feudal Age as soon as you can; you want to build a Stable quickly.

Note: *The Mongols are 50 percent faster than other civilizations when they are used for hunting. Use your opening Scout Cavalry to check for any nearby herds of Deer (as shown in Figure 8-2).*

Feudal Age

The Mongols excel in this Age and in the Castle Age. Build a Stable and start producing Scout Cavalry. While you build a sufficient attack force of about 10 units, use your available Scout Cavalry to check out the enemy position. Pay close attention to the location of their Town Center and any concentration of enemy Villagers.

Figure 8-2 *With your Scout Cavalry unit flushing out prey, the efficiency of your hunters can help you gain an early advantage.*

Building a Blacksmith and researching any advance that aids in Cavalry should be a priority. You should also construct an Archery Range to produce Cavalry Archers, which fire 20 percent faster than regular Archers, for your second wave.

Once you have that initial force of Scout Cavalry, produce more of them for backup, and include Cavalry Archers in this allotment as well. But don't build too many; by now your enemy might be on his way to the Castle Age, and you need to strike fast. Take your initial wave of Scout Cavalry and attack the enemy Town Center. Be sure to set your gather points within the enemy encampment so that your attack continues as troops are built.

Tip: *If the enemy has already advanced to the Castle Age, abort any attack on their base. Instead, concentrate on reaching the Castle Age yourself, upgrading your troops with the Blacksmith, gathering resources, and so forth.*

This first wave might be enough to destroy the Town Center and a handful of Villagers, as shown in Figure 8-3. The additional troops will keep the pressure on while you gather enough resources to advance to the next Age. Your goal here is to employ fast, devastating attacks as quickly as you can. With any luck, the enemy won't know what hit him and will fall under your assault.

Figure 8-3 *The initial force of Scout Cavalry burns the rival Town Center to the ground.*

Castle Age

Your first actions in the Castle Age should be to further upgrade your Cavalry units and build a Castle, Siege Workshop, and Monastery. While the Mongols are still effective in the Imperial Age, they truly rise in power over other civilizations in the Castle Age. Now is the time to gather a great horde, as shown in Figure 8-4.

Figure 8-4 *A good mix of horsemen makes for a swift, terrifying assault.*

Your Monks lack the ability to convert enemy buildings or siege equipment (the Mongols lack the Redemption upgrade), but you will still need them to convert enemy troops and Villagers and to heal your own horsemen. Concentrate on building an army of pure speed and power, avoiding ground troops, as they will slow you down. The army should include Knights, Camels, Cavalry Archers, and the fabled Mangudai Cavalry Archers (the Mongol special unit). Trade to gain the Gold, Food, or Wood you need.

> **Tip:** *Do some scouting before you build more weapons. If the enemy hasn't built a Castle or walls around his village, you shouldn't bother constructing slow-moving siege equipment.*

Assign some troops to form a Box Formation around your Monks, and send them after your swifter horde. Don't create too many Monks; the Mongols

are not the religious type. In fact, Mongolian Monks are some of the weakest in the game. Attack the enemy in force and cripple him. Focus on destroying Villagers, the Town Center, and other unit-producing buildings, and then go for the Houses (as shown in Figure 8-5). Keep the pressure on—do not relent. If the enemy proceeds to the Imperial Age, keep raiding their resources, but you need to advance as well. With any luck, you can end the battle in this Age.

Figure 8-5 *If you have a horde of Cavalry, the hapless enemy Villagers, buildings, and troops will fall before you.*

Imperial Age

While the Mongols are still strong in the Imperial Age, this Age is not their best. Their navies have access to all upgrades (except the Dry Dock), but their Monks lack crucial advances such as Block Printing (+3 Conversion range) and Illumination (which regains faith at a faster rate), and their defenses are not as strong (they have no Keep or Bombard Towers) as those of their opponents.

Worse still, their vaunted Cavalry doesn't include Paladins, Plate Barding Armor (horse armor), and Ring Archer Armor. At this point in the game, you'll need to start using infantry if you want to even the odds. Still, a strong, swift Cavalry unit is useful in conducting raids and hit-and-run attacks, and in harassing the enemy to hamper his power.

Tip: *Do not rely on Monks, except for healing and for converting those who might be assaulting your walls. Lacking the extra hit points, conversion range, and the ability to convert enemy buildings is a severe handicap for Mongolian Monks.*

It is very useful to research your way to gunpowder units, to build defenses, and to continue your assaults. Once you have a sufficient force, backed this time by siege equipment, you can end the fight once and for all.

Unique Unit Tactics: Mangudai

The Mongols specialized in firing arrows from horseback, and the best Cavalry Archers were known as Mangudai. They were known for their speed and strength, often leading enemy troops into ambushes. They were equally adept at hit-and-fade tactics.

The best way to use these powerful troops, and the more powerful Elite version, is to support them with Knights, Light Cavalry, and infantry. They are best suited to destroy siege weapons from afar, attack buildings from a safe distance, and slay Monks and Swordsmen. They are less effective against Archers, Skirmishers, and Light Cavalry.

Figure 8-6 *A horde of Mangudai can slay almost any attacker before they get too close.*

An excellent tactic is to swarm incoming sieges with Mangudai, as shown in Figure 8-6, but

make sure that you support them with Knights or infantry. Avoid using them against specialized Archery units like the Britons' Longbowmen. Since they are fairly cheap to build in relation to other advanced units, they can make up the bulk of your army.

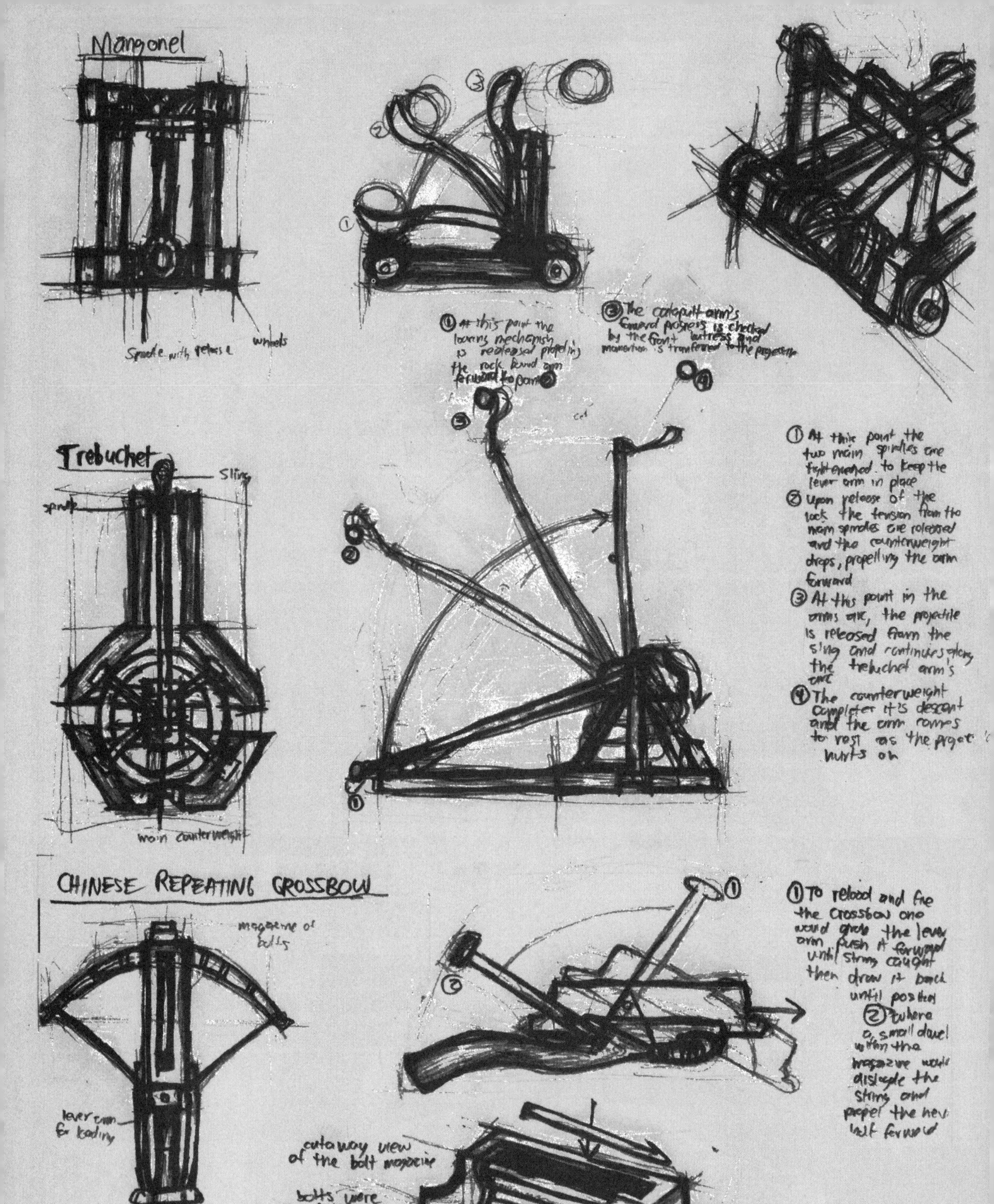
Mangonel
wheels
At this point the catapult arm's forward motion is checked by the front buttress and momentum is transferred to the projectile
Trebuchet
sling
spindle
main counterweight
At this point the two main spindles are tightened to keep the lever arm in place
Upon release of the lock the tension from the main spindles are released and the counterweight drops, propelling the arm forward
At this point in the arms arc, the projectile is released from the sling and continues along the trebuchet arm's arc
The counterweight completes it's descent and the arm comes to rest as the projectile hurls on
CHINESE REPEATING CROSSBOW
magazine of bolts
lever arm for loading
To reload and fire the crossbow one would grab the lever arm, push it forward until string caught then draw it back until position
where a small dowel within the magazine would dislodge the string and propel the new bolt forward
cutaway view of the bolt magazine
bolts were top loaded, and the magazines generally held between 6-10 featherless bolts.

Chapter Nine

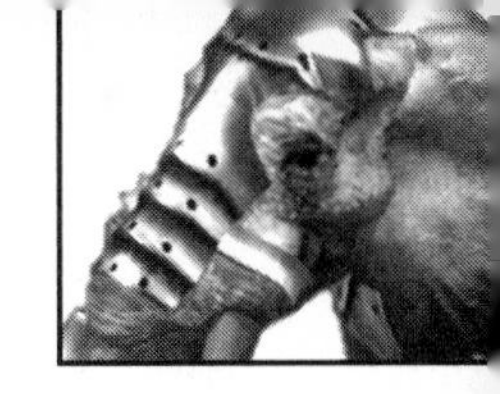

The Persians

The Persian Empire was one of the ancient world's great empires. Boasting such famous rulers as Cyrus the Great, Darius I, and Xerxes, the kingdom became a land of extensive wealth and influence. By the fourth century BCE, however, Alexander the Great and the Hellenes had put an end to Persia's heyday. But shortly after Alexander's death, the Persians were able to regain much of their kingdom. Although the empire never matched its past glories, it remained a major power until the seventh century.

The medieval Persian Empire stretched from the Euphrates River to modern-day Afghanistan. Persia fought the Roman Empire during the third and fourth centuries; a peace treaty ended the war in 364 CE. Two centuries later, after Rome's fall, Persia battled the Byzantines for control of Palestine, Arabia, and the Anatolian peninsula. A truce ended the seesaw battle in 628 CE, but a couple of years later, Muslim invaders assailed Persia's weakened kingdom. By 651 CE, the Persian Empire had fallen to the Saracens.

Maximizing Strengths and Minimizing Weaknesses

If you like brute strength, you'll like the Persians. They have the most powerful melee Cavalry (Persian Paladin) in *Microsoft Age of Empires II* (as shown in Figure 9-1) and the toughest Cavalry unit—the War Elephant. Their naval and archery units are nothing to laugh about either. Additionally, the Persian Town Center and Docks boast twice as many hit points as their counterparts in other civilizations, and to top it off, the Persians also have access to a wide range of economic technologies.

Figure 9-1 *The Persian Paladin is a powerful melee unit.*

Their weaknesses aren't glaring, but they can handicap them against the Byzantines, Mongols, and Turks—in other words, civilizations with powerful Cavalry or siege weapons. Unfortunately for the Persians, they lack some key defensive structures, such as the Fortified Wall and the Keep, and speed enhancements, like the Shipwright and the Treadmill Crane. Although these are not always critical factors, they sometimes play key roles in a civilization's development against hard-hitting opponents.

The Persians also have some more serious flaws: their Monk technologies are feeble, and they lack the ability to convert buildings or other clerics; and Persian defense and building technologies aren't up to par (reference the previous comment on the Fortified Wall and the Keep). Nevertheless, a brawny Cavalry, a capable navy, and an efficient economy—if used properly—can, more often than not, lead the Iranians' ancestors to victory.

How Changes Through the Ages Affect Tactics

The Persians are, in one way, identical to the 12 other civilizations in *Age of Empires II*—as the Ages change, so do they. Tactics that work in the Dark Age

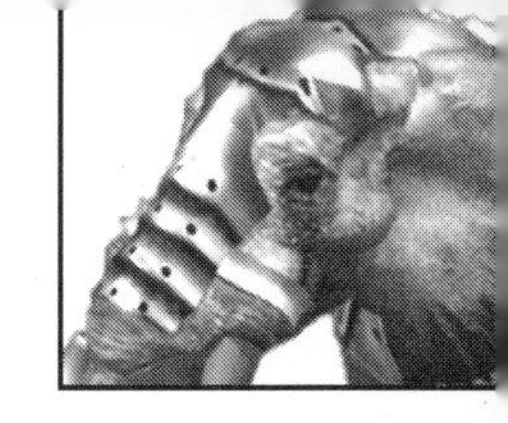

may not work in the Castle Age. Nevertheless, there are some constants in the Persian camp. They have a strong Cavalry and navy, along with access to most economic technologies. Reading the following primer will prepare you to lead these men in any Age, regardless of the civilization's pros and cons.

Dark Age

The Persians lack the gathering and production efficiencies of the Chinese and Frankish civilizations. Although they begin missions with an additional amount of Food and Wood, it's not significant. Therefore, you must create more Villagers in order to keep up with other civilizations. To speed up the collection process, send your Scout Cavalry unit to scope the land for enemies and raw materials.

At this stage of the game, very little sets the Persians apart from the typical *Age of Empires II* civilization. One chief difference, however, is the quicker production rates of the Town Center and Docks. If you are on a map with lots of water, use the Dock production advantage to create a fleet of Fishing Ships (as shown in Figure 9-2). With plenty of Fishing Ships, you'll

Figure 9-2 *Persian Docks' high work rates are ideal for creating lots of Fishing Ships.*

have dominion over Fish Farms in the Dark Age. Don't forget to construct a Mill and Barracks, too. Create some Militia to protect your Villagers from invaders, and raid your enemy's resources.

Feudal Age

Raise a serious army in this Age. Begin by constructing a Blacksmith and investing in all of the technologies there. This research will improve the weapons and armor of your soldiers. Build an Archery Range, and send a group of Archers and Men-at-Arms to attack enemy economic structures. Build some Watch Towers near your settlement. Place a few nearby the enemy site as well. This will prevent opponents from penetrating your village.

Castle Age

Castle Age research is a critical element of victory. Upgrade your soldiers' armor and weaponry at the Blacksmith. Attempt to compensate for your weak static defenses—the lack of a Fortified Wall or Keep—with University studies. (See Figure 9-3.) Research the

Figure 9-3 *University research can help strengthen feeble Persian defenses.*

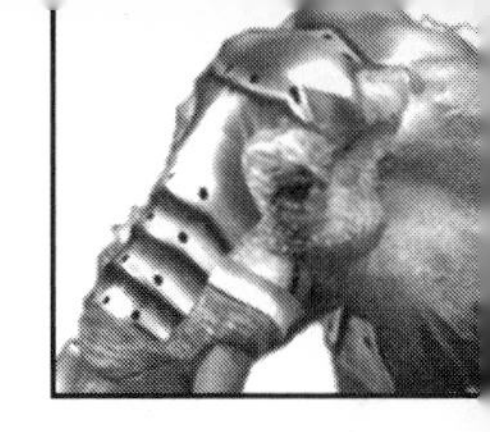

Guard Tower, Murder Holes, and Masonry. Also, continue researching economic technologies like the Heavy Plow, Hand Cart, and Bow Saw.

Use your efficient Docks and ships, upgraded with Careening, to contest control of the seas. War Galleys and Fire Ships are instrumental in eradicating the enemy's fishing trade.

Build a Castle. Create War Elephants, Knights, and Crossbowmen, and send them out to battle. Use the War Elephants to take down buildings. The Knights and Crossbowmen are more efficient for slaying enemy soldiers. Mangonels and Battering Rams are useful for crumbling enemy Walls.

> **Tip:** *The Vikings have a critical weakness; they cannot build Fire Ships. Using your Fire Ships, sink their War Galleys. Without Fire Ships of their own, they will be hard pressed to defend their "big guns."*

Imperial Age

Upgrade your soldiers and equipment for the last stages of battle. Use your strong Cavalry to exploit the opponent's weaknesses. The Saracen and Turkish cavalries are no match for an army of Paladins, Heavy Camels, and Elite War Elephants. Mix these soldiers in with the toughest siege equipment you have to offer: Onagers, Bombard Cannons, and Heavy Scorpions. Archery units like the Hand Cannoneer and Heavy Cavalry Archer are helpful, too. Don't forget to make use of an army of reserves and Guard Towers for defense.

> **Tip:** *The Byzantine Empire was known for its Fortified Walls and numerous Towers, but it was far from invincible—the Turks proved that. A mix of Elite War Elephants, Trebuchets, and Bombard Cannons can bring the walls crumbling down in no time. Persia may have failed to capture Constantinople, but you won't.*

> **Note:** *The Persians often need new economic technologies to stay competitive with the enemy and to build units such as War Elephants. Invest in Stone Shaft Mining, Gold Shaft Mining, the Heavy Plow, and Crop Rotation. These will increase your resources, helping you quickly train military units.*

Direct Cannon Galleons and Fast Fire Ships to eliminate the enemy navy, as demonstrated in Figure 9-4. In tough maritime battles with the Japanese and Vikings, you will need all the extra edges you can get. Don't forget to research Dry Dock; this helps your ships move faster.

Figure 9-4 *Use your strong navy to bombard enemy vessels.*

Unique Unit Tactics: War Elephant

There are three points you need to remember when using the War Elephant. First of all, these units are very powerful. A couple of swings from these trunked juggernauts put most enemies out of commission. Unfortunately, all that power comes with two critical liabilities—War Elephants are extremely slow (in relation to the other Cavalry units), and lots of food is required to create them.

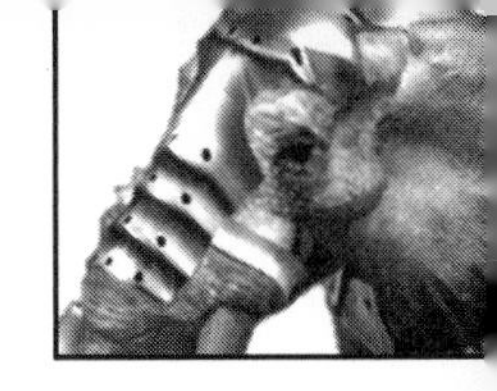

Although they can trample over most competition, their sluggish speed prevents them from catching other "hit-and-run" Cavalry units. It's that inability to deal with enemy Cavalry (and the pachyderm's high cost) that greatly reduces the War Elephant's role. Although they are useful for the defense of your base, they are quite instrumental in protecting more vulnerable units engaged in battle. For example, placing Onagers, Trebuchets, and Archery Range units within a Box formation of War Elephants enables them to attack for longer periods of time. (See Figure 9-5.) It's tough for any unit to penetrate that Wall—as a bodyguard, the War Elephant has no parallel!

Figure 9-5 *War Elephants excel at escorting siege weaponry.*

When attacking enemy villages, send the other Cavalry units to fight the enemy units. Use the War Elephant to help destroy buildings. This tactic is especially beneficial in the Castle Age—before the Trebuchet makes its appearance.

Note: *To improve the speed of the War Elephant, research Husbandry at the Stable. The War Elephant won't travel as fast as the Camels and Horses; however, every little bit helps.*

Figure 9-6 *Elite War Elephants destroy a Town Center.*

Frequently enemy units will try to prevent destruction of their homes by attacking the War Elephant. (See Figure 9-6.) This is, however, an attack you should welcome. When they are placed toe-to-hoof with the opponent, War Elephants can obliterate the enemy Cavalry without even chasing them. The Persians, undoubtedly, knew that Hannibal was on to something years ago!

Chapter Ten

The Saracens

The prophet Mohammed began preaching in 613 AD. Just a few decades later, the religion of Islam swept over the Arabian peninsula. As part of the Jihad—following Mohammed's death in 632—the Saracens conquered Egypt, Palestine, and Syria. (Although the name Saracen specifically referred to a nomadic tribe in Saudi Arabia, it was used by medieval Christians to designate all Arabs.) By the eighth century, Persia, North Africa, Anatolia, and Spain had fallen into Muslim hands. At its height, the Islamic Empire included territories on three continents: Europe, Asia, and Africa. Chief enemies of the Saracens included the Byzantines, the Turks, and European crusaders (for example, the Franks, Teutons, and Britons).

Islamic nations were some of the most prosperous kingdoms of the Middle Ages, providing cultural centers often unmatched by any other civilization in the world. Early leaders set the groundwork for success. Caliph Al-Mamum, for example, founded one of the first academies in Baghdad, opening the doors for intellectual study. From the ninth to the twelfth centuries, the Saracens spearheaded monumental achievements in fields such as astronomy and mathematics. Unfortunately, toward the end of the medieval period, these Islamic nations fell into economic decline.

Maximizing Strengths and Minimizing Weaknesses

The Saracens form a powerful and diverse kingdom. Granted, they lack the brute Cavalry strength of the Persians and Byzantines and the maritime dominance of the Vikings or Japanese; however, the Saracens are still formidable opponents. If they truly have a weakness, it's their lack of quick Imperial Age melee Cavalry (for example, Paladin or Cavalier). Therefore, their strongest melee

Cavalry unit is the slow Heavy Camel (as shown in Figure 10-1). All their other warriors, however, can match whatever their opponents throw at them.

This Arabic civilization has several strong suits. For starters, Saracens can access all archery and infantry units and technology. Additionally, their Archers inflict more damage on buildings than other civilizations' Archers. What really makes the Saracens special, though, are their Monks (pictured in Figure 10-2). Because of their Islamic zeal, these guys have every power and ability afforded *Microsoft Age of Empires II* clerics. Only two other civilizations wield this fully loaded archer/infantry/monk combination—the Byzantines and the Japanese. What sets the Saracens apart from those two civilizations, though, is their hefty allotment of siege equipment. With such a diverse arsenal, this civilization gives gamers a number of strategic options.

Figure 10-1 *The strongest Saracen melee Cavalry unit is the Heavy Camel.*

Figure 10-2 *These Monks have the power.*

How Changes Through the Ages Affect Tactics

Lacking any dominant advantages in the Dark Age, the Saracens start slowly. However, they come on strong in the Feudal and Castle Ages. Make no mistake, the civilization isn't an economic powerhouse (they have no production or gathering advantages), but the Saracens have strong military capabilities. Because of this military strength, they match up well against all civilizations in *Age of Empires II*. They have enough nautical firepower to compete with the Japanese (see Figure 10-3) as well as an abundant supply of siege weapons to help them take down the Walls of the Byzantines.

Figure 10-3 *A fast-attacking Saracen Galley sinks its Japanese counterpart.*

Dark Age

Unlike civilizations such as the Franks, Britons, and Chinese, the Saracens do not have significant advantages in the opening stages of the game. Work rates are not enhanced as with the Britons (faster shepherds) and the Japanese (faster Fishing Boats), and resource stockpiles consist of the standard fare. The goal of any Saracen Dark Age strategy is twofold. First, establish a firm economic system—in other words produce 8 to 12 Villagers to gather Food and Wood. Second, set up a Barracks. If you're on a seafaring map, erect a Dock or two. These will come in handy throughout the game. (Several of the Saracens' advantages, such as quicker Galleys and tougher Transport Ships, come from their maritime strengths.)

Feudal Age

This Age is one of the Saracens' best. A number of the civilization's strengths surface here, including their Market, Transport Ships, and Galleys advantages. If you're having problems establishing resources, build a Market; Saracens have reduced trading costs. Transport Ships have twice the normal amount of hit points and cargo space. And their Galleys can also attack faster than the usual fare.

Note: *Because the Saracens have no resource advantages, you have to research production technologies such as the Horse Collar, Wheelbarrow, and Double-Bit Axe to keep up with your enemies.*

Before attacking, however, research Fletching and Padded Archer Armor at the Blacksmith. Next dispatch your Men-at-Arms and Archers to assault structures. Attack enemy Mining Camps, Lumber Camps, and Markets and sanction their Villagers. This will strain your enemy's economy, making their progression into the next Age more difficult. If you're on a water map, send the Men-at-Arms and Archers abroad using your Transport Ships (as shown in Figure 10-4). Use the Galleys to destroy enemy Fishing Ships and Docks. Don't forget to erect a few Watch Towers to protect your village and resources.

Figure 10-4 *Saracen Transport Ships haul quite a number of warriors.*

Castle Age

When you reach the Castle Age, a surplus of technologies and a new arsenal of weapons enhance your civilization. Build a Monastery and a University, a research Sanctity for your Monks (50 percent increase in hit points), and a Treadmill Crane (20 percent increase in Villager build speed). Have your Blacksmith research Bodkin Arrow while you're at it. This will enhance your Archers' attack points and range. Keep working to enhance your strong suit at this stage; in this case, it's the Archers.

A Siege Workshop will help you prepare for a solid attack. Produce some Cavalry Archers, Mamelukes, and Monks—make sure you put the Monks in the center of a Box Formation—to accompany your melee infantry, Cavalry, and siege units. With a band of new troops, continue to assault the enemy. Use the Monks to heal wounded soldiers and convert enemy structures.

If applicable, send troops aboard Transport Ships to attack the enemy. Establish a beachhead if possible, erecting a Town Center and perhaps a Castle. Send War Galleys and Fire Ships to attack enemy vessels and Docks. Plan on creating additional fleets when playing civilizations such as the Vikings, Japanese, Byzantines, and Persians. In addition, station a couple of War Galleys near your Docks. Because the Saracens don't have Heated Shot technology, they must rely on Ships instead of Towers for coastal protection. Demolition Ships are ideal for this task.

Tip: *Saracen Cavalry Archers are excellent tools for assailing buildings. They deliver as many attack points as the standard Long Swordsman—a powerful unit in his own right. Using some Knights for guards, set the Cavalry Archers and Mangonels to wipe out enemy structures.*

Imperial Age

Some of the Saracens' weaknesses show during this period. The most noticeable, of course, is the lack of fast, hard-hitting melee Cavalry units. This is especially obvious against enemies such as the Byzantines and Persians, who

Tip: *A group of Knights and Mamelukes can't hold back a horde of Paladins forever. This is where the Monks can help out tremendously. Place them behind your Cavalry units (as shown in Figure 10-5). While they're busy protecting the Monks and siege equipment from attackers, instruct your clerics to convert enemy Paladins into your camp. This is one way to bring more diversity to your side!*

have access to three different Imperial Age Stable units. The Saracens, though, have a hefty advantage in siege weapon technology. Build two or three Siege Workshops, producing the best equipment money can buy—Siege Onagers, Siege Rams, and Bombard Cannons. Using your Knights and Elite Mamelukes to guard these weapons, fire away at enemy Cavalry units and whatever else your heart desires.

Figure 10-5 *Use Monks to convert enemy Paladins into the Saracen army.*

Civilizations with more efficient production capabilities and strong navies (for example, the Japanese and Vikings) may give you a hard time in this Age. To defend your villages, set up several Trebuchets along the coast. Their range exceeds that of the Cannon Galleon and Elite Cannon Galleons. Use an assortment of Imperial Age vessels to defend the Trebuchets. This will prevent the enemy from sacking your kingdom. Meanwhile, send Transport Ships full of soldiers to the opponent's town. Force the enemy into a defensive stance—and ultimately into surrender.

Unique Unit Tactics: Mameluke

Mamelukes were slaves trained for battle. In *Age of Empires II,* these soldiers ride upon their camels, flinging machetes at their foes. They work well against all Stable units, including Cavalry Archers. When in large numbers, they're ideal for assaulting Persian War Elephants and Byzantine Cataphracts. Most of the time, however, you'll keep the Mamelukes behind your melee Cavalry units, where they're most effective in helping your Knights and Camels against heavier Stable figures.

> **Note:** *The Mameluke should not attack all unique units. For instance, the Mongolian Mangudai offers similar attack points with further range. The Japanese Samurai must attack at close range. However, due to a high number of attack points and short intervals between strikes, he often bests the Saracens' special figure.*

Although they lack a substantial amount of armor, Mamelukes can be instrumental in defensive situations. Place them on both edges of a pass—especially one with thick brush and trees as in the Black Forest—and direct them to sling away at any unknowing intruder (as shown in Figure 10-6). When used with Knights or Heavy Camels (or both), the Mameluke will help guard Trade Carts, Trebuchets, and airborne siege equipment.

Figure 10-6 *A popular Mameluke ploy: striking down enemies from a pass.*

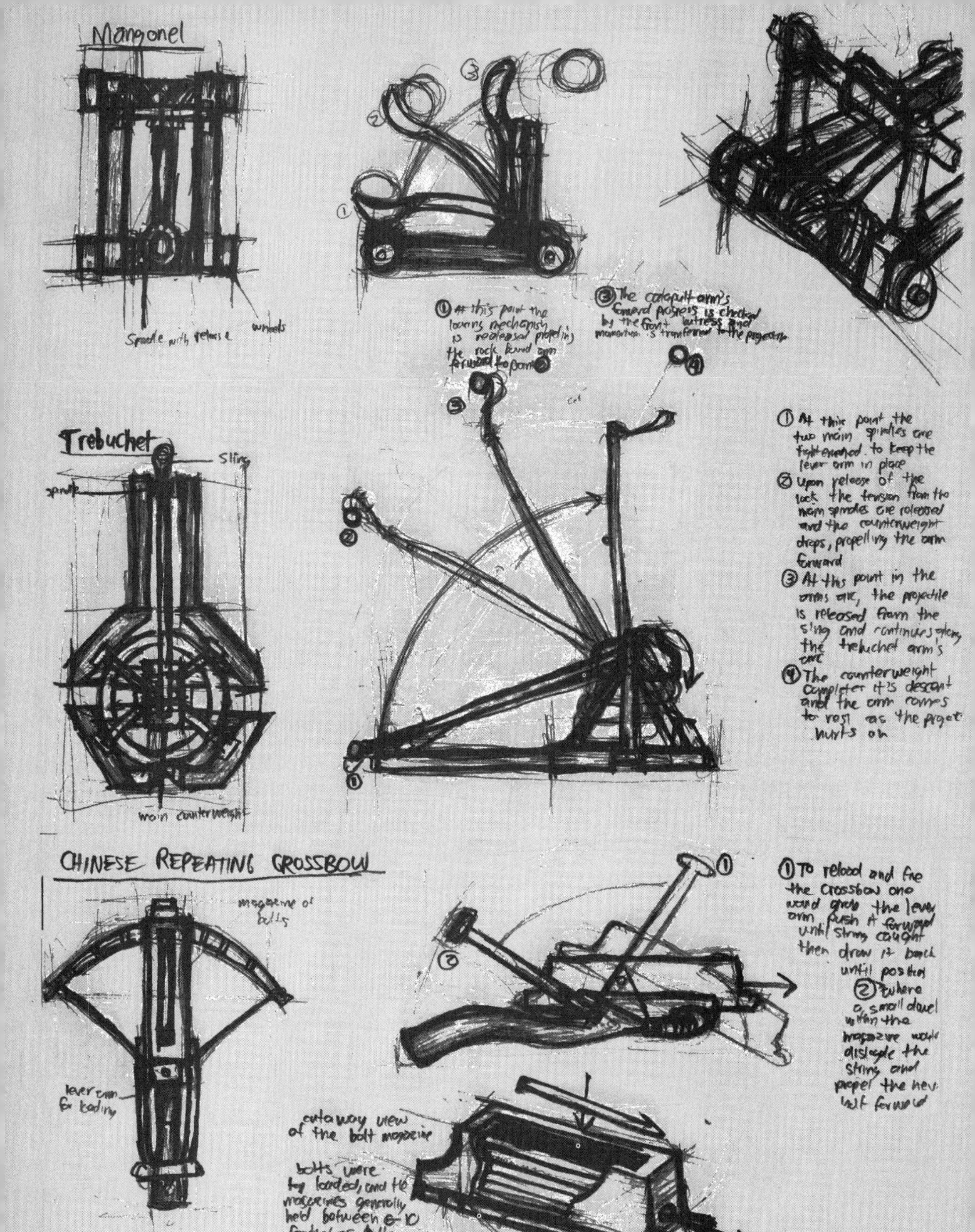
Mangonel
Spindle with release
wheels
① At this point the locking mechanism is released propelling the rock bound arm forward to point ②
③ The catapult arm's forward progress is checked by the front buttress and momentum is transferred to the projectile
Trebuchet
sling
main counterweight
① At this point the two main spindles are tightened to keep the lever arm in place
② Upon release of the lock the tension from the main spindles are released and the counterweight drops, propelling the arm forward
③ At this point in the arms arc, the projectile is released from the sling and continues along the trebuchet arm's arc
④ The counterweight completes it's descent and the arm comes to rest as the project hurts on
CHINESE REPEATING CROSSBOW
magazine of bolts
lever arm for loading
① To reload and fire the crossbow one would grab the lever arm push it forward until string caught then draw it back until position
② where a small dowel within the magazine would dislodge the string and propel the new bolt forward
cutaway view of the bolt magazine
bolts were top loaded, and the magazines generally held between 6-10 featherless bolts.

Chapter Eleven

The Teutons

The Teutons, a people from the area we now call Denmark, invaded the Roman region of Gaul in the first century BCE. They were repulsed, but it was then that their name came to stand for all Germanic peoples.

When the Roman emperor Charlemagne died, the Holy Roman Empire split in two and one portion went to each of his sons. The western portion comprised modern-day France and part of Italy. The eastern portion included Germany, Austria, and northern Italy. Although the western kingdom retained the name Holy Roman Empire, neither side could carry that distinction with the pope's blessing.

In the late twelfth century, the German ruler Frederick I, "Barbarossa," united Germany's duchies and warring factions into what he called the Holy Roman Empire.

Barbarossa was in many ways a military leader but is best known for his ambition, audacity, and political acumen. After uniting Germany's fertile lands, he set his sights on Rome and Italy. Because the pope wouldn't support him, Barbarossa defied the pontiff and declared himself pope. The two promptly excommunicated each other, setting the stage for the Teutonic invasion of Italy.

Barbarossa sacked Milan first and then dealt a crushing blow to the remaining Italian city-states (the Lombard League). When they surrendered, Barbarossa crowned himself the new Holy Roman Emperor—with the pope's blessing.

Having chosen to participate in the Third Crusade, Barbarossa promised to meet the other crusaders in Jerusalem (the all-important Holy Land). His army of 30,000 knights was far too large to travel over water, so he marched them overland to the goal. His joy at reaching the Middle East proved his undoing as he drowned while leaping into the water in full armor. His death marked the end of his empire, but the benefits to Germany in the form of Italian philosophy, science, and art had a lasting influence.

Maximizing Strengths and Minimizing Weaknesses

In *Microsoft Age of Empires II,* the Teutons are Farm-building, defensive, and religious powerhouses during all ages of the game. Although their best units are slow and plodding, they pack a terrific punch and are virtually impossible to defeat using the common "rush" technique in early ages. This is the result of some important production and defensive bonuses that are available to the Teutons without research or construction. (See Figure 11-1.)

Figure 11-1 *Farms are cheap for the Teutons. Use them to feed your defenses.*

The Teutonic Town Center enjoys bonuses to attack damage (+2) and range (+5). Garrisoned Teutonic Towers hold twice as many units and fire twice as fast as normal. As they proceed through the ages, they enjoy strong Farm-building bonuses (Teuton Farms require only two-thirds the amount of Wood that other civilizations use), powerful religious units, and unerring defensive structures.

In short, this is a perfect Wonder-building civilization. But don't count them out of pitched battles or conquests. Teutonic Knights are among the game's most devastating infantry, their Monks enjoy advantages in healing range and have access to all upgrades, and they can generate units at a frenetic rate. Plus, the Imperial Age is technologically kind to them.

It may take a while for their troops to arrive at the battle, but once they do, they conquer.

How Changes Through the Ages Affect Tactics

Despite having some of the weakest Archers and Cavalry in the game, the Teutons are still strong enough to take care of business—if the business is taken care of early enough. They have numerous economic advantages, including inexpensive Farming costs. Of course, the Teutons are known for their defenses, with Towers and Town Centers armed to the teeth. But don't forget about the Monks' extraordinary healing range. If used wisely, these clerics can compensate quite a bit for the weak archers and cavalry.

Dark Age

Given the Teutons' defensive power, you should concentrate on building Villagers and Houses and on gathering resources to advance. Normally you don't need to maintain a defensive army early on; a small group of garrisoned Villagers can wipe out attackers from a very long range even as you gather resources. (See Figure 11-2.)

Figure 11-2 *The attackers come in a large wave but are cut down one by one.*

Concentrate on Food and Wood production, build a Dock so you can fish, and set your sights on Stone and Gold: you'll need them later. Build a Barracks, but don't bother with infantry unless you need to fend off a persistent early attack. Remember, your goal is to advance through the ages as quickly as you can.

Feudal Age

Build a Stable and produce some Scout Cavalry. Explore, and keep an eye out for enemy positions, local resources, and a good perimeter for a stout Stone Wall. Make sure there are ample resources within this perimeter; you'll be hiding there for some time.

Figure 11-3 *Place extra Towers to defend your walls.*

Build more Villagers and mine all the Stone you think you'll need. As soon as you can, build that wall around your camp, placing gates in strategic places. Position Guard Towers to discourage enemy attacks (shown in Figure 11-3), lock your gates, and set your Villagers to amassing a great stockpile of resources, especially Gold and Stone. Begin researching advancements in your Blacksmith, University, and offensive buildings. However, focus more on defensive advancements than offensive. Upgrade your Walls and Towers at your first opportunity.

Position Archers, Cavalry, and infantry near vulnerable areas. As the battle rages, have your Villagers repair Walls. Now isn't the time to build a lot of units, launch attacks, or conduct hampering raids on the enemy. Your advantage lies in defense and research.

Castle Age

Build a Castle as quickly as you can, preferably near your most vulnerable wall (as shown in Figure 11-4). Have some Villagers create more Farms. Your lower Wood cost allows you to trade Wood in your Market (Gold and Stone are

important Teutonic commodities) and build more ships, Archers, and other Wood-based units. After you have your Castle, research Conscription and look toward advancing to the Imperial Age. Don't forget to build a Monastery. Accordingly, if enemy forces breach your Walls and engage your units, take full advantage of the Teutonic Monks' advanced healing range.

Figure 11-4 *Placing your Castle near a potential siege point puts its defensive and unit-generating capabilities where you need them the most.*

Imperial Age

Research the Elite Teutonic Knight and start researching infantry, gunpowder, and defensive upgrades. Use research to make your Monks stronger, faster, and more powerful. Teutonic Monks are some of the most effective clerics in the game, right up there with those of the Byzantines, Japanese, and Saracens. Be sure to give them every advantage possible. While doing all this, do not neglect your resources. For instance, use extra Wood to upgrade your navy and build a fleet to defend Fishing Ships (on sea-based maps). Upgrade to gunpowder and all advancements that aid your combat units and defensive structures. Step up your Gold-gathering efforts; the Elite Teutonic Knight is quite expensive, and you'll need as many of them as you can get.

Determine your ultimate goal. The Teutonic special units are ill-suited for raiding Relics, so consider the Wonder or Conquest victory. Now build a massive army and pursue your goal.

To build the Wonder (shown in Figure 11-5), invest in numerous Guard Towers to protect it. If invasion is your goal, build a good mix of Elite Teutonic Knights, Paladins, Hand Cannoneers, Monks, and Crossbowmen. Take along a few Onagers, Battering Rams, and a Trebuchet or two. Because you've built a stout wall and Guard Towers (and perhaps Bombard Towers) already, you'll find that the Teutonic civilization has an easier time defending the Wonder than the game's other civilizations would.

Figure 11-5 *The Teutonic people are natural defenders, making a Wonder victory an easy option.*

Keep your Villagers gathering resources as you attack the enemy. Order as many units as possible from all offensive structures, and set their gather points to the heart of enemy fortifications. That way, once you reach your unit limit, new units will replace your dead ones and continue marching on the enemy as soon as they are created.

Your Teutonic Knights can take a lot of punishment, so often you'll find that many new units will reach the fight before all the old units are wiped out. This keeps the pressure on as powerful attackers fall, only to be replaced with more.

Unique Unit Tactics: Teutonic Knight

The Teutonic Knight is the game's most expensive—and powerful—infantry unit. (See Figure 11-6.) His plodding speed and high overall cost offset his large number of hit points and strong armor, however.

Deploy your Teutonic Knights against Siege Engines, enemy infantry, and buildings. Because they're too slow to pursue a crafty retreating enemy, it's easy for enemy Cavalry and missile units to trample or pincushion them. Overall, it's best to use them as engineers for dismantling enemy buildings.

With Cavalry and missile unit support, the Teutonic Knight can return to his task of dismantling enemy fortifications with absolute precision. Elite Teutonic Knights should make up the bulk of your assault, backed up by Monks, Siege Engines, Cavalry, and Hand Cannoneers (Skirmishers or Crossbowmen) to ensure everyone's protection (as shown in Figure 11-7). The Monks' range allows them to heal your units *during* the battle!

Figure 11-6 *A good troop of hardy Elite Teutonic Knights makes for a powerful offense and a stout defense.*

Figure 11-7 *With Teutonic Knights in the lead and Monks, Siege Engines, Cavalry, and Hand Cannoneers close behind, this assault can't be withstood.*

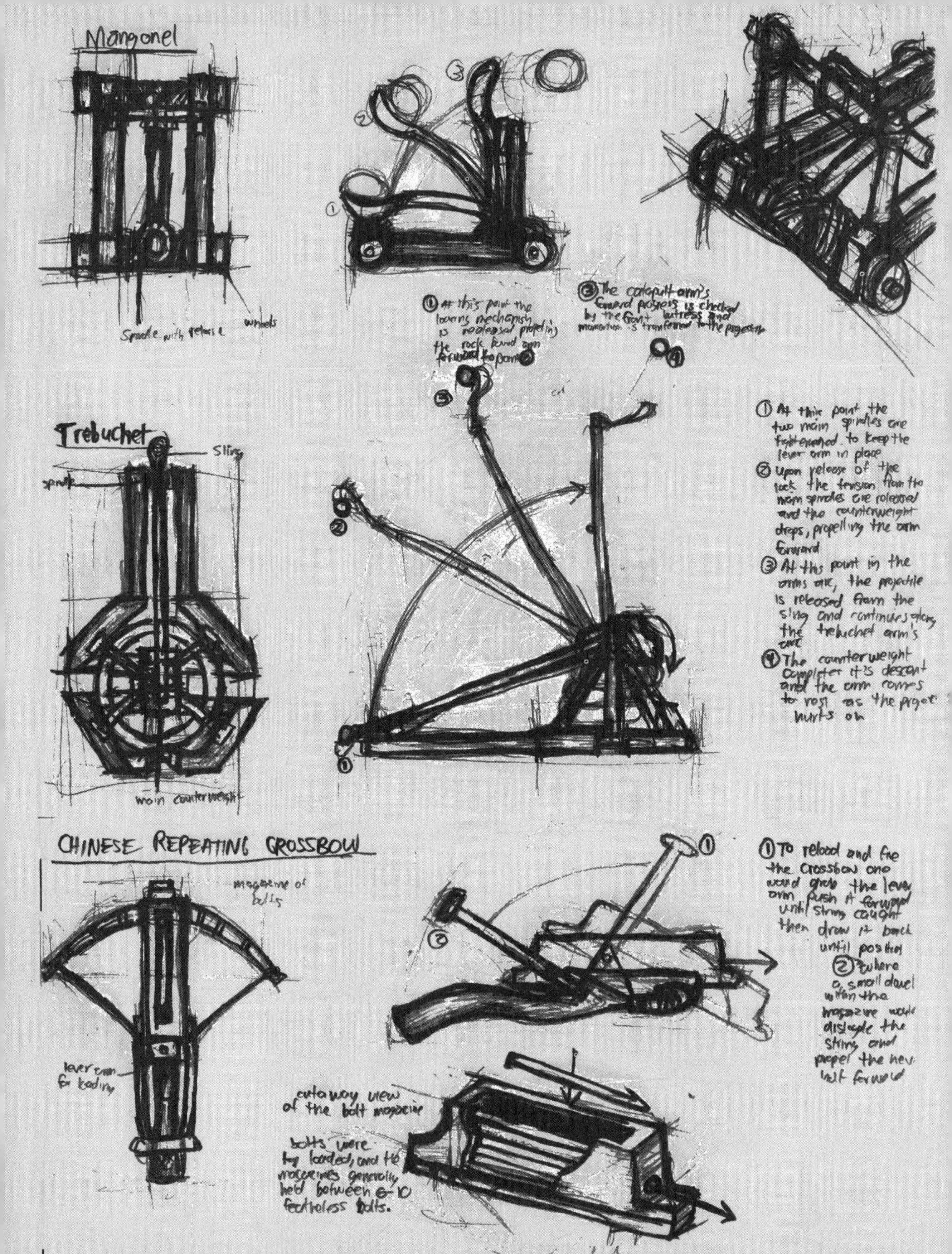
Mangonel
Spindle with release
wheels
① At this point the
The catapult arm's
forward progress is checked
by the front
Trebuchet
Sling
main counterweight
① At this point the
two main spindles are
to keep the
lever arm in place
② Upon release of the
the tension from the
main spindles are released
and the counterweight
drops, propelling the arm
forward
③ At this point in the
arms arc, the projectile
is released from the
sling and continues along
the trebuchet arm's
④ The counterweight
completes it's descent
and the arm comes
to rest as the
hurts on
CHINESE REPEATING CROSSBOW
magazine of
bolts
lever arm
for loading
① To reload and fire
the crossbow one
would grab the lever
arm push it forward
until string caught
then draw it back
until
② where
a small dowel
within the
dislodge the
string and
propel the
bolt forward
cutaway view
of the bolt magazine
bolts were
loaded, and the
generally
held between 6-10
featherless bolts.

The Turks

Not one, but two medieval dynasties were produced by this civilization: the Seljuk and Ottoman Empires. Although the Turks began their reign in the late Middle Ages, they remained a world power until World War I. The civilization began as a nomadic people in central Asia, converting to Islam in the tenth century. During this time, a substantial number of Seljuks became mercenaries for Baghdad's army. By the twelfth century, the Turks had extended their boundaries from the Persian Gulf into the Middle East and Anatolia (the Asian part of Turkey). Their success, however, prompted assaults from two fronts—the Christian Europeans and the Mongols. Weakened by the Crusades, the Seljuk Empire inevitably crumbled to Genghis Khan's troops in the mid-thirteenth century.

The Ottoman Empire lasted much longer—almost six hundred years to be exact. Sultan Osman I united the Islamic peoples of Anatolia during the fourteenth century in a jihad against the Byzantines. In 1453 AD, Sultan Mehmed captured Constantinople, renaming the city Istanbul. The great Turkish architect Sinan built the famous Suleimaniye Mosque there around this time. Although besieged by Mongol assaults, the Ottomans did not succumb to the same fate as the Seljuks. By the seventeenth century, the empire included Arabia, Asia Minor, Egypt, North Africa, and parts of the Balkan Peninsula.

Maximizing Strengths and Minimizing Weaknesses

The Turks emphasize the use of gunpowder and firearms more than any other civilization. They are also strong architecturally and defensively. Furthermore, the Turks field an impressive Cavalry (even though they lack the Paladin) and have a number of economic technologies at their disposal. Of course, all this comes with a few drawbacks. Turkish Monks do not possess important Imperial Age techniques such as Block Printing and Illumination, and the civilization also lacks a diverse arsenal of siege equipment.

Note: *The Turks are the only civilization with access to all static defensive structures and technologies. These features come in handy when dealing with siege weapon powerhouses such as the Saracens and Mongols.*

Overall, though, the Turks easily overcome any deficiencies they might have. For example, the entry of a gunpowder unit, the Janissary, in the Castle Age more than compensates for the lack of units like the Pikeman and the Elite Skirmisher in that same period. Additionally, the Bombard Cannons fill the siege weapon holes left by the Onager's absence. In fact, since Turkish gunpowder units also have more hit points than those in other civilizations, the Turks are always a threat on the sea and on land (as shown in Figure 12-1). In short, the Turks are a blast for anyone who longs to mix lots of gunfire with sword-wielding fun.

Figure 12-1 *The Turks' Janissaries are only one example of the civilization's powerful gunpowder units.*

How Changes Through the Ages Affect Tactics

No other civilization can train their gunpowder units as fast as the Turks. Additionally, the Turks are the only civilization with a gunpowder unit in the Castle Age. With these advantages, it's easy to overlook the general power of the Turk civilization. Overall, the Turks are one of the most well-rounded civilizations in *Microsoft Age of Empires II,* ideal for single or multiplayer matches.

Dark Age

The Turks do not have any ready-made enhancements for gathering or producing food. Their only strength in the first two Ages lies with the collection of Gold. Turkish Gold miners work significantly faster than miners in other civilizations. On maps low in resources this is quite an advantage. In those situations, send out two Villagers to mine from Gold sites (as pictured in Figure 12-2). Be sure to escort them with a Militia unit or two. This mining gives you an economic advantage over the competition. Always keep in mind the "golden rule"—those with the Gold make the rules. After all, a hefty Gold supply is key to building troops.

Figure 12-2 *Turkish Gold miners give new meaning to "Gold Rush."*

Feudal Age

After you advance as quickly as possible to the Feudal Age, you should improve production and gathering techniques by researching staples like the Wheelbarrow, Horse Collar, and Double-Bit Axe. Meanwhile, build a Blacksmith, and then research Fletching there. Continue mining Gold, not only filling your coffers, but also keeping the shiny stuff out of the enemy's hands. To sum up all of this in five simple words: research, mine Gold, and research.

Research, though, is not enough to win; other aspects are intrinsic to victory on the battlefield. Your basic goals in this period are to attack the enemy's economic structures and Villagers and to advance to the next Age quickly, but not before the appropriate technologies are researched. Dispatch

Note: *Place Watch Towers near Gold sites. They are the best guards in the business and can easily shoot down enemy Villagers seeking riches to plunder.*

Men-at-Arms and Archers to attack enemy Villagers. Destroy peripheral buildings like Mining Camps, Lumber Camps, and Markets. Although this may not seem like much, little things like these are crucial to hindering the enemy's progress—even militarily.

Castle Age

The Turks have one major advantage on their side during this period—the Janissary. This unit is the only gunpowder unit in *Age of Empires II* available this early in the game. The Janissary packs quite a punch and has the longest range of nonelite Imperial Age archery units. Used wisely, this unique unit is effective against some of the most deadly of forces, including the Japanese Samurai and Celtic Woad Raider. Yes, it requires nearly 150 percent more resources than the Crossbowman does, but it inflicts three times the damage.

The ideal goal is to keep opponents from acquiring gunpowder technology as long as possible. You can do so by hindering the enemy's economic progression. Basically, you want to accentuate your strengths as much as possible, while distancing those same traits from the enemy. For example, if you can fight a war with Elite Janissaries and Bombard Cannons while your opponent only has Crossbowmen, your enemy won't be standing for very long (as shown in Figure 12-3). Use your Janissaries, Monks, Knights, and Long Swordsmen to initiate the beginning of the end.

Figure 12-3 *Which would you rather fire with—bullets or arrows?*

Imperial Age

This is do-or-die time. What you have to *do*, of course, is keep producing gunpowder units. In themselves, though, they are not enough. Elite Janissaries, Hand Cannoneers, and Bombard Cannons need protection. Champions and Cavaliers should be guarding them at all times. A good force mix is the key. Yes, Janissaries are powerful, but they are also expensive. Unless you have control of the seas, your Elite Cannon Galleons will require some support. Have Fire Ships accompany each vessel just in case a Demolition Ship scurries nearby (as shown in Figure 12-4). Protect your "guns" from pesky units, as you have bigger game—Town Centers, Castles, Docks, and Wonders—to worry about.

Note: *Use the free Light Cavalry upgrade to send troops quickly into enemy territory. These troops are great for demolishing buildings or Villagers—or just disrupting the enemy's concentration.*

Note: *Don't forget the basics. Continue researching technologies at the University, Monastery, and Blacksmith. These will be crucial if the enemy happens to be aggressive and relentless.*

Figure 12-4 *A Fire Ship chases down a Teutonic Heavy Demolition Ship.*

Tip: *When playing enemies like the Saracens, send a special fleet of Cannon Galleons to search for and destroy all Transport Ships—a key strength of the Arabic civilization. Research the Dry Dock and Shipwright to help in nautical efficiency.*

Note: *Don't forget the cardinal rules at this stage of the game. First, hamper the enemy from progressing to the next Age. Next, concentrate on damaging the enemy's resource gathering and production efficiency. Finally, constantly assault the enemy, never giving them time to rest or build up forces.*

Due to the siege weaponry strengths of some rivals (for example, the Mongols, Saracens, and Teutons), the building of Walls and Keeps may be necessary to thwart the enemy's offensive progress. Stationing Trebuchets inside your fortress provides additional help. Just remember, though, not to concentrate too much on defending your territory. It's been said many times but always bears repeating—*the best defense is a good offense*. When the enemy begins pounding at your fortress, attack their village with more force. Something has to give; just don't let it be you.

Unique Unit Tactics: Janissary

Note: *The Elite Janissary's range equals that of the Siege Onager and is the farthest of all the unique units. Furthermore, the Elite Janissary delivers more attack points than any other unique unit, with the exception of the Persian Elite War Elephant.*

Tip: *Although Janissaries are weak, various improvements at the Blacksmith such as Padded Archer Armor, Leather Archer Armor, and Ring Archer Armor will keep them alive a bit longer.*

Janissaries (pictured in Figure 12-5) were slaves used by Turkish leaders for combat and were known for their training and devotion to the Ottoman cause. In fact, a horde of over 10,000 Janissaries was responsible for the fall of Constantinople in 1453 AD. They are quite effective against all types of units, but they are especially so in battles against standard infantry and Monks. When they are standing behind a line of melee Cavalry units, they can even take down Berserks, Teutonic Knights, and Samurai.

Providing ample protection for your Janissary is the key to using this unique unit effectively. Janissaries are as weak as any foot Archer, and as a result, they are *always* in need of defense. An ideal formation consists of positioning some Janissaries—with a couple of Monks by their sides—behind a group of Heavy Camels (as shown in Figure 12-6). Since the Heavy Camels are just guards and provide the same number of hit points as Cavaliers, there's no need to squander extra resources on a horseman. Besides, the Monks can continually heal wounded Camels while engaged in battle. Before you know it, you'll be reenacting the siege on Constantinople.

Figure 12-5 *Several Janissaries guard a Gold site.*

Figure 12-6 *A winning combination: Monks, Janissaries, and Heavy Camels are a tough group to beat.*

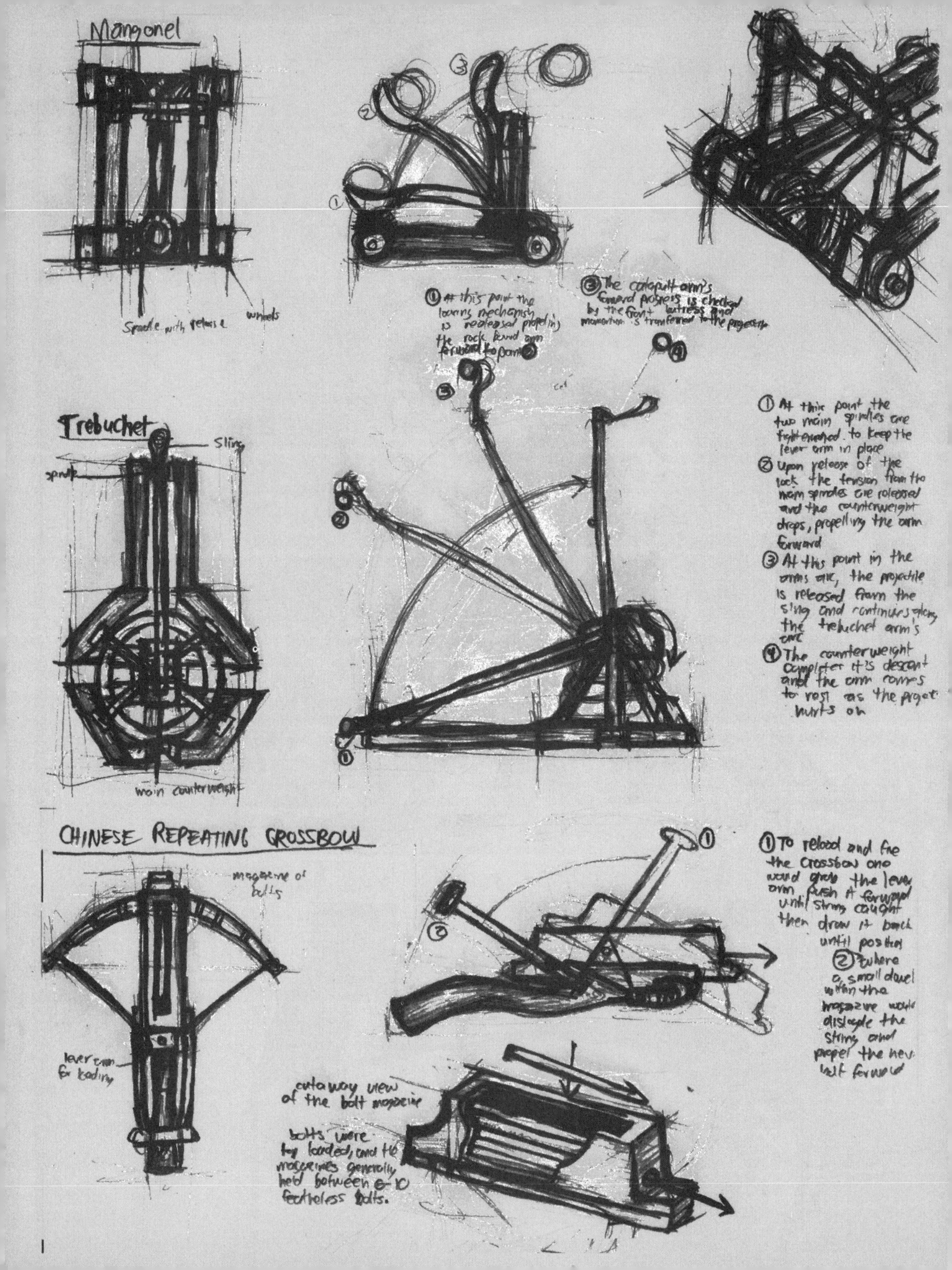

Mangonel
Spindle with release
wheels
③ The catapult arm's forward progress is checked by the front buttress and momentum is transferred to the projectile
Trebuchet
Sling
spindle
main counterweight
① At this point the two main spindles are tightened to keep the lever arm in place
② Upon release of the lock the tension from the main spindles are released and the counterweight drops, propelling the arm forward
③ At this point in the arms arc, the projectile is released from the sling and continues along the trebuchet arm's arc
④ The counterweight completes it's descent and the arm comes to rest as the projectile hurts on
CHINESE REPEATING CROSSBOW
magazine of bolts
lever arm for loading
① To reload and fire the crossbow one would grab the lever arm push it forward until string caught then draw it back until position ② where a small dowel within the magazine would dislodge the string and propel the new bolt forward
cutaway view of the bolt magazine
bolts were top loaded, and the magazines generally held between 6-10 featherless bolts.

Chapter Thirteen

The Vikings

Nordic settlements existed over several hundred years BCE; however, it wasn't until the late eighth century that this civilization became a major player in world history. Their cousins, the Lombards and Goths, had already made their presence known with the fall of the Roman Empire. The Vikings, though, unlike their Germanic brethren, were not restrained to just land raids. They invaded a variety of territories, including Iceland, England, Normandy, Russia, and Palestine. For nearly two centuries, tales of plundered coastal villages and images of dragon-headed Longboats had struck terror into Europe. All of this would change, though, with the Vikings' religious conversion.

The Norsemen had a habit of adopting the customs and beliefs of the cultures in which they settled. Consequently, by the eleventh century, Christianity had reached Denmark, Sweden, and Norway—the lands from which these peoples had originated. Deterred by the new faith and the establishment of larger kingdoms, Viking barbarism soon ended. Nevertheless, ideas from this northern civilization remained. This is true today not only of Scandinavia, but also of Slavic, German, French, and English-speaking cultures. Some of the most obvious influences include the names for several days of the week, which were derived from the titles of Norse deities.

Maximizing Strengths and Minimizing Weaknesses

Generally speaking, the Vikings are the weakest civilization in the game. Despite harboring a strong navy, a significant deficiency of technology and units in the Castle and Imperial Ages hinders these people in land battles. For instance, the Vikings' Cavalry (pictured in Figure 13-1) is the most ineffective of any within *Microsoft Age of Empires II*. This is exacerbated by the Norsemen's

Figure 13-1 *The Cavalier is the only Imperial Age Cavalry unit in the Viking arsenal.*

inability to produce land-based gunpowder units (for example, the Bombard Cannon and Hand Cannoneer). And don't look for spiritual guidance from the Viking Monks; their abilities pale in comparison with those of the Saracens and Byzantines.

Nevertheless, winning in situations where your navy cannot strut—or sail—its stuff is not impossible, just difficult. The Nordic civilization has some advantages worth considering, though. For instance, the Vikings are the only civilization with two unique units: the Longboat and the Berserk. The latter complements the durable infantry, which has over 25 hit points, while the Longboat technology assists the Vikings with cheap, durable ships. This reduced cost allows the Vikings to build plenty.

Figure 13-2 *A group of Long Swordsmen battle an enemy Archery Range.*

The Vikings have to act early—if not, they won't last long. Use your infantry to constantly target enemy structures and Villagers (as shown in Figure 13-2). Try to keep your opponent at least an Age behind you. If the

enemy is able to research and construct Hand Cannoneers and Paladins, you're going to have your hands full.

Note: *The Vikings are the only civilization incapable of producing a Fire Ship. Of course, the more powerful Longboat makes up for this deficiency.*

How Changes Through the Ages Affect Tactics

Some civilizations, such as the Japanese and Byzantines, are well equipped for battle on land or sea. Others are not. The Vikings fit the latter category. They have a formidable navy but their army lacks important technologies and sophistication. The Vikings' only chance of winning a land-based contest is to attack and destroy the enemy early.

Dark Age

Note: *When you're playing as the Vikings, try to ally with another civilization. You'll want to do this because the Vikings can use the help, and because during team play, Viking Docks require significantly fewer resources to construct.*

You have three basic objectives in this period. First, explore as much of the map as possible. Use your Scout Cavalry on land and a fleet of Fishing Ships to search the sea. Next, fulfill the requirements for advancing to the Feudal Age. Generate several Villagers for building two Dark Age structures and collecting Wood and Food. Finally—if possible at this time—dispatch a group of Militia to destroy enemy buildings and Villagers.

Feudal Age

The Feudal Age marks the emergence of the Vikings' special attributes. Infantry units now have additional hit points, and the Vikings have access to their inexpensive warships. The Vikings also receive free Wheelbarrow technology, something that greatly improves gathering efficiency. Such enhancements make resource management easier while allowing the Vikings to mount early attacks.

Figure 13-3 *Viking Galleys cost less than their opponents' counterparts.*

Continue attacking the enemy, using Men-at-Arms to demolish economic structures and Archers for handling Villagers. Build Galleys to seize control of the sea (as pictured in Figure 13-3). The earlier you dominate the waterways, the more smoothly the game will run. Meanwhile, research Fletching at the Blacksmith, and add Gold and Stone to your must-haves list. Trade for the appropriate resources at the Market, and upgrade quickly to the Castle Age.

> **Note:** *As with the other twelve civilizations, you can only produce unique units once a Castle has been constructed. This applies to the Vikings and their two different unique units produced at two different sites. Therefore, although the Berserk is produced at the Castle and the Longboat is constructed at the Dock, both require you to build a Castle first.*

Castle Age

This is perhaps the strongest period for the Vikings. They have more warships available in their arsenal than in the previous Age, and infantry come with a greater number of hit points than similar units in other civilizations. Not one—but two—unique units make appearances. And although Castle Age Stables do not have access to Husbandry or Camels, the degree of difference here between the Vikings' Cavalry units and those of other civilizations is minimal. Needless to say, your main goal in the Castle Age is to

attack the enemy unrelentingly. Just don't forget to build a Monastery, University, and Siege Workshop. Equipment from the Siege Workshop will make the infantry's job a lot easier.

Imperial Age

Naturally, you should try to reach this Age as quickly as possible, but you never want to see your opponents get here. It's extremely difficult to defeat the enemy once they attain a hefty Cavalry, powerful Monks, and various gunpowder units in their arsenal. Therefore, land-based battles against civilizations like the Byzantines, Chinese, and Saracens in their Imperial Age are rarely pretty. The only way you can win is to accentuate your strengths in infantry and siege weaponry. The building of additional Siege Workshops and Barracks helps you do just that.

The Vikings are more suited for sea battles. Although they lack Fire Ships, they have Demolition Ships, Cannon Galleons, and the famous Longboats. With reduced costs for warships, the Vikings can produce killer boats in a lot less time than the enemy. Only the navies of the Byzantines, Japanese, and Turks compare in strength and efficiency. To use the ships to your advantage, have the Demolition Ships defend your coastline against enemy vessels. Then use the Elite Longboats to sink the opposition's Transport Ships and Fishing Ships (as shown in Figure 13-4), and use the Cannon Galleons to bombard enemy buildings and armies.

Figure 13-4 *A fleet of Elite Longboats sinks an enemy Transport Ship.*

Unique Unit Tactics: Longboat

Longboats are the most famous symbol of Nordic civilization. These sturdy ships, carved with monstrosities upon the bow, were responsible for making the Vikings some of the best pirates in history. Manned by oarsmen, the Longboat was capable of traversing shallow river basins and landing on nearly all types of coastlines. Likewise, the game's Longboats can make their way through shallows and tight spots (as shown in Figure 13-5).

Figure 13-5 *A Viking Longboat navigates through shallows.*

Think of the Longboat as a War Galley capable of flinging multiple arrows. The Elite Longboat's features are comparable to those of the Galleon. Both ships are more aptly suited for taking down Demolition Ships than the Fire Ship is. In fact, a group of Longboats can extinguish a Fire Ship quite easily. Most of the time, they should be used to protect Cannon Galleons and to scourge the seas of enemy Transport Ships and Fishing Ships.

Note: *Technologies that are useful for improving Longboats include Fletching, Bodkin Arrow, Bracer, and Ballistics.*

Unique Unit Tactics: Berserk

Like a warrior ravaged with fits of madness, the Viking Berserk of *Age of Empires II* terrorizes settlements with his brute strength and ferocity. Berserks are known for two distinct characteristics—their high number of attack points and

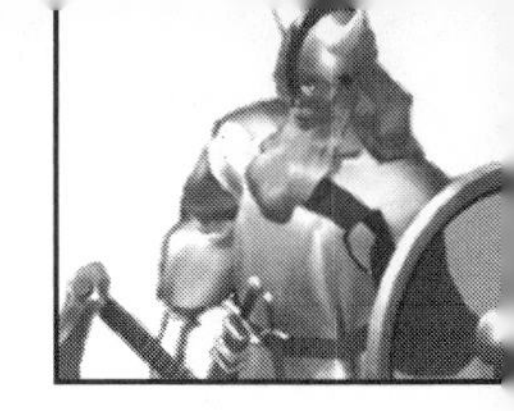

the ability to heal themselves. The latter feature is quite a boon considering the frail Monks in the Viking camp.

One of the primary ways to use the Berserks' self-healing powers involves rotating the unit as follows: Form two groups of Berserks. Send one group to fight while the other rests (see Figure 13-6). Pull the wounded soldiers out to heal while rotating the others into the fray. Continue the rotation as needed. This method saves time and resources in creating new Berserks. Furthermore, the enemy never gets a chance to rest.

Note: *The Elite Berserk dishes out almost as many attack points as the Teutonic Knight. Unfortunately, the Berserk's armor, unlike that of the Teutons' unique unit, is roughly the equivalent of tinfoil.*

Figure 13-6 *A group of Berserks heal themselves.*

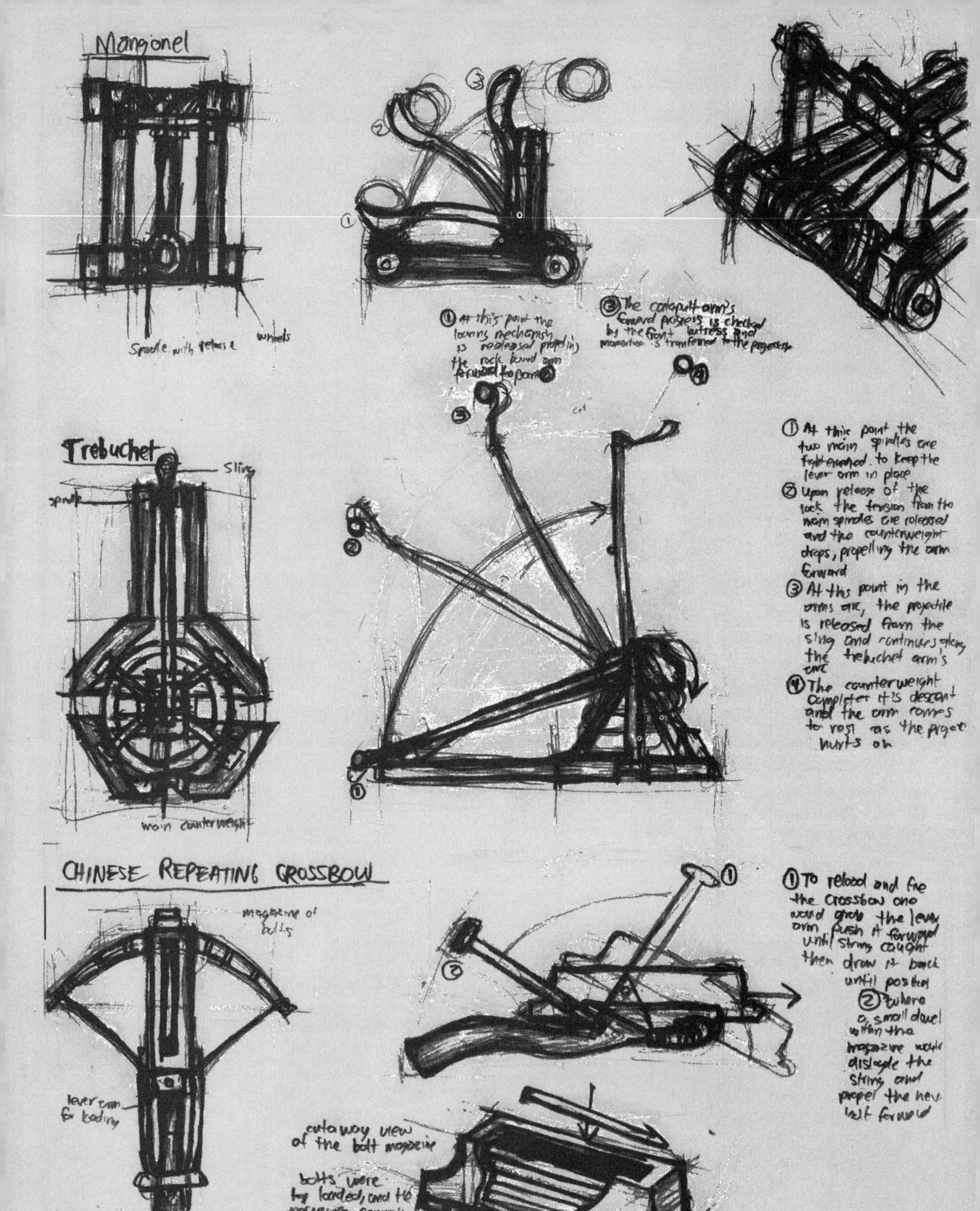
Mangonel
Spindle with release
wheels
① At this point the
mechanism
the rock
③ The catapult arm's
forward progress is checked
by the front buttress and
Trebuchet
Sling
spindle
main counterweight
① At this point the
two main spindles are
to keep the
lever arm in place
② Upon release of the
lock the tension from the
main spindles are released
and the counterweight
drops, propelling the arm
forward
③ At this point in the
the projectile
is released from the
sling and continues along
the trebuchet arm's
arc
④ The counterweight
completes it's descent
and the arm comes
to rest as the
hurts on
CHINESE REPEATING CROSSBOW
magazine of
bolts
lever arm
for loading
① To reload and fire
the crossbow one
would the lever
arm push it forward
until string caught
then draw it back
until position
② where
a small dowel
within the
magazine
dislodge the
string and
propel the
bolt forward
cutaway view
of the bolt magazine
bolts were
loaded, and the
magazines generally
held between 8-10
featherless bolts.

Part II

Inside the Age of Kings—Analysis and Tactical Tips

Warriors do not march into battle without their weapons, armor, and food. Neither should gamers attempt to play without the equipment they need to win. But in this case the equipment is not weapons, armor, and food; it's knowledge, experience, and statistics.

Think of these next two chapters as your rucksack, holding your war-fighting tools. It's here that you'll not only learn the basic tactics that lead to victory but also glean the information you need to properly employ those tactics.

Chapter Fourteen

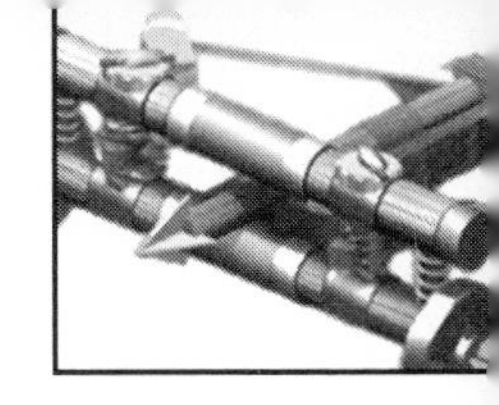

The People and Weapons of Kings

Many strategy guides provide a laundry list of game units, buildings, and other assorted features. Many games, however, don't have the high-quality user manual that *Microsoft Age of Empires II: The Age of Kings* has. The user guide contains numerous pullout cards, manual pages, and game screens that are devoted to describing and categorizing. I won't try to duplicate the manual's cut on each unit here. Instead, I'll lay down some unit-specific strategies for your gaming perusal.

Infantry

If it walks on foot and doesn't fire arrows, it's infantry. At least according to *Age of Empires II,* and hey, if it's good enough for this game's designers, it's good enough for me. Infantry includes three subcategories: the melee units (shown in Figure 14-1), the Pikeman-types, and the unique units. Let's look at each.

Figure 14-1 *A group of melee units.*

Melee Units

Melee units, as shown in Figure 14-1, are your basic infantry. Their cost remains constant throughout the Ages, making them a better buy as time goes on. These units excel in two areas: razing enemy buildings and protecting your own vulnerable units. All infantry receive an attack bonus when they battle buildings, so they are a logical choice to send into these types of battles. They also work well in the front line of an Archer-backed Line Formation, or as the box around two or three Monks. Archers are some of the toughest rivals for the infantry, as are the heavier Cavalry units.

Name	Cost	Hit Points	Attack Points	Armor/ Pierce Armor	Range	Speed
Militia	60F, 20G	40	4	0/0	0	Slow
Man-at-Arms	60F, 20G	45	6	0/0	0	Medium
Long Swordsman	60F, 20G	55	9	0/0	0	Medium
Two-Handed Swordsman	60F, 20G	60	11	0/0	0	Slow
Champion	60F, 20G	70	13	1/0	0	Slow

Spearman, Pikeman

These are the ultimate "Cavalry-away" unit, as shown in Figure 14-2. They are death to ponies, Camels, and Elephants alike. Note that they are best used in a formation with melee-type units such as Militia and Swordsman. If they are grouped with melee units in a Line Formation, the game will alternate columns of Pikeman-type units with columns of melee units. As a result, your melee units will be protected from both melee units and Cavalry.

Figure 14-2 *Pikemen are bad news for Cavalry.*

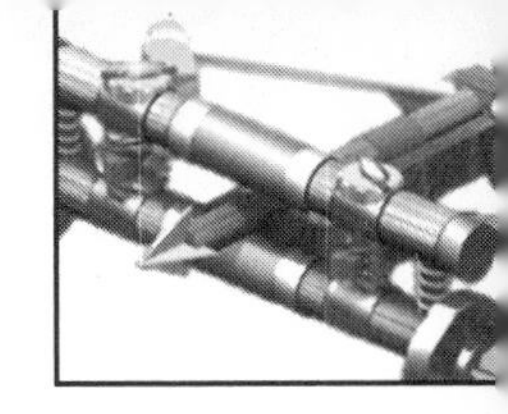

Name	Cost	Hit Points	Attack Points	Armor/ Pierce Armor	Range	Speed
Spearman	35F, 25W	45	3	0/0	0	Medium
Pikeman	35F, 25W	55	4	0/0	0	Slow

Infantry Unique Units

These are the toughest foot soldiers in the game. If you need a building taken down, an enemy formation decimated, or a building guarded, these will often be your first choice. (See Figure 14-3.)

Figure 14-3 *A group of infantry unique units on a coffee break.*

Berserk

Name	Cost	Hit Points	Attack Points	Armor/ Pierce Armor	Range	Speed
Berserk	65F, 25G	48	9	0/0	0	Slow
Elite Berserk	65F, 25G	60	14	2/0	0	Slow

Berserks are the only self-healing units in the game. Use this ability wisely. They are also the weakest unique unit. They work best when they are able to rotate to the rear to heal themselves. They also work well protecting your ranged units and assaulting buildings.

Samurai

Name	Cost	Hit Points	Attack Points	Armor/ Pierce Armor	Range	Speed
Samurai	60F, 30G	60	8	1/0	0	Slow
Elite Samurai	60F, 30G	80	12	1/0	0	Slow

The Samurai are the consummate unique-unit killer. This unit not only inflicts a significant number of hit points with each swing of the sword, but it swings that sword more quickly than any other infantry unique unit. Use the Samurai to actively seek out and destroy enemy unique infantry—unless it is the Woad Raider. They have no problem fighting this Celt, but they may be too slow to catch him. Of course, Samurai are not weaklings in their own right and work well in a Line Formation or destroying buildings. However, they are also more expensive to produce than other Castle Age infantry.

Teutonic Knight

Name	Cost	Hit Points	Attack Points	Armor/ Pierce Armor	Range	Speed
Teutonic Knight	85F, 40G	70	12	5/2	0	Slow
Elite Teutonic Knight	85F, 40G	100	17	10/2	0	Slow

The Teutonic Knight is a tank on legs. Easily the toughest foot soldier in the game, a handful of these can wreak havoc on numerous Two-Handed Swordsmen. Unfortunately for those playing as the Teutons, this quality has a price. The Teutonic Knights are also the most costly foot soldiers in the game. It's best to sprinkle these lightly in your melee unit formations, or send them on raids against enemy economic structures.

Throwing Axeman

Name	Cost	Hit Points	Attack Points	Armor/ Pierce Armor	Range	Speed
Throwing Axeman	55F, 25G	50	7	0/0	3	Slow
Elite Throwing Axeman	55F, 25G	60	8	1/0	4	Slow

Throwing Axeman are an anomaly—a melee unit with a ranged attack. These guys have the added ability to battle buildings and the range to do it from a couple of tiles' distance. Make no mistake, however—they are not Teutonic Knights. Although stronger than typical Archer-ranged attack units, they are no match for a Two-Handed Swordsman in a toe-to-toe confrontation. On the plus side, Throwing Axemen are the cheapest of all unique units, making them somewhat dispensable.

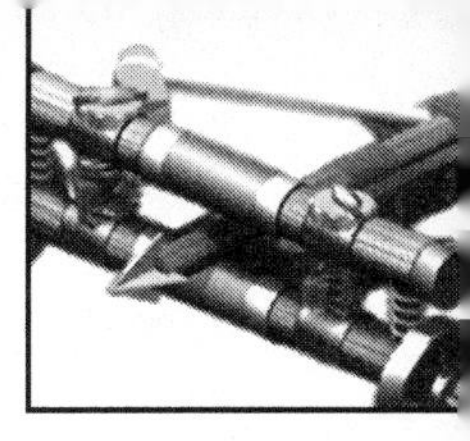

Woad Raider

Name	Cost	Hit Points	Attack Points	Armor/ Pierce Armor	Range	Speed
Woad Raider	65F, 25G	65	8	0/0	0	Medium
Elite Woad Raider	65F, 25G	80	13	0/0	0	Medium

The Woad Raiders' unique attribute is speed. Yes, they are stout fighters, but they are the only infantry unit with a Medium speed rating. This makes them ideal Villager hunters. The Villagers, who crawl about the map (their game speed is set to Slow), cannot avoid the Woad Raiders' swords and will fall within two whacks of an Elite Woad Raider. Use Woad Raiders to form elite economic raiding parties focused on the enemy Villagers.

Huskarl

Name	Cost	Hit Points	Attack Points	Armor/ Pierce Armor	Range	Speed
Huskarl	80F, 40G	60	10	0/4	0	Slow
Elite Huskarl	80F, 40G	70	12	0/6	0	Slow

The Huskarl is resistant to Archers' arrows. Its unique (at least for an infantry unit), piercing armor enables it to close in on and destroy enemy Archers before the arrow slingers can pincushion their bodies.

Archers

Archers are your basic foot- and hoof-propelled ranged weapon units, shown in Figure 14-4. They come in four varieties: foot Archers (including the Hand Cannoneer), horse Archers, Skirmishers, and Archer unique units.

Figure 14-4 *A smorgasbord of Archer types battle some approaching infantry.*

Foot Archers

Name	Cost	Hit Points	Attack Points	Armor/ Pierce Armor	Range	Speed
Archer	25W, 45G	30	4	0/0	4	Medium
Crossbowman	25W, 45G	35	5	0/0	5	Medium
Arbalest	25W, 45G	40	6	0/0	5	Medium
Hand Cannoneer	45F, 50G	35	17	1/0	7	Medium

When used properly, these fighters are a huge force multiplier. String several Archers behind a line of melee infantry, plop the whole formation on high ground, and you have a heck of a defense.

Archers also make great interdiction units. Send small bands of them to the fringes of the enemy's camp and attack Villagers as they transit to the woods, Farms, or Mines. Remember that crippling an enemy's economy is the most effective way to bring him to his knees.

Cavalry Archer

Name	Cost	Hit Points	Attack Points	Armor/ Pierce Armor	Range	Speed
Cavalry Archer	40W, 70G	50	6	0/0	3	Fast
Heavy Cavalry Archer	40W, 70G	60	7	1/0	4	Fast

Cavalry Archers are best used as fast Archers. They often serve the same purpose in a Line Formation with Heavy Cavalry as foot Archers do in a similar Line Formation with melee infantry. Obviously, Cavalry Archers are great for raiding parties and super for wiping out Villagers. However, avoid foot Archers and enemy Heavy Cavalry like the plague.

Skirmisher

Name	Cost	Hit Points	Attack Points	Armor/ Pierce Armor	Range	Speed
Skirmisher	25F, 35W	30	2	0/3	4	Medium
Elite Skirmisher	25F, 35W	35	3	0/4	5	Medium

Skirmishers are to Archers as Pikemen are to the Cavalry. Use these folks to take out enemy projectile pushers. They have the piercing armor to take a few

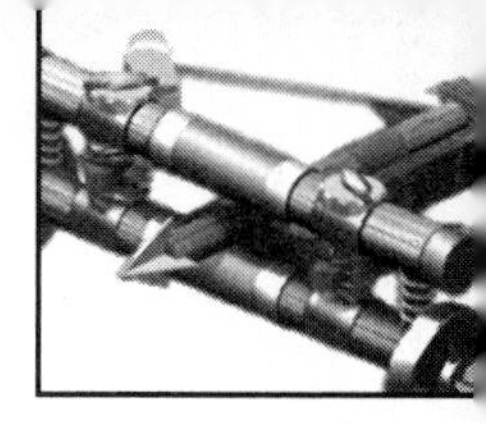

Archer hits and keep on ticking, *and* they receive a bonus when attacking Archers. Pure and simple, these folks were made for tromping Archers.

Archer Unique Units

Archer unique units are a devastating force. Each of these units has specific bonuses that make them a fearsome enemy. Some, like the Chu Ko Nu, fire much more rapidly than typical Archers, while others, like the Long Bowman, have a long reach. Whatever their specialty, these are some of the most useful warriors in the game.

Chu Ko Nu

Name	Cost	Hit Points	Attack Points	Armor/ Pierce Armor	Range	Speed
Chu Ko Nu	40W, 35G	45	8	0/0	4	Medium
Elite Chu Ko Nu	40W, 35G	50	8	0/0	4	Medium

Although the Chu Ko Nu's mediocre attack and range would seem to make them a weak unit, they have an attribute that makes them quite strong indeed—they fire *much* more rapidly than the Archers in other civilizations. Their rapid-fire capability not only makes them devastating but also makes them a good value. Five Chu Ko Nu can lay down as much feather as twice the number of Arbalests.

Janissary

Name	Cost	Hit Points	Attack Points	Armor/ Pierce Armor	Range	Speed
Janissary	60F, 55G	35	15	1/0	8	Medium
Elite Janissary	60F, 55G	40	18	2/0	8	Medium

A darn fine "Archer," the Janissary has two drawbacks: it's expensive—one of the most expensive unique units—and its accuracy decreases with range. Nevertheless, its crushing attack and excellent range make it a natural back-line inhabitant, and a not-too-shabby building breaker.

Longbowman

The Longbowman is an excellent unit. It's inexpensive and has the longest range of any Archer not powered by gunpowder. The unit's drawback is its attack, which at a meager five to six points is the same as a Crossbowman or an Arbalest. Even so, the Crossbowman and Arbalest can't damage what they can't reach, and the Elite Longbowman has the reach on both units.

Name	Cost	Hit Points	Attack Points	Armor/ Pierce Armor	Range	Speed
Longbowman	35W, 40G	35	6	0/0	5	Medium
Elite Longbowman	35W, 40G	40	7	0/1	6	Medium

Mangudai

Name	Cost	Hit Points	Attack Points	Armor/ Pierce Armor	Range	Speed
Mangudai	55W, 65G	60	6	0/0	4	Fast
Elite Mangudai	55W, 65G	60	8	1/0	4	Fast

The Mangudai are the bane of enemy siege weapons. Not only do the Mangudai have the speed to sweep around the enemy flanks, but they also have the power, range, and bonus to destroy the siege weapons once they arrive in their location. When they are not busy destroying Onagers, the Mangudai make great units to harass and kill enemy Villagers.

Figure 14-5 *A tired Villager and pious Monk confer on what tragedy might befall them next.*

Miscellaneous Foot Folk

The Villager and Monk, shown in Figure 14-5, don't fit into a convenient category. Accordingly, we gave them their own.

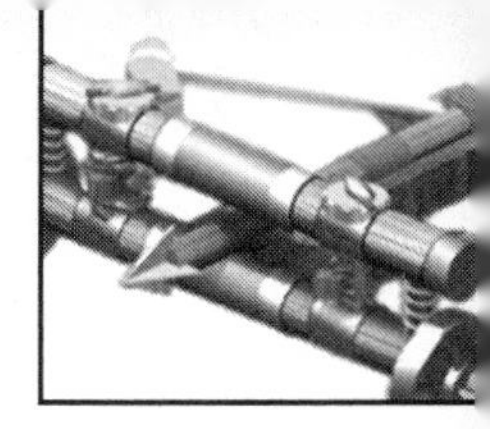

Monk

Name	Cost	Hit Points	Attack Points	Armor/ Pierce Armor	Range	Speed
Monk	100G	30	0	0/0	9	Slow

Monks are insidiously valuable. As I've said before, their conversion ability is alluring, but they are often more useful in the center of a Box Formation healing the warriors that surround them.

Villager

Name	Cost	Hit Points	Attack Points	Armor/ Pierce Armor	Range	Speed
Villager	50F	25	3	0/0	0	Slow

Create lots of Villagers and protect them. Provide every technical upgrade available for them. The Villagers are the weakest units in the game, but the resources they gather are the key to your success.

Cavalry

Cavalry (as shown in Figure 14-6) are the mobile warriors of medieval times. They may be used for anything from shock troops to light, fast raiders. In this section, we'll discuss three types: horse Cavalry, Camels, and unique units.

Figure 14-6 *A reunion of famous Cavalry folks.*

Horse Cavalry

Name	Cost	Hit Points	Attack Points	Armor/ Pierce Armor	Range	Speed
Scout Cavalry	80F	45	3	0/2	0	Medium
Light Cavalry	80F	78	7	0/2	0	Fast
Knight	60F, 75G	100	10	2/2	0	Fast
Cavalier	60F, 75G	120	12	2/2	0	Fast
Paladin	60F, 75G	160	14	2/3	0	Fast

The horses are a disparate lot. Light Cavalry and Scout Cavalry are great at galloping around the enemy flanks and falling on the opposing Archers or siege engines in the rear areas. Heavy Cavalry, such as Knights, Paladins, and Cavaliers, are great for annihilating enemy foot soldiers. The Paladin and Cavalier are successful at destroying buildings. They don't receive any bonuses for this, but their 14-point attack is significantly better than most infantry's attack rating. But don't forget, the horses hate Pikemen.

Camel

Name	Cost	Hit Points	Attack Points	Armor/ Pierce Armor	Range	Speed
Camel	55F, 60G	100	5	0/0	0	Fast
Heavy Camel	55F, 60G	120	7	0/0	0	Fast

Camels are good for one thing—killing Cavalry. Their attack is weak against buildings, and their lack of armor makes them vulnerable to infantry and Archers. They can, however, severely injure a horse.

Cavalry Unique Units

Obviously the most powerful Cavalry available, these unique units are a benefit to any army. Read on to learn some tips for employing them.

Cataphract

Name	Cost	Hit Points	Attack Points	Armor/ Pierce Armor	Range	Speed
Cataphract	70F, 75G	110	9	2/1	0	Fast
Elite Cataphract	70F, 75G	150	12	2/1	0	Fast

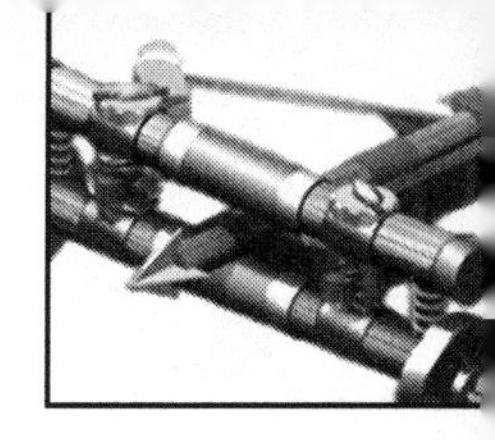

Cataphracts are perhaps the best infantry killers in the game, aside from area effect siege weapons. They are fast, so they close in quickly before the enemy can run away, and they can easily escape when the need arises. On the downside, they are very expensive. Form small raiding parties (for example, five to six Cataphracts) of these units to descend on unsuspecting bands of enemy soldiers.

War Elephant

Name	Cost	Hit Points	Attack Points	Armor/ Pierce Armor	Range	Speed
War Elephant	200F, 75G	450	15	1/2	0	Slow
Elite War Elephant	200F, 75G	600	20	1/3	0	Slow

The War Elephant is the ultimate armored building demolition machine. Elephants don't inflict as much damage as siege engines, but they are much tougher. They are also a heck of a lot more expensive. In all, they are one of the weakest "buck per bash" unique units in the game.

Mameluke

Name	Cost	Hit Points	Attack Points	Armor/ Pierce Armor	Range	Speed
Mameluke	55F, 85G	65	7	0/0	3	Fast
Elite Mameluke	55F, 85G	80	10	1/0	3	Fast

I love these guys. Think of them as Throwing Axemen on Camels. They are lethal to enemy Cavalry and work best when placed behind a line of Heavy Camels.

Siege Weapons

Siege engines are the artillery and heavy weapons of medieval times. I divide them into two types: area effect weapons, which launch ammunition that affects a wide area on impact, and anti-building, siege engines that are best used against enemy fortifications (as shown in Figure 14-7).

Area Effect Weapons

Name	Cost	Hit Points	Attack Points	Armor/ Pierce Armor	Range	Speed
Scorpion	75W, 75G	40	12	0/6	5	Slow
Heavy Scorpion	75W, 75G	50	16	0/7	5	Slow
Mangonel	160W, 135G	50	40	0/6	7	Slow
Onager	160W, 135G	60	50	0/7	8	Slow
Siege Onager	160W, 135G	70	75	0/8	8	Slow

Area effect weapons are most successful against enemy foot soldiers and Archers. These machines destroy anything you can catch in the open. They are not so impressive when fighting the faster enemies in the game, although researching Ballistics improves this capability. They perform well when placed behind your lines in support of a fixed defense, but remember—friendly fire isn't friendly. A burst from an Onager is so strong that it will kill friend as well as foe, so it's best to target the enemy Archer in his rear areas to avoid accidentally killing your own troops.

Figure 14-7 *A Trebuchet launches on an enemy fortification.*

Anti-Building Weapons

Name	Cost	Hit Points	Attack Points	Armor/ Pierce Armor	Range	Speed
Bombard Cannon	225W, 225G	50	40	2/5	12	Slow
Battering Ram	160W, 75G	175	2	0/180	0	Slow
Capped Ram	160W, 75G	200	3	0/190	0	Slow
Siege Ram	160W, 75G	270	4	0/195	0	Slow

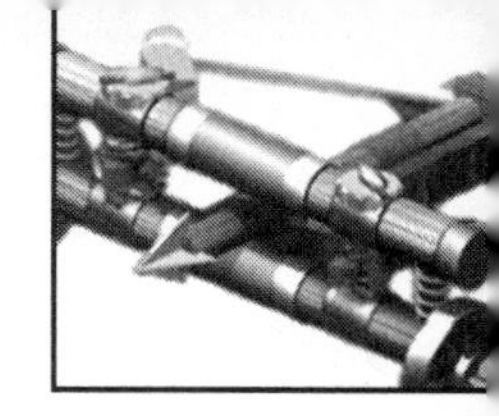

Name	Cost	Hit Points	Attack Points	Armor/ Pierce Armor	Range	Speed
Trebuchet (packed)	200W, 200G	150	0	2/8	0	Slow
Trebuchet (unpacked)	200W, 200G	150	200	1/150	16	Slow

Obviously, these units are meant for destroying buildings. Protect the Ram types with infantry or Cavalry, as they are sure to draw a crowd. Try to employ the others—especially the Trebuchet—at range. A single Trebuchet, used wisely, can dismantle an entire camp. By the way, if you are on the receiving end of one of these siege weapon's attentions, the best way to escape is to quickly send out some of your Cavalry to destroy them.

Ships

Ships, shown in Figure 14-8, serve several useful functions in *Age of Empires II.* They fish and protect ships that fish, they transport troops, and they bombard shore facilities. There are four categories of ships: Miscellaneous, Galleys and Galleons, Fire Ships and Demolition Ships, and unique units.

Figure 14-8 *A fleet is an impressive weapon.*

Miscellaneous Ships

Name	Cost	Hit Points	Attack Points	Armor/ Pierce Armor	Range	Speed
Fishing Ship	75W	60	0	0/4	0	Medium
Trade Cog	100W, 50G	80	0	0/6	0	Fast
Transport Ship	125W	100	0	4/8	0	Fast

These ships need to be protected, as each ship has an important mission in the game. And of course, it's important to protect the Fishermen and the food they reap. The Trade Cogs, on the other hand, are basically Trade Carts with sails. The farther they travel, the more money they make. Unfortunately, distant travel is fraught with danger. Make sure you escort them with Fire Ships and Galleys.

Galleys and Galleons

Name	Cost	Hit Points	Attack Points	Armor/ Pierce Armor	Range	Speed
Galley	90W, 30G	120	6	0/6	5	Fast
War Galley	90W, 30G	135	7	0/6	6	Fast
Galleon	90W, 30G	165	8	0/8	7	Fast
Cannon Galleon	200W, 150G	120	35	0/6	13	Medium
Elite Cannon Galleon	200W, 150G	150	45	0/8	15	Medium

The Galleys and Galleons are sea attack units with the most extensive ranges. Yes, Fire Ships can shoot a couple of tiles, but that is puny compared to the Elite Cannon Galleon's 15-tile range. Use the Cannon boats to demolish shore facilities, and use the Galleys for sea control. Make sure that you escort both with Fire Ships.

Fire Ships and Demolition Ships

Name	Cost	Hit Points	Attack Points	Armor/ Pierce Armor	Range	Speed
Fire Ship	75W, 45G	100	2	0/6	2	Fast
Fast Fire Ship	75W, 45G	120	3	0/8	2	Fast
Demolition Ship	70W, 50G	50	110	0/3	0	Fast
Heavy Demolition Ship	70W, 50G	60	140	0/5	0	Fast

These are anti-ship ships. Both are too fast for Galley and Galleons' weapons to track them with any accuracy. They are great for sneaking up on those powerful ships and bringing them down. The Demolition Ships are also devastating weapons against Docks. And you can get all of this damage for about a third of the cost of a Cannon Galleon. What a deal!

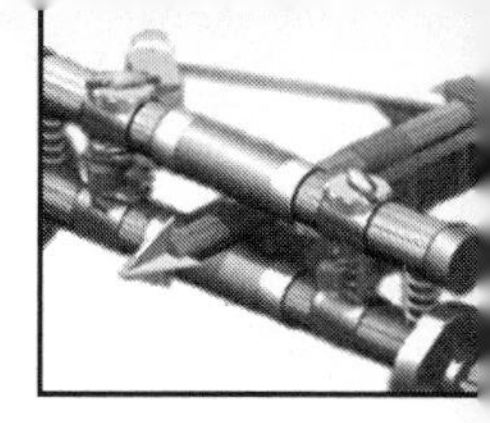

Unique Units

Name	Cost	Hit Points	Attack Points	Armor/ Pierce Armor	Range	Speed
Longboat	100W, 50G	130	7	0/6	6	Fast
Elite Longboat	100W, 50G	160	8	0/8	7	Fast

These Ships are an excellent choice if you want to control the sea. They are relatively inexpensive, so Vikings can field a formidable fleet of these quick and capable Ships. Equally adept at both anti-ship and anti-shore combat, Longboats are a valuable addition to the fleet.

Buildings

All immobile units—from Walls and Fish Traps to Monasteries and Wonders—are buildings. Microsoft divides the buildings in *Age of Empires II* into two categories: economic structures and military structures. The first category comprises resource-related facilities and advanced technology and cultural centers. Military structures consist of everything else—defenses and military unit production facilities. For your convenience, the following buildings are grouped under four subcategories.

Resource-Related Facilities

Name	Age	Cost	Hit Points	Attack Points	Garrison	Range
Town Center	III	275W	2400	5	15	6
House	I	30W	900	0	0	0
Mill	I	100W	1000	0	0	0
Mining Camp	I	100W	1000	0	0	0
Lumber Camp	I	100W	1000	0	0	0
Dock	I	150W	1800	0	0	0
Farm	I	60W	480	0	0	0
Fish Trap	II	100W	50	0	0	0
Market	II	175W	2100	0	0	0

You might be the best general in the world, but without resources you're not going to make it very far. Consider two things in regard to these buildings (as shown in Figure 14-9): proximity and basic technologies. To reduce the travel time of your Villagers from distant Gold, Stone, and Lumber sources to the Town Center, build Stone Camps and Lumber Camps near those sites. Plant Farms near the Mill and Town Center. As far as your most basic technologies—those that affect gathering abilities at the Mill and Town Center—are concerned, research as many of these as possible. Tools like the Wheelbarrow, Horse Collar, and Trade Cart will quicken the collection process greatly.

Figure 14-9 *An economic stronghold of Imperial quality.*

Advanced Technology and Cultural Centers

Once a hefty stockpile of resources and an efficient production system are in place, it's time to worry about the advanced technology and cultural centers. Blacksmiths and Universities are important for researching weapon upgrades—always a must for victory. Because of their value, it's best to situate these buildings next to armed structures such as Towers, Castles, and Town Centers. These will provide adequate protection from invaders.

Technology and Cultural Centers

Name	Age	Cost	Hit Points	Attack Points	Garrison	Range
Blacksmith	II	150W	2100	0	0	0
Monastery	III	175W	2100	0	10	0
University	III	200W	2100	0	0	0
Wonder	IV	1000W, 1000S, 1000G	4800	0	0	0

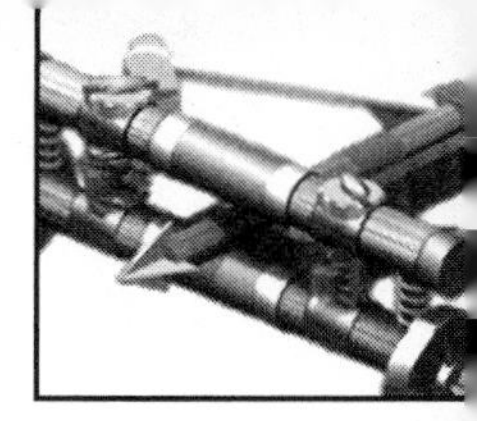

Defenses

Defenses are probably the least important subcategory. Aggressive play is often more important to winning than building a fortress is. However, rather than wasting resources on such defenses as Walls, it's better to invest in constructing Towers near the outer edge of your town. You should also place them at Gold sites and near enemy territory. You'd be surprised how many enemy Villagers can be slain this way.

Defenses

Name	Age	Cost	Hit Points	Attack Points	Garrison	Range
Palisade Wall	I	2W	250	0	0	0
Gate	II	30S	2750	0	0	0
Stone Wall	II	5S	1800	0	0	0
Fortified Wall	III	5S	3000	0	0	0
Outpost	I	25W, 25S	500	0	0	0
Watch Tower	II	125S, 25W	1020	5	5	8
Guard Tower	III	125S, 25W	1500	6	5	8
Keep	IV	125S, 25W	2250	7	5	8
Bombard Tower	IV	125S, 100G	2220	120	5	8

Military Unit Production Facilities

These buildings (shown in Figure 14-10) are in charge of producing warriors. The only structure capable of defending itself, though, is the Castle. Protect the other buildings not by erecting Towers, but by garrisoning infantry inside each of these structures. When a horde of enemies approaches, dispatch

Figure 14-10 *These buildings are responsible for creating your army.*

your units to clean up the ruckus. Note that troops cannot be garrisoned in the Barracks, Stable, Archery Range, and Siege Workshop unless a Gather Point is set on these buildings while the units are being created.

Military Production Facilities

Name	Age	Cost	Hit Points	Attack Points	Garrison	Range
Barracks	I	175W	1200	0	10	0
Stable	II	175W	1500	0	10	0
Archery Range	II	175W	1500	0	10	0
Castle	III	650S	4800	11	20	8
Siege Workshop	III	200W	2100	0	0	0

Technologies

Many of us today can't imagine life without technology. Well, medieval people did not have our technological conveniences, but they knew what it took to win a war. And you'd better believe—just like today—technology was the bottom line in staging successful campaigns. So get your Blacksmith hammering, your Monks converting, and your eyeballs scanning if you're planning on becoming the next Charlemagne.

Building Technologies

Name	Age	Cost	Notes
Town Watch	II	75F	+4 building LOS
Town Patrol	III	300F, 200G	+4 building LOS
Masonry	III	175W, 150S	Increases building HPs/armor
Architecture	IV	200W, 300S	Increases building HPs/armor
Treadmill Crane	III	200W, 300S	+20% Villager build speed
Hoardings	IV	400W, 400S	+1000 Castle HPs

Building technologies have three functions: expand a structure's line of sight, make edifices sturdier, or increase Villager building speeds. Although many contests can be won without these aids, they do make things a lot easier.

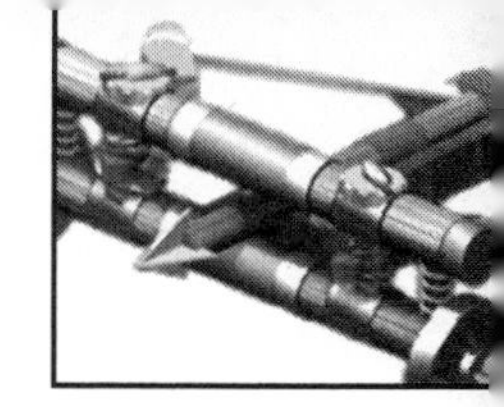

Against tough, aggressive opponents, investment in Masonry and Architecture at the University (shown in Figure 14-11) is not a bad idea. Hoardings is essential in Regicide matches, when the King is protected by being stashed inside his Castle.

Figure 14-11 *Research building technologies at the University to make structures sturdier.*

Economy and Trade Technologies

Name	Age	Cost	Notes
Loom	I	50G	+15 Villager HPs; +1/+1P armor
Wheelbarrow	II	175F, 50W	+10%Villager speed; +25% Villager capacity
Hand Cart	III	300F, 200W	+10% Villager speed; +50% Villager capacity
Gold Mining	II	100F, 75W	+15% gold-mining speed
Gold Shaft Mining	III	200F, 150W	+15% gold-mining speed
Stone Mining	II	100F, 75W	+15% stone-mining speed
Stone Shaft Mining	III	200F, 150W	+15% stone-mining speed
Double-Bit Axe	II	100F, 50W	+20% wood-chopping speed
Bow Saw	III	150F, 100W	+20% wood-chopping speed
Two-Man Saw	IV	300F, 200W	+10% wood-chopping speed
Horse Collar	II	75F, 75W	Farm +75 food
Heavy Plow	III	125F, 125W	Farm +125 food; +1 Villager food capacity
Crop Rotation	IV	250F, 250W	Farm +175 food
Coinage	II	150F, 50G	Decreases tribute fee to 20%
Banking	III	200F, 100G	No tribute fee
Guilds	IV	300F, 200G	Decreases trading fee to 15%
Cartography	II	100F, 100G	See ally LOS and exploration
Conscription	IV	150F, 150G	+33% unit creation speed at Barracks, Stable, Archery Range, and Castle
Spies/Treason	IV	200G per enemy Villager/ 400G per use	See enemy LOS and exploration/ see enemy King's locations
Sappers	IV	400F, 200G	Villagers +15 attack vs. buildings

All resource gathering and production technologies are a must. Don't expect to win a single mission without economic and trade technologies like the Wheelbarrow, Hand Cart, and Gold Mining. Trading technologies are not as important for civilizations with built-in resource enhancements as for those without. However, they come in extremely handy for those situations in which you find yourself with an imbalance of goods. Trading for Gold at the Market (shown in Figure 14-12) is often necessary in Death Matches. Spies/Treason is an indispensable technology when playing Regicide matches.

Figure 14-12 *Trade technologies at the Market can increase your Gold.*

Monk Technologies

Name	Age	Cost	Notes
Fervor	III	140G	+15% Monk speed
Sanctity	III	120G	+50% Monk HPs
Redemption	III	475G	Convert buildings (except Walls, Gates, Town Centers, Monasteries, Castles, Farms, Fish Traps, Wonders), all siege units
Atonement	III	325G	Convert other Monks
Illumination	IV	120G	+50% Monk rejuvenation speed
Faith	IV	750F, 1000G	+50% conversion resistance
Block Printing	IV	200G	+3 conversion range

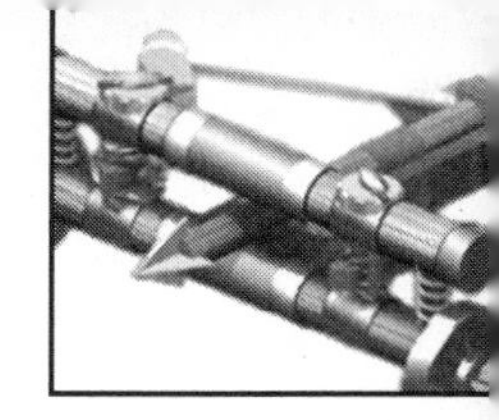

Not all civilizations have access to these technologies. In fact, only the Byzantines, Japanese, Saracens, and Teutons can use all seven of these abilities. Try to research as many of these technologies as possible. Because of the Monk's slow speed, Fervor and Sanctity gained at the Monastery (shown in Figure 14-13) are always wise choices. Conversion aids, such as Redemption and Block Printing, are ideal for special operations.

Figure 14-13 *Research Fervor at the Monastery to jump-start your slowpoke Monks.*

Infantry Technologies

Name	Age	Cost	Notes
Tracking	II	75F	+2 infantry LOS
Squires	III	200F	+10% infantry speed
Scale Mail Armor	II	100F	+1/+1P infantry armor
Chain Mail Armor	III	200F, 100G	+1/+1P infantry armor
Plate Mail Armor	IV	300F, 150G	+1/+2P infantry armor
Forging	II	150F	+1 infantry/Cavalry attack
Iron Casting	III	220F, 120G	+1 infantry/Cavalry attack
Blast Furnace	IV	275F, 225G	+2 infantry/Cavalry attack

Infantry technologies are important but not critical advancements. Certainly, if you have enough time, you'll want to research every technology available to your civilization, including the infantry technologies at the Blacksmith (shown in Figure 14-14). On the other hand, you should concentrate your research first on economics and second on technologies that enhance the most units.

Figure 14-14 *Researching infantry technologies at the Blacksmith can help these folks fight better.*

Missile/Siege Technologies

Name	Age	Cost	Notes
Fletching	II	100F, 50G	+1 attack/range for Archers, Cavalry Archers, Galleys, Longboats, Town Centers, Castles, Towers
Bodkin Arrow	III	200F, 100G	+1 attack/range for Archers, Cavalry Archers, Galleys, Longboats, Town Centers, Castles, Towers
Bracer	IV	300F, 200G	+1 attack/range for Archers, Cavalry Archers, Galleys, Longboats, Town Centers, Castles, Towers
Padded Archer Armor	II	100F	+1/+1P Archer and Cavalry Archer armor
Leather Archer Armor	III	150F, 150G	+1/+1P Archer and Cavalry Archer armor
Ring Archer Armor	IV	250F, 250G	+1/+2P Archer and Cavalry Archer armor
Ballistics	III	300W, 175G	Track moving units
Murder Holes	III	200F, 200S	No minimum Tower/Castle range (except Bombard Towers)
Heated Shot	III	350F, 100G	+50% Tower attack vs. Ships
Chemistry	IV	300F, 200G	+1 missile attack (except gunpowder units); enables gunpowder units to be researched
Siege Engineers	IV	500F, 600W	+1 siege range (except Rams); +20% siege unit attack vs. buildings

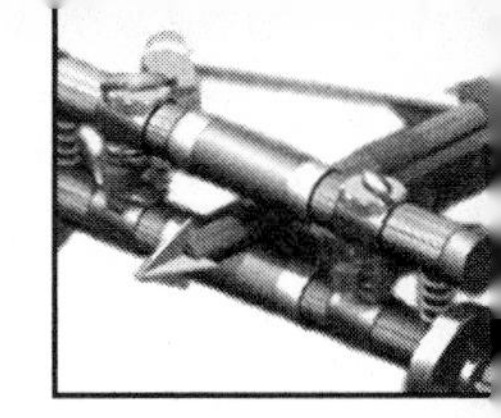

Missile and siege weapon technologies are second only to economic technologies. Many of the missile technologies offered at the Archery Range (shown in Figure 14-15) affect multiple units and multiple types of units, making it significant research. The four most important are Fletching, Bodkin Arrow, Bracer, and Ballistics.

Figure 14-15 *Upgrades at the Archery Range not only help Longbowmen, but they aid Galleys as well.*

Cavalry Technologies

Name	Age	Cost	Notes
Husbandry	III	250F	+10% Cavalry speed
Scale Barding Armor	II	150F	+1/+1P Cavalry armor
Chain Barding Armor	III	250F, 150G	+1/+1P Cavalry armor
Plate Barding Armor	IV	350F, 200G	+1/+2P Cavalry armor

Cavalry technologies fall into the same category as the infantry technologies—they are nice to have but not critical. Perhaps the most important is Husbandry, which is available at the Stable (shown in Figure 14-16). The Cavalry's strength is speed, so

Figure 14-16 Speed upgrades found at the Stable are the best for Cavalry.

anything that enhances that is useful. There is nothing better than a horde of fast Cavalry.

Ship Technologies

Name	Age	Cost	Notes
Careening	III	250F, 150G	+1P armor; +5 Transport Ship capacity
Dry Dock	IV	600F, 400G	+15% Ship speed; +10 Transport Ship capacity
Shipwright	IV	1000F, 300G	-20% Wood to build Ships

Figure 14-17 *Building a fleet of Ships is cheaper after researching Shipwright at the Dock.*

Ship technologies are more important for seafaring civilizations such as the Japanese than they are for other civilizations. Shipwright—available at the Dock (shown in Figure 14-17)—is the most significant Ship technology to invest in. It allows you to save money on Ships, which in turn allows you to build more.

The Final Upgrade

Okay, that's it—the quick tips on the people, places, and things of *Age of Empires II: The Age of Kings*. Continue reading to learn how to put all of this information to use in a game of *Age of Empires II*.

Chapter Fifteen

Building Block Strategies

Microsoft Age of Empires II is a tough game, but that's what makes it so darn addictive. Simple games come and go, but it's the challenging games that stay on hard drives month after month. To play well, you need more than a walk-through that shows where to position your troops and in what order to conquer your enemies. You need a strong grasp of the basic techniques necessary to prosper and succeed in the Age of Kings.

That's what this chapter is all about. In previous chapters, I have often told you when and where to attack a Castle, formation, or other enemy objects, but—unless it was a unique situation—I haven't said how. Well, this is where I say how. So come along; it's time to learn how to win the battles you need to fight and build the buildings you need to win.

Economics and Technology

It's strange that a game about military conquest often hinges on economics and technological research. Ignoring the economic facets of life in *Age of Empires II* will lead to defeat as surely as attacking a horde of Pikemen with Heavy Camels will. Here are a couple of tips to keep those proverbial Pikemen at bay and your city booming (as shown in Figure 15-1).

Figure 15-1 *A booming economy is the key to victory.*

Villagers Rule

Villagers are *the* most important units in the game. Without them, nothing can be built, farmed, or repaired. That may seem obvious, but nevertheless, one of the most common mistakes real-time strategy neophytes commit is not producing enough Villagers. To put it simply, don't scrimp. When you're playing a mission that requires unit production, summon enough Villagers to rapidly grow your economy.

Note: *So, how many Villagers is enough? Unfortunately, it varies depending on the type of mission and the Age. The more sophisticated the Age, the more expensive the units, and hence more Villagers are required. While there is no rule written in Stone—Stone is too expensive to write on—a little bit of common sense goes a long way. If you are drumming your fingers on the keyboard, washing your monitor, or falling asleep while you are waiting for enough resources to be gathered in order to build your next unit, you need to have more Villagers (as shown in Figure 15-2) collecting those resources.*

The following list gives you basic guidelines as to how many Villagers you'll need to support a medium to large economy:

Dark Age	8 Villagers
Feudal Age	13 Villagers
Castle Age	19 Villagers
Imperial Age	25 Villagers

Certainly, it's possible—depending on the particular mission, resources, and civilization—to succeed with less or to require more Villagers, but the above numbers are good baseline figures.

Now that you know how many Villagers to produce, what should they be doing once you have them? In general, 40 percent of the Villagers should be gathering Food, and the rest should be equally distributed between collecting Gold, Wood, and Stone. These percentages will change

Figure 15-2 *It takes quite a few Villagers to support an economy.*

depending upon the Age, the mission, and your own troop preferences. For example, seafaring missions require more Wood, and Imperial Age missions require more Stone. Melee units, such as the Long Swordsman, Man-at-Arms, Two-Handed Swordsman, Champion, Knight, Pikeman, Spearman, and Skirmisher, all require Food, as shown in Figure 15-3. Archers—and their many subcategories—do not. Neither do the multiple types of siege engines.

> **Note:** *You should also avoid scrimping on the Villager-related research. That research, like the Villagers it enhances, is the most important research in the game. Research the Loom as soon as you begin the game. By the same token, the Wheelbarrow and Horse Collar should be the first technologies your scientists study upon entering the Feudal Age.*

Figure 15-3 *It takes a lot of chow to keep the troops going.*

Food is used for more research and unit-building than any other type of resource, so it's critical to keep a steady supply flowing into your Mills. Don't, however, underestimate the power of Gold. By trading in the Market, you can turn a healthy supply of Gold into any commodity that you desire.

> **Tip:** *Gold is a valuable resource. It is, however, difficult to make it the mainstay of your existence. It's best to use Gold to buy the extra materials needed for research or for advancing to the next Age.*

And Buildings Are Their Weapon of Choice

A significant factor in an empire's economy is the placement of buildings. How quickly Villagers move, chop, dig, and hunt is governed by their civilizations and their upgrades, but how far they have to move is governed by their master—in other words, you.

Place destination buildings adjacent to their raw resources. Mining Camps should touch the Gold or Stone supplying them, Mills should be plopped in

> **Tip:** *Don't forget the Markets. Not only do they allow you to buy and sell commodities, but they also generate income through trade routes. Unfortunately, it doesn't really help to build your Market adjacent to an ally's Market. Yes, the Trade Cart will make more trips between the two Markets, but it will also generate less income per trip. The Market's best location, as shown in Figure 15-4, is close to your Gate (if you have one) but not so close as to draw the fire of unfriendly siege weapons.*

the middle of the Farms and herds, and Lumber Camps work best when they are adjacent to the forests from which they gather Wood.

What to Do, What to Do

Well, you know where to put your buildings, but which buildings should you place first? As with everything else in *Age of Empires II,* there is no simple answer, but there are some sound rules to follow. Build your economy first. Don't worry about erecting a Barracks until you have the buildings needed to run the economy. If your Town Center is located adjacent to all the resources, you won't need to build anything—at least not at first. On the other hand, the closest forest might be quite a few tiles away from you. In that case, building a Lumber Camp adjacent to those woods should be the first order of the day.

Figure 15-4 *Place Markets close to your Gates, but not too close.*

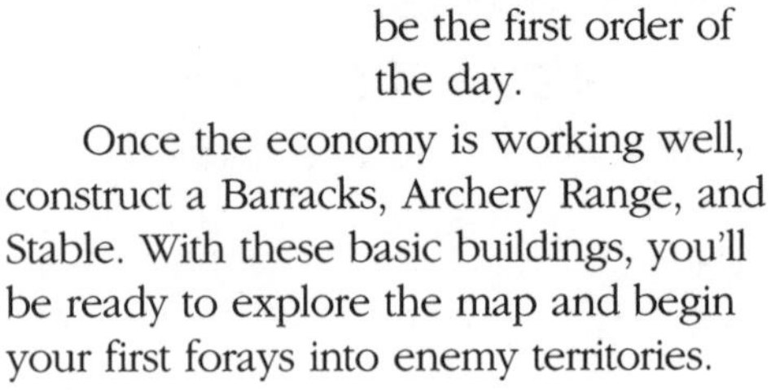

Once the economy is working well, construct a Barracks, Archery Range, and Stable. With these basic buildings, you'll be ready to explore the map and begin your first forays into enemy territories.

> **Tip:** *The more Villagers you have constructing a building, the faster it will be erected. Each Villager cuts the build time by 33 percent, so although using more Villagers always helps, you will reach a practical point of diminishing returns where additional Villagers could be better employed elsewhere. Three Villagers is sufficient for most jobs. Double that number if you're building a Wonder.*

What to Research, What to Research

In *Age of Empires II,* there are almost as many research paths as there are players. What you research can often be a matter of personal preference. Nevertheless, there are some important research points to remember.

As I said before, general economic upgrades are the most important items to research in the early game. Anything that speeds production—across the board—is an important technology. In missions where you begin with few resources other than Villagers, research Wheelbarrow and, once the Mill is built, Horse Collar technologies. By the same token, study Hand Cart, Heavy Plow, and Crop Rotation when available. Food is a nearly universal need, so any technology that increases its availability is valuable.

Perhaps the next most important research topic is Gold Mining and Gold Shaft Mining. Gaining this technology enhances access to material that helps you in every facet of your civilization. Gold is the universal product; increasing its availability helps universally.

If playing with allies, the most important Feudal Age technology is Cartography. Knowledge is a weapon, and knowledge of the map's layout is a valuable weapon indeed. If you have no allies, the most valuable Feudal technology is Fletching. I'm not saying this just because I have a weakness for Archers—although, when they are properly guarded, they are an excellent Feudal unit—but rather because the Fletching technology affects the most units. In the Feudal Age, Fletching enhances Archers, Watch Towers, and Town Centers. Upgrading to the Castle Age adds the Cavalry Archer and War Galley to the list (for applicable civilizations). Similarly, Ballistics is the crucial topic of study during the Castle Age. Ballistics research allows all units—Crossbowmen, Cavalry Archers, Mangonels, Scorpions, War Galleys, Fire Ships, and the plethora of ranged attack unique units—to more accurately target moving units.

Moving into the Imperial Age, players should target their Universities at Chemistry research. No, it doesn't affect the most units—that award goes to Bracer technology—but Chemistry is the research basis for three of the most virulent weapons in all of *Age of Empires II:* the Bombard Tower, the Elite Cannon Galleon, and the Bombard Cannon.

Fighting the Good Fight: Combat

Sooner or later you are going to fight. To win the game, you must force your will on the other player, and to do that, you must fight. Although the tactics in *Age of Empires II* are as varied as the units and terrain they fight on, there are nonetheless some basic tenets of combat.

Know Your Civilization

All *Age of Empires II* civilizations are created equally. They are not, however, created identically. That makes the game fun, but it also makes it a challenge. To be successful, you must know the civilization you lead. For example, English Longbowmen have an awesome range, yet Saracen Archers—due to the civilization's advantage—inflict more damage on buildings. Byzantines, with their buildings' hit point advantage, appear to be strictly defensive. Their Monks, however, heal their targets faster than Monks of any other civilization, making their charges harder to kill.

The advantages of battle do not end when the arrows stop flying. You need to plan how best to use a civilization's advantages. Asking the Mongols to farm for their Food is inefficient; their Villagers are much better at hunting (as shown in Figure 15-5). The Japanese are similar; their Fishing Ships collect Food quickly, so it would be wasteful to attempt to feed the Japanese population with farm produce. Spend some time with the game's excellent user manual, and study the civilization you intend to play.

Figure 15-5 *The Mongols are hunters—not farmers.*

Know Your Troops

Not only is it important to know your civilization, but you must know your troops. This includes both the troops specific to your chosen civilization and the generic soldiers to which each civilization has access. The game comes with an excellent reference card that gives you a great deal of information.

Again, unlike many first-generation real-time strategy games, *Age of Empires II: The Age of Kings* doesn't lend itself to mindless horde attacks. Twenty Swordsmen inflict less damage on a troop of mounted Knights than 10 Pikemen do. Conversely, those Pikemen are little more than targets for a handful of Men-at-Arms backed by a few Archers.

Rules of Thumb for Ground Units

It's confusing, but here are some simplified rules of thumb to help you use the right unit for the right job.

- Sword swingers, who include Militia and all their upgrades, are good for destroying buildings, slaying Cavalry, and protecting your ranged units. With the notable exception of the Samurai, Huskarl, and Woad Raider, they are pretty lame Archer killers. There are more special units in this category than in any other. Samurai attack more frequently than any other infantry unit and are death to other unique units. On the other hand, the Teutonic Knights have a slower attack that causes greater damage to the unlucky recipient. The Franks' Throwing Axeman is the only infantry unit with a ranged attack, making it effective against Archers and Swordsmen alike, while the Viking's Berserk heals itself.

> **Tip:** *Don't underestimate or ignore the Berserk's healing ability. Two formations of Berserks are a formidable opponent to any enemy. One formation fights while the other heals. When the first formation gets injured, you can direct it to retreat and bring forward the formation that was healing itself.*

- Spear wielders, who include Spearmen and Pikemen, are top-notch against Cavalry (as shown in Figure 15-6) but weak against most other units. They work well on the outside of an Archer-centered Box Formation, where they can keep Cavalry units at bay while the Archers stuff the enemy horses with arrows.
- Skirmishers are one of the best units to take down Archers. Don't forget, however, that better Archers are

Figure 15-6 *A line of Pikemen is a formidable opponent for any Cavalry unit.*

also a smart way to slay enemy arrow slingers. If your Archers have a range advantage over the opposition's Archers, you can eliminate them with relative impunity.

- Archers, including Chu Ko Nu, are good against most anything that their arrows can touch. They are especially successful when they are battling against foot soldiers (Skirmishers excepted). A good anti-Archer tactic is to engage the bowmen in combat with your infantry and Archers, and then sweep around the enemy's flank with your Cavalry and fall on the enemy Archers. No Archer lasts long against melee-type Cavalry.
- Cavalry are a disparate lot. Cavalry Archers, Mangudai, and to a large extent Mamelukes, can best be described as speedy Archers, while other Cavalry forces have a variety of roles. Light Cavalry are the bane of Archers, Monks, and siege weapons. The Light Cavalry's speed enables them to ride around the opposing army's flanks and swoop down on the hapless rear echelon units (such as Archers, Monks, and siege engines). Heavy Cavalry, such as the Knight, Cavalier, Paladin, and Cataphract, are great against non-Pikeman infantry and other Cavalry. The heavy units are super for crushing Archer formations—they can close in rapidly and are poison to the Archers once they are adjacent to them. Finally, use Camels against European Knights.
- Elephants are a unique breed. They are lethal to tightly packed formations of infantry. On the other hand, they suffer the same disadvantages as most mounted units when they are squaring off against Pikemen. Use them to lead an assault, but only when no Pikemen are present.
- Siege engines come in two distinct varieties: those that are good against flesh and those that are good against Wood (and Stone). The Scorpions, Mangonels, and Onagers are examples of the former. Keep them behind your front lines and use them to bombard dense formations of enemy troops. These war machines can decimate 30-man Box Formations in little more than a couple of shots.

Tip: *The only defense against area effect siege weapons is Cavalry, especially Mangudai. If the Scorpion family of weapons is ravaging your formations, you must flank the enemy lines with Cavalry and then hack the enemy siege engine to bits.*

- Rams, Bombard Cannons, and Trebuchets are examples of the Stone killers. Use these weapons to take down the opponent's town. The Trebuchet should be kept well back and used to eliminate Bombard Towers. Bombard Cannons are great against Keeps and Guard Towers

(as shown in Figure 15-7), while the Rams—which must be escorted to prevent their destruction—must directly ram the Walls they are to destroy.

- Monks and Hand Cannoneers (including Janissaries) are the odd men out in this unit categorization. Monks are a valuable and often underutilized unit. When converting, attempt to convert the most powerful enemy unit in your range. I call this getting your money's worth. Although the conversion feature is seductive, it is not the Monks' only power.
- Monks automatically heal any nearby friendly units that are injured. In fact, allied Monks even heal nearby allies, which is one of the only ways that computer allies can directly support your forces. Place Monks in the center of Box Formations, and they will do their level best to keep the rest of the formation—including each other—in fighting trim. A Berserk box filled with Monks is a scary sight.
- Hand Cannoneers are powerful, and while they are inaccurate at longer ranges (greater than five tiles), they kick kilt in the range of two to three tiles. Janissaries are somewhat more accurate, but they share the same basic properties as the Hand Cannoneers. Sprinkle both in your formation to destroy melee units, such as Swordsmen, before they get too close to your Archers.

Tip: *Villagers also make good Monks, in the sense that they can "heal" buildings. Frequently the bad guys will focus their attack on one side of a large building. Meanwhile, on the far side of the building, a couple of friendly Villagers with repair orders can fix up the structure as fast as the enemy tears it down, making the building invincible and wasting the enemy's time while you garner a force to destroy him or her.*

Figure 15-7 *Several Bombard Cannons can rapidly level a Keep.*

Nautical Notes

Taming the seas is crucial for the Japanese, but it is also extremely important to any of the other folks in *Age of Empires II*. The seas produce food, the seas allow trade, and the seas provide a route to outmaneuver your opponent. The fighting is similar to land battle, with a few notable differences. Let's take a look at the combatants.

Note: *Unlike Villagers, who stand idly on barren Farms, Fishing Boats will flee an empty Fishing Trap and seek a new trap from which to harvest food.*

Tip: *When you are exploring, whether with Ships or Cavalry, it's a great time to use the Patrol feature in* Age of Empires II. *Select the two explorers, click the Patrol button, and hold down the Shift key while right-clicking several areas in the mini-map. Release the Shift key and right-click in your camp. Your scouts will not only explore the area, but they will also continue to Patrol the countryside, providing advance warning of enemy incursions.*

Tip: *Always seek a manner of attacking your opponent to which he or she cannot respond. If enemy Cavalry is wasting your Bombard Cannons, try attacking the enemy's Keeps from the sea. Cannon Galleons have a longer range and are very resistant to Cavalry attack...unless the enemy ponies learn to swim.*

- Fishing Ships do just what their name indicates. On predominantly water maps, such as the Archipelago, their contribution to the economy is crucial. The Fish Traps they build provide much more Food than Farms, and their tenders, for example Fishing Boats, take no Food to produce. Of course, they can also fish without traps.
- Galleys are scouts and should be used as such. Whenever possible send them exploring in pairs. One is just too easy a target.
- Fire Ships and Demolition Ships are the formation-busters of the sea. Both are faster than the Galleons they face. And although they are at a distinct disadvantage when the Galleons can engage them in battle from afar, they are trouble for the Galleons at a close range. Accompany your Galleons with at least a couple of Fire Ships.
- War Galleys and Galleons are the bread and butter of naval warfare, and the heart of any fleet. War Galleys have good range, Galleons have darn good range, and the versions equipped with Cannons—especially the Elite Cannon Galleons—have nearly the best range in the game, second only to the Trebuchet. Although the Cannon Galleons are not the best ships for gaining control of the

sea—the Fire Ships close in and destroy unaccompanied Galleons—Once the seas are yours (as shown in Figure 15-8), the Cannon Galleons are the best shore-bombardment platforms available.

Figure 15-8 *A powerful fleet is an awesome weapon.*

Know Your Battles

You have to know how to gather resources, you need to know the best technologies to research, and you need to understand the civilization and troops you are gaming. Nevertheless, when all is said and done, you need to know how to win battles. Here are some tips to keep you on the winning side.

Might Is Right

Don't mess around with onesies and twosies, at least not when it comes to the smaller units such as Cavalry, Archers, and melee units. For example, if you stand a Knight in open terrain and attack him with a single Archer, the Archer might wound the Knight, but the Knight will definitely kill the Archer. Let's say you then bring up another Archer to battle the Knight—you'll get the same result. At about the fifth Archer, you'll slay the Knight. Score: Knight 4, Archers 1. The way to negotiate this battle is to take the five Archers it took to eliminate the Knight and attack him with all five at once. Chances are that their combined might will level the Knight before he can kill the first Archer. The point is simple: attack in mass whenever possible.

Note: *Attacking in mass is not always the best way to fight, however. Attacking a Keep in mass is not a good idea when you have a single Trebuchet that can take it out from a distance.*

Range Is Your Friend

I don't know about you, but the computer can select and move its units much faster than I can select and move mine. Accordingly, I try to avoid situations where both the computer and I are simultaneously moving and clicking units, as the computer often wins. It's always a good idea to use your troops as a single sledgehammer rather than as many ball-peen hammers. You do, however, want to avoid those chaotic situations in which the entire battlefield is in turmoil.

One method to avoid those chaotic situations is to employ weapons with greater range than those the enemy employs. If the folks in black hats have a Guard Tower, destroy it with a Bombard Cannon. If the enemy has a Keep, eliminate it with a Trebuchet (as shown in Figure 15-9) or Elite Cannon Galleon. Whenever you can keep your troops out of harm's way, you should do so.

Note: *Don't expect your opponents—whether human or computer—to sit by idly while your Trebuchet dismantles their Keep. Smart players will rush you with whatever they have. It's important to have a staggered line of Swordsmen-types, Archers, and Pikemen ready to repel any counterattack.*

Ambushes

You should set ambushes whenever possible. I did this several times to conquer the sixth mission in the Joan of Arc campaign. Here's how: Form a group consisting of whatever Swordsman-types, Archer-types, and Pikeman-types you have available. Place several Monks behind them (if they are available). If you have Scorpions or the like, place them a bit farther back in your group. Cavalry should be held in reserve as a counterattack force.

Figure 15-9 *Trebuchets are the best long-range weapons in the game.*

Now send some bait to the enemy. Light Cavalry works well for this purpose. Ride into an enemy position, and make them chase you. Lead them back to your waiting troops, and they'll bash their unprepared selves against your wall of humanity. Always strive to lead the enemy into your waiting swords rather than running into theirs.

Tip: *If possible, anchor one side of the formation to a patch of woods. This protects the anchored side and reduces the area that the enemy can attack.*

Hit Them Where They Aren't

Frequently—especially in the scripted missions—you'll be confronted with a seemingly unassailable position. Don't panic. Use scouts to gather information about the enemy position. Most fortresses have a weakness, which is an area where clever employment of ranged weapons can open a hole in a fortress that might allow your troops to swamp the enemy's defenses.

Remember, you rarely have to kill all your opponents to win a game. The smart warrior is not the one who crushes enemies and captures objectives, but the warrior who avoids enemies and still captures objectives.

Diversionary Attacks

Both computer and human opponents alike react to attacks. Hey, if someone yells at you, you yell back. This is no different in *Age of Empires II*. If a base is assaulted, the defenders respond. You can use this to your advantage.

More often than not, a small attack (from 10 to 15 units) draws all a base's defenders to the site of the attack (as shown in Figure 15-10). If you then swarm the opposite side of the base, you can catch the defenders in the jaws of a pincer and destroy them.

Figure 15-10 *Defenders have no way of knowing whether attacks are real or a diversion.*

Conversely, you can mount a major attack on one side of the base and trot to the other and snatch a Relic or whatever prize you are after.

Form It Up!

Formations are a human's great advantage against the computer. You'll rarely see a computer opponent employ them as well as humans do. Let's take a look at the different formations and when to best use them.

- Line: The Line Formation is the classic medieval formation. *Age of Empires II* intelligently places units in their appropriate places in the line. This is an excellent formation for protecting ranged units such as Archers from their nemesis, the Skirmisher. Line Formations place the melee units, such as Men-at-Arms, in front and the Archers to the rear.
- Staggered: A Staggered Formation is a Line Formation that has been slightly spread. It's good for blocking a slightly wider piece of land than a similar Line Formation. It also limits casualties from area effect weapons such as the Scorpion.
- Box: The Box Formation is great for protecting weaker units such as Monks, Bombard Cannons, or Trebuchets. Place a variety of units, such as Pikemen, Swordsmen, and Archers, in the formation in addition to the units you are protecting.
- Flank: The Flank Formation splits the grouped units into two smaller formations. It's a good formation for catching enemy units in the crossfire between two factions of Archers. It can also be useful for melee units to avoid the enemy's front line units and instead attack the Archers in their rear ranks.

The Final Tip

Those are the basics. The final tip is to practice using them. And what better place to start than the campaigns. So grab a sword, turn the page, and let's go!

Part III

The Game of Kings—Final Walkthroughs and Strategies

If Part II was the potatoes of this book, this part is the meat. The main course of any strategy guide is the mission walkthroughs and specific game strategies. The following chapters are a gourmet's dream. They include step-by-step campaign walkthroughs, strategies for Random Map, Regicide, and Death Match games, and serious multiplayer tips.

If you don't have game, this is the place to get it. When you're finished reading these walkthroughs, you'll be a Saladin or a Joan of Arc in your own right.

Chapter Sixteen

Single-Player Empires

Microsoft Age of Empires II is more than just another real-time strategy game. Not only are the graphics, artificial intelligence, and tactical options top notch, but the game is also a bit of a history lesson. Nowhere is this more evident than in its masterfully constructed campaigns. Each campaign tells a story, teaches some history, and provides a fine set of missions. But no one said that having fun would be easy. Some of these scenarios are tough nuts to crack, but you have the right tool in your hands, so read on.

The Joan of Arc Campaigns

It is a war that has lasted for one hundred years, and the French have lost nearly every battle. Soon the English and their allies in Burgundy will conquer all of France. The heir to the French monarchy is too cowardly to ascend to the throne. The French army is wounded and tired and has given up all hope. But in the darkest hour, a young peasant girl declares that she intends to save France.

Mission One: An Unlikely Messiah

Objectives:

- Escort Joan from the camp at Vaucouleurs to the Chateau of Chinon.
- Ensure that Joan survives.

Hints:

- France's enemies are Britain and Burgundy. Be on the lookout for their forces.
- Do not expect much assistance from the demoralized Army of France, but be alert for any soldiers who might be inspired to join your ranks.
- Protect your two Knights. They are your best fighters and know the lay of the land.

Walkthrough:

Joan, a nineteen-year-old peasant girl, has received visions from patron saints for several years. She has announced her divine mission to the weary French soldiers—to rescue the war-torn land from England and its ally, the forces of Burgundy. First, though, this young lady and soon-to-be heroine must be escorted from the Vaucouleurs camp to the Dauphin's station in Chinon.

Chinon lies directly west of the encampment. The two Knights are Joan's primary protection. Have them lead her through Vaucouleurs, finding soldiers interested in her cause. Not everyone will join. For instance, the Spearmen guarding the Pavilions show no desire whatsoever to help. However, four Men-at-Arms and four Crossbowmen enthusiastically join the mademoiselle's entourage (as shown in Figure 16-1).

Figure 16-1 *Joan and her entourage leave the Vaucouleurs camp.*

Place the soldiers in a Defensive Stance before venturing from the base. Situate the Men-at-Arms in the front with the Crossbowmen slightly behind. Keep the Knights and Joan at the end of the train. The road forks northwest (around Vaucouleurs) and southeast. A Scout Cavalry warns you of a nest of Burgundians to the northwest. Unfortunately, he will not aid your cause any further.

> **Tip:** *Walk up to every French soldier. Often your party has to be within relatively close range to "inspire" others to fight for your cause.*

A pair of Wolves lie near the southeast trail. If you stray too close, the Wolves will attack, so be prepared to slay the beasts. Just south of this spot, a battle is in progress—but not for long. The English have wiped out some more French troops. Wait in the pass until the enemy troops retreat to the east. Once they are gone, continue south past the French Outpost.

The trail curls northwest. Just past the destroyed bridge, at a fork in the trail, a band of Highwaymen await you. Slay them, and then head along the left branch of the trail, leading north.

A Burgundy base is ahead. Send everyone but the Knights and Joan to attack the entrance gate. A few enemy infantry units will come out to attack. Slay them and continue hacking down the gate. Head through the base until you reach the shallows west of the base. You're not out of the woods yet. You need a ship, and some more Burgundians are patrolling the area ahead.

Send a diversion west, following the trail, to occupy the enemy's attention. Meanwhile, move the Knights and Joan south along the coast to the Dock that lies just ahead. Load them into the Transport Ship and sail southeast. When you reach the fork in the river, navigate the ship south (as shown in Figure 16-2), past the cliffs. Unload the passengers at the French settlement. Some Crossbowmen and Scorpions will join you there. Use them to attack the enemy War Galley.

Head across the shallows and onto the path. Send everyone except the Knights and Joan to take down the scattered

> **Tip:** *It's a good idea to place the Crossbowmen and Men-at-Arms in Aggressive mode again. Keep the Knights and Joan as a separate group, in a Defensive Stance and in Box Formation. They do not need to fight unless it's absolutely necessary.*

> **Note:** *The only way to cross into the Chinon region is through the Burgundy fortress. The river and surrounding forests make travel into the area impossible except by ship.*

Figure 16-2 *Transport Ships head for the Chinon Chateau.*

> **Tip:** *There's usually more than one way to skin a cat. For instance, you can also lure the War Galley down the other river fork using an empty Transport Ship. This decoy distracts the enemy vessel, while your other Transport Ships pass by.*

enemies. Once the enemies have been cleared away, have the group follow the path to where it is decorated with banners. Cross the bridge and enter the Dauphin's palace. He will be enthralled by the courage and patriotism of this young peasant girl named Joan.

Mission Two: The Maid of Orléans

Objectives:

- Joan must survive.
- The Cathedral in Orléans must remain standing.
- Escort Joan to Blois so that she can command the French army.

Hints:

- Hurry to Orléans before the English can cause much damage. Be wary of British forces south of the river, but don't forget to rendezvous with your army in Blois.
- Once the supplies arrive in Orléans, you will be able to build up your forces. Frankish Knights are useful for taking care of British Longbowmen and siege weapons. Frankish Castles are inexpensive and provide an excellent defense.
- Use your Market to trade for resources until you can venture outside the city.
- British Castles have large garrisons. It is best to assemble a large attack force before attempting to storm them.
- Farms in Orléans are located west of the city, but as they are outside the city Walls, they are vulnerable.

Walkthrough:

Joan, fitted in armor and carrying Charlemagne's sword, rides on horseback. She is accompanied by the Duke D'Alençon, four Knights, two Two-Handed Swordsmen, and a Scout Cavalry. Place the soldiers in two groups. The four Knights and both Two-Handed Swordsmen should lead. Place Joan, the Duke, and the Scout Cavalry behind this group. Head northwest on the trail leading out of the base camp.

Challenge the Burgundy Light Cavalry and Knights up ahead—one at a time. Keep Jeanne d'Arc (as the French call her) out of the fray by placing her in a Defensive Stance. The first group should be able to take out the enemy

with few or no casualties. Pick up your army and supplies up ahead, in Blois (as shown in Figure 16-3). If your men need healing, seek the Chinon Monk, who resides just beyond the base camp.

> **Note:** *The Chinon Monk outside the Monastery only wishes you luck at first. However, he comes in handy later. In fact, to completely heal your Knights, direct them back to the cleric for healing. Sometimes he even follows your soldiers up the trail.*

Head out of the northeast Gate of Blois; go toward Orléans. Northeast of Blois is a Dock that is off the beaten path, just above the Gold site. Load the Trade Carts, D'Alençon, and Joan onto the two Transport Ships. Just north of the Dock lies Orléans on the opposite shore. When you reach Orléans, unload the troops and cargo, and then take them inside the city.

Figure 16-3 *The Wagons in Blois need to be shipped to Orléans.*

Orléans is equipped with a Mill, a Market, two Stables, a Barracks, a Blacksmith, and several Watch Towers. From the Orléans Town Center, progress to the Castle Age. Meanwhile, have the Blacksmith research Fletching, a technology that will improve the attack points and range of your towers. Send several Knights and Crossbowmen from Blois to guard the Dock.

> **Note:** *Orléans only accepts the Trade Carts once they are steered to the Town Center. This will give the base 1000 points in Food and 1500 points in both Wood and Gold.*

Although the city just received fresh supplies from Blois, Orléans is still running low on Food. Go to the Market, trade some of your Gold for Food, and then trade some of your Wood for Gold. This will suffice until you gain access to the Farms west of Orléans. Next, create

> **Note:** *This scenario gives you plenty of Market experience. It's kind of a juggling act that varies with the building process. For instance, you may trade Gold for Food, only later to sell Wood for Gold because your Gold stockpiles are low.*

Figure 16-4 *Use the Farms to the west of Orléans for Food.*

three Knights from each of your two Stables. Order the three Villagers to build a Siege Workshop.

Send the Orléans Knights to destroy the British Outpost that is northwest of the city. Have them guard the pass so that you can send Villagers to cultivate the western Farms just below the pass (as shown in Figure 16-4). Produce more Villagers to cultivate the Farms. Research the Wheelbarrow and Hand Cart at the Mill to help out with gathering efficiency.

> **Tip:** *Once the Walls of the British fortresses are knocked down, send the Battering Rams to attack the Guard Towers. Next, destroy the Town Center and military structures. Finally, with the help of your Knights, crush the Castles.*

As you accumulate Villagers, distribute them throughout the area west of Orléans, and construct a Mining Camp and a Lumber Camp. Meanwhile, have the Siege Workshop create several Battering Rams. Send the Knights to battle the British Longbowmen stationed toward the north of the city. Next, use the Battering Rams to attack the northern British fortresses. A couple of Knights are able to defeat any infantry that might give you problems. Orléans will soon be saved.

Mission Three: The Cleansing of the Loire

Objectives:

- Destroy at least three British Castles.
- Ensure that Joan survives.

Hints:

- Make sure you have enough siege weapons before assaulting the English Castles.
- The area across the river and to the east should have ample resources to begin your town.

Walkthrough:

Load your crew into the two Transport Ships and steer them down the river until you come to the fork. Head slightly north, and then disembark on the lower eastern shore. This will take a couple of trips. While shipping the others, have the Villagers build Farms, Houses, and a Town Center. Gather as many supplies as possible, stressing Food and Wood at the beginning.

> **Note:** *The southeast is full of resources, including Fish, Gold, Stones, and Sheep. And best of all, there are no enemy compounds in this area.*

Erect a Dock near the coast, but don't waste time building combat vessels. Just create a couple of Fishing Ships and have them plant Fish Traps throughout the river. Use the other Villagers to build Farms and herd Sheep. Once you have sufficient resources, erect a Blacksmith and a Stable. Next, upgrade to the Castle Age. Some Burgundians might try to infiltrate your area through the shallows. Use the Demolition Ships to kill them while they are still crossing the shallows.

> **Tip:** *If you do not order the giant La Hire and some Knights to take down Burgundy's Watch Tower (the only enemy structure in the southeastern corner), your Builders won't get much building done. The Tower's fire will kill the Builders before they have time to erect a structure.*

Train some Cavaliers at the Stable and send about ten or twelve of them into the Burgundy village directly northwest of your camp. Accompany the Cavaliers with several Crossbowmen to assist them. Demolish the Guard Towers first, since they propose the biggest threat. Next, reduce all of their other buildings to rubble. Meanwhile, place the Crossbowmen on top of a hill to kill any British or Burgundy Villagers parading about.

> **Note:** *The Burgundy site is not well guarded, as there are no fortress Walls. You will encounter few combatants, and overall, the attack should be easy, with few or no casualties on your side. If your soldiers suffer some wounds, heal them in a newly built Castle.*

Once the area is clear, have your Villagers construct a Castle on the site where the Burgundy village once stood. Next, add a Siege Workshop and a University. Research appropriate ballistic technologies. Building a Stable is not always necessary; however, I recommend it here for training additional Cavaliers that are often needed to lay siege to enemy Castles (as shown in Figure 16-5). After construction on the Siege Workshop is complete, order it to construct several Mangonels. It's time to take down the enemy fortresses.

Figure 16-5 *Use Cavaliers or Knights to destroy British Castles.*

The basic strategy for sacking all three Castles in this mission goes as follows:

- Attack the Guard Towers and Castle Gates with Mangonels. They offer much more firepower than the Cavaliers.
- Use the Cavaliers or Battering Rams to hack away at the Castle—the structure has no close-range defenses; however, its long-range defenses allow it to fire away freely at attacking Mangonels.

Tip: *Mangonels do not have enough hit points to take on a Guard Tower without repairs (as shown in Figure 16-6). When the siege weapon is around 30 percent, pull it out of battle and have a Villager repair it. In a few seconds, the Mangonel will be like brand-new.*

When invading each of the Castles, some enemy soldiers may rush out to attack. Use the Cavaliers to defeat them. A line of Crossbowmen is ideal for backup in those situations. Just make sure that you don't forget to protect the siege equipment.

Invade the Castles, starting with the one the farthest northwest and moving southeast. You want to keep your distance from Fastolf's Army as long as possible. Of course, this won't be long enough. After your troops destroy the first British Castle, Fastolf and his men march to the area to handle the chaos. For

the most part, his army consists of Cavaliers. Luckily for you, they have some distance to travel before they confront your men.

Escort all of your Mangonels within the Walls of the fortress you've just taken. Station some Cavaliers where the Gate used to be. This will prevent Fastolf from destroying your siege equipment. Next, station another group of Cavaliers outside the Castle with a line of Crossbowmen on a hill behind them. Use the Mangonels to put as many Britons to rest as possible. The Cavaliers and Crossbowmen can take care of the remaining British troops.

Once Fastolf and his army have been defeated, continue sacking the British Castles in the same manner as you did with the previous one. Before you know, it the Loire will have three fewer British settlements, and Joan will be on her way into French legend.

Figure 16-6 *Be prepared to repair your Mangonels when bombarding Guard Towers.*

Mission Four: The Rising

Objectives:

- Travel west to help reinforce the French town. Be wary of opposition along the way.
- Ensure that Joan survives.

Hints:

- Gaining control of the river might be a good strategy, but do not squander your resources needlessly on ships.
- Chalon is the closest and most vulnerable of the three English-occupied villages. Making an example of them early could help even the odds for you in the long run.

- Remember your objectives. It is not necessary to level the cities; you only need to force the English to withdraw.
- Wall off all shallows to slow enemy invaders.

Walkthrough:

Joan is accompanied by Monks, Scout Cavalry, Knights, Crossbowmen, and Men-at-Arms. Your destination is on the trail. Unfortunately, a band of British troops is up ahead, too. South of the trail are several Chalon Guard Towers, which contain French forces allied with the Britons. Since these will be easier to defeat than the British troops, you must find these first—and avoid the British at all costs.

First, place all of your Knights in one group. Order everybody else into a group with Joan. Send the Knights forward, and have them head south along the forking trail. Direct them to level a nearby Guard Tower (as shown in Figure 16-7) and continue west. Another Guard Tower is stationed just below a patch of trees. Demolish that Guard Tower, and then continue west, deviating off the beaten path. When you spot the next enemy tower, you know what to do.

Figure 16-7 *The Franks hack away at a Chalon Guard Tower.*

Proceed north along the path near where the last tower once stood. Turn right at the crossroads. When the road forks again, head north and dismantle the final Chalon Guard Tower. After destruction of the towers is complete, head to the nearest Town Center. You can slay the band of British guards that attacks you from the east with your Knights and Men-at-Arms.

Tip: *Garrison the Crossbowmen inside the Town Center. Place your melee units a short distance south of your Town Center. That way the Britons will attack the Town Center, and your men can ambush them from behind.*

Once you've cleared out the Britons, order the Monks to heal your wounded soldiers. Produce Villagers from the Town Center, and have them gather Food, Wood, Gold, and Stone. Direct Builders to erect a Dock, Stable, Siege Workshop, and University. Produce a couple of Knights at the Stable and then have them destroy any remaining British Scout Cavalry to the west. Build some Mangonels at the Siege Workshop. Now the territory south of the river is cleansed of enemy infestation, and you can advance to the Imperial Age.

Have some Villagers construct three Guard Towers near the shallows. Build a Galleon and attack the Chalon Knights from the river, careful to avoid the four rushing enemy Scorpions. Try to trick the enemy into advancing close to your newly built Guard Towers and Mangonels, where they will soon fall. Next, send about ten Cavaliers into the Chalon area. Destroy the buildings and the remaining Crossbowmen. When British Knights and Longbowmen begin to descend from the north, tackle each one at a time, and they will be history.

Bring in a Builder to construct a Castle in the region just above the shallows. Next, order the Monks to enter this area and heal the Cavaliers. Once their strength is replenished, send the Cavaliers east to defeat the British soldiers and demolish any buildings in the area. Create a Trebuchet to take care of the Castle (as shown in Figure 16-8).

Figure 16-8 *The Trebuchet can really do some damage to the Castle.*

You've done a nice job, but the Britons aren't budging. The only thing to do is eradicate their northern fortress. Use Mangonels—in a Box Formation with Knights—to crush the enemy Keeps. When Britons begin to swarm outside the gate,

> **Tip:** *Scour the wilderness for enemy Longbowmen and Knights, who are scattered about in insignificant numbers. Next take down any structures you find; this part of the mission culminates in the destruction of the Town Center and Castle.*

use your 10 Cavaliers to stop them. Next, set up the Trebuchets, and devastate the Town Center and Castle. Once you sack the Cathedral, the British will wave the white flag.

Mission Five: The Siege of Paris

Objectives:

- Ensure that Joan survives.
- Refugee Villagers in Paris are attempting to escape English tyranny. Rescue at least six of the refugees and escort them to the Chateau of Compiègne (the square between the flags).
- Rendezvous with the King's reinforcements in Paris, just south of the river bridge.

Hints:

- Don't try to defeat every British unit. Focus on your objectives.
- Guard your siege weapons. Towers will be a big problem if you don't.
- If you are faced with overwhelming opposition, run away!

Walkthrough:

Joan and her new companions Lord de Graville and Jean de Lorrain have a sizable army at their disposal. And they will need it, as this mission is not going to be easy. The very first move you make in this mission can get you into some serious trouble. You can follow the trail into the Castle entrance, but that's not the best idea. It's heavily fortified with two Gates and several Keeps. Besides, two enemy Monks and some Elite Longbowmen and Onagers will harass your soldiers if you pursue that plan.

Don't knock on the front door; this is like announcing that you've come to crash their party. Surprise them by entering Paris off the beaten path. Head northwest along the edge of the map. You will not encounter any opposition here, just some Farms, Houses, and wilderness. Place a Trebuchet toward the middle of this section to take down the Wall (as shown in Figure 16-9). Use a group of Pikemen and Crossbowmen for defense, but bring everybody else nearby.

As soon as you put a gaping hole in the fortress, some enemy troops will sneak out and attack. Bombard the Mangonels with your Trebuchet. French Pikemen and Crossbowmen can take out the other enemy units. At this point,

have all your forces infiltrate the Walls. Some enemy units are stationed to the right of your entry. Use the Bombard Cannons to crush the enemy Cavaliers and Crossbowmen.

Figure 16-9 *Set up a Trebuchet to create a hole in the northwestern Wall.*

Navigating through the defended streets can be tricky, and avoiding enemy Towers is almost impossible. Since protecting Joan is vital to the operation, have the Paladins surround her, her companions, and the Trebuchet. To be extra careful, direct the group into a Box Formation with everyone guarding Joan.

> **Tip:** *Place all of your units in No Attack Stance. This will prevent them from wasting time trying to destroy British Guard Towers.*

Order the Pikemen and Crossbowmen into another group. They will be in charge of protecting the refugees. Once they have liberated the French prisoners, hurry out of the area. British Galleons patrol the river and aren't hesitant about shooting. Rendezvous with the King's reinforcements at the Monastery just south of the bridge.

> **Tip:** *Although you have to stay relatively close to the river, you also need to keep out of harm's way. Choose the paths between the Houses on your route to the bridge. Unfortunately, the King's ship you're about to rendezvous with has brought only two soldiers from a lower age to help you. Rotten scoundrel!*

Hurry both groups across the river, keeping everyone in No Attack Stance. If you continue east, near the Cathedral you will find some Franks eager to join your party. Use the band of Militia and Throwing Axeman, along with the Heavy Scorpions to thwart the charging Britons from the northwest. Meanwhile, erect a

> **Tip:** *You have to be careful here. Lots of open areas around the city end up being blocked in by forests. The safest bet is to knock down a section of Wall near the Gold. This will allow a successful exodus.*

Trebuchet to put a hole in the Wall through which your troops can escape (as shown in Figure 16-10).

Head southeast down the trail. Compiègne lies ahead on the first left. Unfortunately, Burgundy forces are waiting to attack on both sides of this road. Before continuing, reorganize your party. Distribute the remaining Paladins, Crossbowmen, Pikemen, and Militia into two groups, placing them in Aggressive Stance. Send one group to the right and the other to the left. While they're busy battling the Burgundians, send Joan, her companions, and the Refugees straight down the middle of the road into the Gate. Victory is yours.

Figure 16-10 *Joan leads the exodus out of Paris.*

Mission Six: A Perfect Martyr

Objectives:

- Ensure that the Trade Cart carrying the French flag survives.
- Plant the French flag (loaded in a Trade Cart) on the hill in Castillon that is already covered with flags.
- Rendezvous with the French artillery, commanded by Jean Bureau.
- Rendezvous with the French army, commanded by Constable Richmont.

Hints:

- Most of the land here is occupied. You have to displace Burgundy in order to build a town. Don't knock down all of Burgundy's Walls—you can use them for your own defense.
- Longbowmen are powerful, but Bombard Cannons are better!

Walkthrough:

Figure 16-11 *Meeting Constable Richmont and his entourage.*

You begin in a small clearing in the northeast section of the map, with a Trade Cart escorted by Guy Josselyne. Head southeast, and go around the trees and across a small creek. You are greeted by Constable Richmont and his sizable entourage (as shown in Figure 16-11). Cross the river at the shallows and you'll find Jean Bureau and the French artillery awaiting you.

Take a few moments to place your troops into manageable "war parties." Group the foot soldiers—Arbalests, Champions, and half of the Hand Cannoneers—together. Place them into a Line Formation and give them Stand Ground orders. Put the Bombard Cannons and the other Hand Cannoneers in another group. Make a third group consisting of the Light Cavalry and another containing all but two of the Paladins. Put the Trebuchets, Trade Cart, Villagers, Constable Richmont, Jean Bureau, and the remaining Paladins into a Box Formation. Now you're ready to rock.

Place your formations south of the Burgundy fortress. Take out the enemy Guard Towers and Trebuchet with your Trebuchets and Bombard Cannons. Protect the Bombard Cannons and Trebuchets with the Arbalests, Champions, and Hand Cannoneers. Continue your attack on the Burgundy fortress until you destroy the Town Hall. Once you have the resources found in the Town Hall you can proceed to the next phase of our plan.

Move the foot soldier group so that the trees south of the Burgundy fortress secure the formation's southern flank. Move the Bombard Cannon formation behind them. Place both Cavalry groups in the general area—just south of the Burgundy fortress Walls—and keep the Trade Cart group behind them all (as shown in Figure 16-12).

Send the Light Cavalry to the river crossing directly west of your position. Fly into the British troops and obliterate any ranged-attack siege engines you

Figure 16-12 *This is how the French should look shortly before they ambush the British.*

find. Run back to your lines. The Brits will normally follow you and battle your foot soldiers. This will be their last mistake. The combination of the foot soldiers' swords, guns, and arrows, mated with the Bombard Cannon's balls devastates their attack. Once the attack has failed, creep northeast along the river until your Bombard Cannons can eradicate the Keeps guarding the river crossing.

After the river crossing Keeps are eliminated, station the foot soldiers north of the crossing, facing north. There is usually a Burgundy detachment north of the crossing, and you want to be ready when they come out of the Woods.

Once the Burgundy troops are down, cross the river, unpack the Trebuchets, and take out the two Bombard Towers west of the crossing. Repeat this procedure with the next Bombard Tower that is north of the first two. Now move all of your folks to the middle of the northwest edge of the map. Use your Trebuchets to take out the Castle and the Guard Towers that you find there.

Build a small village with the resources plundered from Burgundy. You'll need a Town Center, Market, Mining Camp, and a Barracks. Have the Villagers

Note: *We are going to ignore some of the game's hints for this mission. It is no doubt solid advice that might lead to victory, but I believe victory can be bought at a much cheaper price. We will, for all intents and purposes, ignore the*

Tip: *Take your time and make sure you keep the foot soldier formation in front of the Bombard Cannons. Place the Cavalry in reserve and use them to sweep behind enemy lines and attack any siege engine units.*

Tip: *Be careful, these Burgundy troops are often accompanying some powerful siege engines. Use your Cavalry to destroy the siege machines.*

mine under the watchful eyes of your remaining Cavalry. Advance the Trebuchets, foot soldiers, Bombard Cannons, Trade Cart, and one Light Cavalry (to increase the line of sight for siege weapons fire) toward the British fortress southwest of your position. You'll see a tan path of barren earth that leads to it.

Demolish the fortress's Bombard Towers with the Trebuchet, and punch a hole in the Wall with your Bombard Cannons. If you're running short on soldiers, have your Barracks create Pikemen and Long Swordsmen. Escort the Trade Cart with your foot soldiers onto the hill with the flags, and the mission will finally come to an end. France is saved!

The Barbarossa Campaign

Can the will of one man forge an empire? Frederick Barbarossa attempts to force the squabbling German fiefdoms into his Holy Roman Empire, which he then must defend from the machinations of the Italian city states and the Pope in Rome. And should he accomplish all of those feats, there is always the third Crusade to wage.

Mission One: Holy Roman Emperor

Objectives:

- Capture four Relics from the six German duchies.

Hints:

- Because the Empire faces so many enemies, it would be wise to dispose of one or two early, before they become a real threat.
- Remember, only Monks can transport and garrison Relics.
- Take care to have a Monk nearby to transport the Relics you locate.
- You can tell if an enemy Monastery has a Relic garrisoned inside if the Monastery has a flag perched on top of it. The only way to recover Relics inside an enemy Monastery is to destroy the Monastery.

Walkthrough:

Frederick Barbarossa must unite the German nations if he is to have any hope of becoming Emperor of the Holy Roman Empire. The easiest way for him to do this is to lead a large army into these kingdoms and take their Relics. Once four Relics are taken, the fiefdoms will fall into line behind the new Emperor.

Tip: *Completely defeating each kingdom in turn is time-consuming, requires multiple attacks, and is inefficient. You should destroy only Swabia entirely, as the Swabians will impede your progress when attacking Saxony. Conduct swift raids, aim for Monasteries, and steal the Relics with single-minded efficiency.*

It is not important how much damage you do, how many resources you gather, or how many enemy nations you force to submit; victory rests upon the four Relics. The scenario begins with Barbarossa in possession of a Castle, a Monastery, a handful of Villagers, and a small group of fighting units. Create a few Monks, and set the rest of your Villagers to resource gathering and House building.

The minute you have your first Monk, have your attackers escort him west and then south into the camp of Burgundy (as shown in Figure 16-13). Destroy any opposition, steal the Relic, and return home. Replace your losses by generating more attackers.

Figure 16-13 *Barbarossa's stalwart guards escort the Monk toward the unprotected borders of Burgundy.*

As soon as you have a decent-sized force (ten or so Cavalry units, ten or more Infantry, and several siege units), head northwest to demolish the Swabian temple and steal their Relic. Be careful, though, as they possess a few Monks. Once you have the Relic, bring it back and build a Wall with a gate between the forests north of your village. Use Monks to convert all northern attackers, and be aware of siege-equipped Bavarian troops assaulting your Castle from the south. Your Castle should be able to defend itself against all attacks, although a Guard Tower or two wouldn't hurt. Gather resources until you have a

Tip: *Since you only need four Relics to be victorious, do not waste your time fighting the tougher groups, like the Austrians and Bavarians. Just place Guard Towers near those settlements to keep the enemies from becoming pests when you are fighting the other groups. For example, build Guard Towers on the river shallows between you and Bavaria. These frustrate the attacks of that prolific nation.*

grand army with more than a few Mangonels, Scorpions, and Battering Rams. Head northwest again and obliterate Swabia completely. Continue traveling northwest until you reach the Walls of Saxony. Destroy these Walls, steal the Relic just north of the Saxons' Town Center, and return home.

After that, raid and take the Relic of the Bohemians (shown in Figure 16-14), who also lack a Wall and are located between the Saxons and the Austrians (northeast edge of the map). Once you have four of the Relics in your possession, the entirety of Germany is yours to command.

Tip: *A good general strategy is to attack a main structure, such as a Castle, to distract enemy troops once a Relic is stolen from a Monastery.*

Figure 16-14 *As his troops distract the hapless Bohemians, Barbarossa's Monk steals the Relic.*

Mission Two: Henry the Lion

Objectives:

- Defeat Poland.

Hints:

- The German states of Bavaria and Saxony are "feeding" the armies of Barbarossa and Henry the Lion. Defend these helpless states at all costs.

Walkthrough:

You begin this scenario with three allies, one enemy, a built-up camp, some resources, a small army, and no Villagers. You are dependent upon Saxony and Bavaria and must guard their unprotected Villagers from the Polish threat. Be careful, though; the Lion is preparing to pounce upon you. Begin creating troops and send them to the two allies. Make sure you build a few siege weapons and send them away as well. Leave your troops within the towns of your two allies. When your army is large, and you've accepted the "gifts" of your allies, send your troops north toward the Polish lands, but keep an eye on them and be quick to react, as Henry the Lion will soon betray you.

Once you destroy the first Polish Castle, Henry announces his ambitious intentions—to become emperor himself. Pull all your men back and crush the cowardly Lion as quickly as you can, destroying all his troops. A Walled area in the extreme west guards a Relic and a group of captive Villagers. (See Figure 16-15.) Carefully approach the area and knock a hole in its defense. Use a Monk to take the Relic therein, and use those freed Villagers to good advantage.

Figure 16-15 *Barbarossa wreaks vengeance upon the treacherous Henry the Lion.*

Now begin gathering resources in earnest, building siege equipment, and sending scouts to find the Polish positions. You need to destroy two or more Castles and various Polish units and buildings (as shown in Figure 16-16).

Figure 16-16 *Barbarossa's men destroy the hapless Polish Castles with impunity.*

Mission Three: Pope and Anti-Pope

Objectives:

- Convert the Cathedral in Milan.

Hints:

- You are going to need Villagers to provide a suitable offensive.
- The town of Crema is providing Milan with supplies. Perhaps you should take care of them early.

Walkthrough:

This mission places you in yet another precarious position, but you have the tools needed to survive and Milan and her allies aren't in an attacking mood yet. Build some Fishing Ships, start fishing, and then build some more Villagers and gather resources. Take your combat units and a couple of Monks southeast, and punish the Cremians for supplying Milan.

> **Tip:** *Use your Monks to convert the Villagers of Crema and use other attackers to steal their Sheep.*

Begin researching and preparing for a sea assault. Advance to the Imperial Age and research all technologies relating to gunpowder. Once you have a large and advanced force, build some Cannon Galleons and as many Transport Ships as you think you'll need to transfer your army. You should also construct some Fire Ships for defense of the fleet. Use the Cannon Galleons to knock down the Wall directly across from your allies. Break down the Wall (as shown in Figure 16-17), and send your ships back to escort the transport fleet to that beachhead.

Figure 16-17 *Breach the Wall to soften defenses and make the invasion a safer proposition.*

Land your troops, defending the boats from enemy ship assaults, and take out the Frankish installation on that peninsula. Unload some Villagers and build a Barracks, Archery Range, Stable, Siege Workshop, Monastery, and perhaps a Castle there. Produce an army and several Monks, and then attack Milan (southwest of your current position) in force. Target and destroy all troop buildings, Town Centers, and Guard Towers. However, keep an eye on your men; *do not* let them destroy the Cathedral.

Figure 16-18 *The devout Monks of Barbarossa convince the Monks of the Great Cathedral that Barbarossa is indeed the Holy Roman Emperor.*

Send your Monks over to the Cathedral and convert it. Once it is yours, Milan falls before you (as shown in Figure 16-18).

Mission Four: The Lombard League

Objectives:

- Construct a Wonder within the city Walls of Padua, Venice, or Verona.

Hints:

- The Lombards have a head start on you, so build defensive structures until you can train an army.

Walkthrough:

The scenario opens with a massive sea and land assault on your Town Center and your Walls in the south; a short distance east of your city, you have a fleet of Fishing Ships, Fire Ships, War Galleys, and troop-laden Transport Ships waiting to join you. Sail one of your Transport Ships from your Dock and rendezvous with the rest of your fleet. Take the fleet south, but avoid the fighting. Aim

for that island connected by shallows to your besieged base. Unload your troops, build a new Town Center, and start gathering resources. Use your combat vessels to guard your Fishing Ships, as shown in Figure 16-19. Once you've collected enough resources, build some Walls or Guard Towers to block both of the river's shallows.

Figure 16-19 *Protect your fishing ships from seaborne assault, for the enemy is tenacious.*

Once you've established your defenses, build a massive army. At around this time, Henry the Lion will betray you once again (some people never learn). When your army is ready, destroy him.

Advance your troops northward and begin creating as many Villagers as you can. Attack Verona, which is situated northeast of Henry's former base. Once you are inside their Walls, send for your Villagers, amass resources, and build your Wonder. Before you build the Wonder, make sure your site is defended by as many Guard Towers as you can afford (as shown in Figure 16-20). Let the Wonder stand for the allotted time and you win.

Figure 16-20 *Guard Towers and troops protect your workers as they work wonders on enemy soil.*

Mission Five: Barbarossa's March

Objectives:

- At least ten troops must survive to reach the Hospitaller camp.

Hints:

- There are few safe places to land along the Anatolian peninsula. Directly across from Constantinople is one of the safest landings.
- Do not destroy enemy ships you might use—you are not going to be able to build your own in this mission.

Walkthrough:

Should you travel south to Gallipoli or south and west to Constantinople? If you opt for Gallipoli (as shown in Figure 16-21), you'll find the going easy, but once you arrive you'll be attacked by a massive fleet of Saracen ships. It is likely that all of your transports will be sunk before you can even load them!

Tip: *There are two paths you might take to commandeer some ships. One involves the guarded port of Constantinople, and the other passes through the peaceful village of Gallipoli. Gallipoli (to the south) is* much *harder.*

Instead, proceed to the gates of Constantinople, but hang back, set up your Trebuchets, and then take one Knight and approach the gate. The Byzantines will refuse to aid you, so you must force them by threatening the Hagia Sophia Wonder by stationing troops next to it.

Figure 16-21 *Gallipoli is a small town with danger lurking by its coast.*

Once you've broken a hole in the defense, send your troops directly to the Hagia Sophia Wonder within the city. Its leaders will relent, and you'll have a shiny new navy. Quickly move every available

troop onboard the Transport Ships, and leave your Trebuchets behind to distract the marauding enemy that sometimes storms the gates at the last minute.

Sail quickly, using your attack ships to defend the transports, but not to pursue or engage the enemy. Find the cliffs to the east, and hug them as you continue southward until you find the beach. Unload quickly, keeping to the eastern cliffs, and move your men northeast as fast as you can, letting the empty ships occupy the attacking navy.

> **Tip:** *Use your Trebuchets to knock out all the Bombard Towers; this will save your men's lives. Destroying the Castle from a distance is also prudent. Do not attack the Dock yet, as you need those ships for your own army!*

> **Tip:** *Future events will be much easier to handle if you have at least one of your Onagers intact. In fact, without that unit, the scenario that follows is almost impossible.*

Move your troops northeast around the cliffs, then southwest, skirting the Woods, and crush the Seljukian enemies you find there. Now head due south, looking for a Wooded passage to the top of the cliff. You know you've found it when a soldier mutters, "If only we had a way to knock down those trees." There is. Use that Onager to attack the ground there (as shown in Figure 16-22). If you cannot go this way, because you have no Onager, you'll have to hug the cliff and proceed south, but that's a tougher route.

Figure 16-22 *The plucky siege tool saved the day by making a path where there was none before.*

After you punch your way through the trees, climb to the top of the cliff and then head straight south until you reach the edge of the map. Keep going southwest along the edge of the map, hopefully with at least ten men in tow, until you reach the Hospitaller camp.

> **Note:** *If you do try to go through Gallipoli and you survive, you'll find some marooned Frankish Crusaders and a Trebuchet waiting to be picked up on an island between you and the mainland. Go ahead and add them to your army.*

Mission Six: The Emperor Sleeping

Objectives:

- Do not allow the Dome of the Rock to be destroyed.
- Deliver the body of Barbarossa to the Dome of the Rock in Jerusalem.

Hints:

- Use your available time (10 minutes) to orchestrate an efficient attack. Position your Pikemen around War Elephants and your Paladins around siege weapons.
- You can pass through the Saracen and Persian gates as long as you are allied with them.
- Invest heavily in siege weapons—particularly Capped Rams.
- Convert Persian War Elephants to gain valuable assault units.

Walkthrough:

It is best to fight defensively for the first stretch of this arduous scenario. Generate Villagers, chop down the forest separating you from the water to the north, mine Gold and Stone, and build buildings. As soon as the 10-minute countdown is close to an end, build a Wall that stretches from the forest in the east to the cliffs in the west. Then start building *many* Guard Towers. Send out your Paladins, Pikemen, and quite a few Monks, and scatter them among the Tower defense (as shown in Figure 16-23). Use your Monks to convert enemy siege equipment and, most important, the massive Elephants.

Figure 16-23 *With this many Guard Towers, a stout Wall, and Monks to rob the enemy of its best soldiers, you cannot lose.*

Once you reach the Sheep, build Farms, a Dock, and some Fishing Ships (use Fish Traps as well). Build your army, and then send them and the wagon bearing the Emperor southwest to meet up with Richard the Lionhearted. Bust a hole in the Walls outside Jerusalem, south of where the hapless and foolish Richard attacks. Break into Jerusalem, and carefully eliminate all Bombard Towers and troops that might be nearby. Carefully escort your wagon, and the pickled Emperor (as shown in Figure 16-24), to the holy Dome of the Rock in the south corner of the city. The Empire may soon fall, but Barbarossa fulfills his promise! Victory is yours.

Note: *Richard the Lionhearted's assault is pathetic, but it serves as a diversion if you then attack the single Wall to the south of his attack.*

Figure 16-24 *Frederick Barbarossa's men keep his honor intact by escorting him to the end of the third Crusade.*

The Genghis Khan Campaign

The nomadic tribes of the Asian steppes spent centuries entangled in their own petty feuds until united under Genghis Khan. Within years, a highly disciplined army pours out of Mongolia to embark on a campaign of world conquest. But how can a tribe of horse Archers possibly overcome the military might of Persia and Eastern Europe, let alone the technologically advanced empires in China?

Mission One: Crucible

Objectives:

- Wait for instructions from Genghis Khan.
- Ride forth to each of the Mongol tribes and convince them to join the Khan's army.
- Make an example of any tribes that openly war against you by destroying them.

Note: *Your overall objective is to get four tribes to ally with Khan. To gain the allegiance of a tribe, you have to meet the conditions set by that tribe.*

Hints:

- You can change Diplomacy settings whenever you want, but don't be surprised if the other tribes respond to your actions.
- Only Monks are able to transport Relics.
- The Kereyids are known as the most religious of the tribes, and they may have a few Monks near their camp.
- Use the Objectives button to keep track of new objectives or those that have changed.

Walkthrough:

Genghis Khan has sent you forth to gain the allegiance of as many tribes as you can and to pulverize those who are disloyal. If you check your Diplomacy settings, you will see that you are allied with all of the tribes but the Kara-Khitai, who feign neutrality until you come within range.

To begin the round of negotiations, send your troops northwest along the river to the Ungirrads' camp. The Ungirrads tell you that their price for allegiance is a Relic.

Swing west toward the Tayichi'uds, and parlay with them as well. You learn that they are at war with the Naiman and will join you only if the Naiman are destroyed.

Now head east a short distance and then north to the Kereyids, and speak with them. Because the cold has hurt their food supply, their price for allying with Genghis Khan is twenty Sheep. Although there are Sheep all around the map in small groups, fortunately the Kara-Khitai have a pen full of Sheep just to the northeast, and you have the muscle to steal their flock.

Once you kill the three guards on duty, round up the nine Sheep in the pen, and send them to the Kereyids' camp. Send your troops there as well, but fan them out on the way back, picking up the other eleven required Sheep from the small groups to the southeast and southwest of the pen.

Tip: *When the Sheep are accepted by the Kereyids, their collars will turn blue. If the Kereyids don't swear allegiance, check for any Sheep that have not moved to the camp. If there are Sheep in the camp whose collars haven't changed, move them directly beside the Kereyids' Sheep and they should change color.*

When the Kereyids have their twenty Sheep, you'll gain some troops and two Monks (as shown in Figure 16-25). Use the Monks to heal all your units to full strength, and then give them a few Light Cavalry as guards and move them out of harm's way.

Figure 16-25 *Those Monks make this mission a whole lot easier.*

Send the bulk of your forces east across the river and then north to the Naiman camp (as shown in Figure 16-26). Along the way, when you see a group of two Kara-Khitai, destroy them and wait: a Mangonel will arrive shortly. It's important to clear this path so you won't lose your Monks when they follow. Also, watch out for the three Kara-Khitai Watch Towers near the center of the map.

Figure 16-26 *Parlaying with the Naiman.*

In the Naiman camp, you learn that they have an equal hatred for the Tayichi'uds, and that the Naiman's condition for joining Khan's horde is the same: the utter destruction of their hated enemy. Although the Naiman are a bit stronger than the Tayichi'uds, neither force can hope to stop you, so save yourself some travel time, and wipe out the Naiman clan.

Tip: *Don't overlook the Naiman unit to the north when you attack, or you'll have to come back to finish him off.*

When the Naiman have been dispatched, bring your Monks over with their guard. Have the Monks heal your main force, and then march everybody to the southeast. Move past the box canyon with the Sheep, and enter the gap in the trees just beyond. There you find a Relic guarded by three Wolves. Turn them into pelts and grab the Relic with one of your Monks.

Next, send everybody over to talk with the Uighurs just to the southeast. You find that their price for joining the alliance involves killing a powerful Wolf named Ornlu who lives on the plateau to the east. As a veteran Wolf fighter, this will prove a simple task. When you're done you'll gain the allegiance of the Uighurs, five Camels, and a gift of fire arrows.

Send the Camels and the rest of your forces to the south along the southeast side of the map, toward your original starting position. Once there, send half your forces and the Monk with the Relic to the Ungirrads' camp, and the other half to the Tayichi'uds' settlement. You will gain the allegiance of each, and victory will be at hand.

Mission Two: A Life of Revenge

Objectives:

- Prevent the tent of Genghis Khan from being destroyed.
- Kill the traitor Kushluk.

Hints:

- To persuade the Tayichi'ud Villagers to join you, kill all of their soldiers.
- The Mongols do not yet know how to make siege weapons.

Walkthrough:

After you've completed the first mission, wait a few seconds for your men to regroup, and then follow the advice of the Horseman who found the

Tayichi'uds. Kill all Tayichi'ud soldiers but spare their buildings, as soon they will all be yours (as shown in Figure 16-27). Create Villagers and start hunting, chopping Wood, and building a Palisade Wall to protect your Town Center. This Palisade Wall should buy you some time if and when your enemy mounts an attack. They will usually try to attack the Town Center first and then the tent of Genghis Khan.

Figure 16-27 *Attack and slay all military units to convert the Tayichi'uds to your cause!*

Tip: *There is a huge herd of Deer in the southeast corner. Carefully guide as many Villagers as you can spare all the way there and gorge yourself upon the meat.*

Be sure to hunt at every opportunity; the Mongols are good at it. Scout out the enemy position and find herds of Deer. Gather resources, advance as far and fast as possible, and then mount an attack into enemy territory.

Once you are ready to attack, proceed into the enemy camp and destroy the Walls, replace or heal the wounded, and strike deep into the southwest. Kushluk himself will lead the attack; slay him and the uprising will end (as shown in Figure 16-28).

Figure 16-28 *There is the cowardly Kushluk—pursue him and slay him!*

Mission Three: Into China

Objectives:

- Conquer the Tanguts, Hsi Hsia, Jin, and Sung.

Hints:

- The Great Wall will give you trouble without siege equipment. Fortunately you can capture some northeast of the wall.
- Your initial base can defend you for a short time, but soon you have to push into China to find resources.
- The Chinese nations will put aside their differences to fight a common enemy. You must fight all four at once, lest one gain the upper hand.

Walkthrough:

Lasso your troops (shown in Figure 16-29) and move them to the east. Continue until you find a river fork and launch an attack against the Villagers milling about. When you reach the eastern part of the village, some Villagers, a Battering Ram, and a Mangonel join you. Build your own Town Center and important buildings, and start gathering resources. Advance your technology as far as possible and move near the northwestern edge of the Great Wall (shown in Figure 16-30). Build a Castle, Barracks,

Figure 16-29 *Use these men wisely, for they will reap large initial benefits.*

Stable, Siege Workshop, and Archery Range there, and begin producing troops. Use Trebuchets and siege equipment to shatter the wall when ready. After a hole is made, move through and go southwest until you come across some Bombard Cannons that defect to your side. Wreak havoc on the enemy where you find them.

A coordinated assault against all your enemies isn't necessary—provided you have momentum and are ready to board transports to take out the Jin on their island (to the far east). Also, farming and fishing should keep the resources on your side of the wall plentiful for quite some time.

Figure 16-30 *They don't call this the Great Wall of China for nothing!*

Tip: *Trebuchets are the best way to attack the Great Wall out of reach of those pesky Keeps that line it.*

Mission Four: The Horde Rides West

Objectives:

- Defeat the Khwarazm Empire.
- Defeat the Russians.
- Set the two Trade Carts containing assassins close enough to the Khwarazm Shah to strike.

Hints:

- Your two armies are divided and will not be able to meet until they reach Samarkand.

- If your assassination attempt fails, the leadership of the Shah will guarantee that the Persians are a much more deadly enemy.
- The Persians are expecting their gift. If they do not receive it soon, they may eventually declare war on you.

Walkthrough:

You are charged with assassinating the Shah of the Khwarazm Empire, and the deed itself is simple. The timing, however, is critical.

You start with two Town Centers: one to the north and one to the southeast. Your assassins wait near the southeastern Town Center. Though your treacherous attack will spring from there, the southeastern village is ill suited for defense and will soon run short of Wood. Use it instead as a resource engine, gathering all the Gold, Wood, Stone, and animal foods that you can, but do not build any buildings other than mines. You'll be abandoning the town later, and there's no sense wasting time and Gold on urban renewal.

In the north, scout out the area—especially west—and find the gaps and cuts in the woods that you can later fill in with Stone Walls to keep your main town free from interference. As you scout, keep in mind these three objectives: protecting your growing settlement, keeping the Russians from nosing around, and funneling an enraged Persian army into the teeth of your future defenses.

While you're scouting the west, destroy the two Merkid horsemen and make sure their village is clear. They have a good deal of Gold, and that may come in handy later. Additionally, some of their buildings might be of use when you develop Monks who can convert them.

Also keep an eye out for trails that the Russian Villagers are using. If you find one, place a few units on it and slaughter the Villagers as they come by. There is no sense in letting the Russians get any stronger than necessary.

When the production rate of your Stone Mine in the southeast is strong, start blocking off the paths to your northern town, adding towers if you can afford it. The key is to make sure you leave one small path toward your village, which can accommodate a bristling army of defenders at its far end.

> **Tip:** *When you're building your defenses, don't forget to plan for an onrushing herd of bloodthirsty War Elephants. They're not going to stop until you make them.*

Keep gathering resources in the southeast as fast as you can, and generate units, buildings, and technological advances in your fortification to the north. Advance to the Imperial Age when it is possible. When you have your town

sealed off—with the exception of one entrance—build a Castle at the end of the only remaining entrance. Leave plenty of room to move troops and Siege Engines past. Build a force of Mangudai and Trebuchets, and throw in a few upgraded Guard Towers while you're at it.

The key is to have your northern defenses in place before the southeastern area has been picked clean. Once the southeastern area is clean, send the Trade Carts on their mission to the Shah, and start building a fast-moving attack force backed up by Trebuchets in your northern town. You'll want to be ready to attack and destroy the Russians when the Shah is killed. Don't rush ahead, and don't kill the Shah before you have a potent storehouse of resources. You should upgrade the units you plan to use in your attacks, and you should have enough resources to field two large armies in a very short amount of time.

> **Tip:** *When the southeastern area has been cleared and you're swinging into attack mode, it would be suicide to send your Villagers north via the Persian territory to the west. Instead, send them north to the northeastern edge of the map, and then move them over the plateau and down the other side. They'll be stuck between a forest and some cliffs, but it's a perfect place to build a Lumber Camp, freeing up Lumberjacks in the north.*

When your Trade Carts are in place for the attack and your forces are massed and ready to go on the offensive, put your nefarious plan into action and assassinate the Shah by moving your Trade Carts directly in front of him. When he falls, start your troops for the Russian settlement to the southwest, and attack any units you can without taking too much damage yourself. Bring up Trebuchets in the rear and pound the Castle and other forces into dust as fast as you can.

When you've passed through the Russian village, keep heading southwest along the northwest edge of the map, until you run into a lakeshore. Swing southeast at that point and follow the shore to the back gate of the Khwarazm fortress, slaying Villagers and defensive units as you go. Try to keep your Mangudai supported by Cavaliers or Knights, and don't leave your Trebuchets alone in your dust. You're going to want to raise a big stink when you get there—not a little commotion.

> **Note:** *You don't want to bring a healthy army into battle against the Russians. This fighting force is going all the way down to the Khwarazm back door and giving it a kick. If you're not in good shape when you get there, you'll be cut to ribbons in no time.*

When you're in place at the western gate on the northwestern wall of the Khwarazm city, do your best to entice the Persian forces to come out and attack.

Shelling their Town Center and other buildings with Trebuchets works quite nicely, but whatever you do, make them come out to get you—don't go into the city on this assault.

Tip: *Your advantage is your speed. You can run circles around most of the Persian units, but they're very tough in a close fight. Keep moving!*

Once you get the Persians' attention, they'll come out in force. You're not going to be able to stop them, but you should inflict as much damage as possible on this wave of attackers. Kill and convert as many of them as you can before your forces are destroyed. As you lose units, start rebuilding them immediately; your second attack should bring the Khwarazm to their knees.

Note: *This is a one-two punch. You must not try to attack until the Persians have thrown themselves in the teeth of your defenses. When the ground is littered with dead and dying Khwarazm, it is time to attack!*

While you're waiting for the enemy to attack, send out a few speedy scouts to locate the oncoming War Elephants and their Knight escorts. Position your siege engines, Archers, Mangudai, and other units in a ring around the end of the funnel you've left for them to find, and when the Persians come through, let them have it with everything you've got. Be aggressive, and try to wipe them out as fast as you can. You're going to be sending the next wave of attackers right back the way they came, and the sooner you can get their carcasses out of the way the better (as shown in Figure 16-31).

Figure 16-31 *Excellent! The War Elephants attacked the Guard Tower and never knew what hit them!*

When you've beaten back the angry Persian attackers, head out the way they came, but take a more direct route to the back gate. Try to bring along some Siege Onagers—if you have

them—and Trebuchets, but get the Mangudai moving fast right off the bat. You want to take control of the back gate, blow it open, and then flood in and obliterate anything that moves. When the slower troops catch up to you, you can use them to destroy the buildings.

You'll encounter some resistance, but the Shah's main fighting force will already have been destroyed, so you should be able to clean out the fortress as you go. If you keep some Elite Skirmishers defending the Trebuchets, you should be able to use the Mangudai to slay roaming defenders. Continue the attack until the Khwarazm Empire is no more (as shown in Figure 16-32).

Figure 16-32 *A second wave of Mongolian troops seals the fate of the Khwarazm Empire.*

Mission Five: The Promise

Objectives:

- Capture the Bohemian flag, the Polish flag, and the German flag.

Hints:

- Don't spend all of your Stone at the Market. You're going to need it.

Walkthrough:

Build up a small base and some decent units as fast as you can. You don't have to immediately build a Wall between you and the Polish building to the southeast; such a Wall prompts attack. Instead, once you have a small army, attack the Poles. They have some Knights and quite a few Mangonels nearby, which you should destroy. Once you have an army strong enough to demolish a Castle, attack and defeat the Polish, as shown in Figure 16-33.

Figure 16-33 *Good King Wenceslas looked down and saw his Castle burning!*

Start working on advancements and build a huge and powerful army. Farm, fish, chop, and mine all that you can. Then attack south, destroying the Germans first. As you march on the Germans, beware of the scattered enemy units that enjoy attacking the siege weapons at the tail end of your army. Destroy Castles, Town Centers, Guard Towers, and all the other units that you find. Flag ownership is determined by your proximity, so make sure you get close enough to them to claim your share (as shown in Figure 16-34).

Tip: *If you want a small boost to your army, look to the southwest of the Bohemian base. You'll find a Temple, a Monk, and some Huskarls just waiting to aid you.*

Now head west from your base camp and scout out the Bohemian position. Construct a field base consisting of Barracks, an Archery Range, and Stables nearby and attack the Bohemians in force. Watch out for the enemy Siege Onagers located on the cliffs surrounding the main gates; they can do massive damage to your army. Destroy them and the Castle and Eastern Europe will fall to the son of the Great Kahn!

Figure 16-34 *Mongol soldiers capture the German flag.*

Mission Six: Pax Mongolia

Objectives:

- Survive until Subotai's reinforcements arrive.
- Defeat Hungary.

Hints:

- Because of the ice on the Sajo River, it is impossible to build ships.
- Use the Saboteurs wisely; you cannot train any more.
- Siege Onagers can flatten forests.

Walkthrough:

The Teutons have been preparing for war, and now they advance. Reinforcements are on the way, but they will not arrive before the defense of your settlement has been decided. You must defend with all of your might, yet be prepared to abandon your village if your forces are overrun.

Send your Villagers to mine all the Stone they can in case you must abandon your home; you'll need it if you're on the run. Change all of your troops to a Defensive Stance, and then group your Light Cavalry together and move them toward the set of Guard Towers that are nearest your Town Center. Hold your Cavalry in reserve for the Scorpions, which will be along soon enough. Move your Saboteurs north, out of harm's way, but within striking distance of any units that might make it to the heart of your encampment.

Now group your Mangudai together and move them quickly to the bridge. You'll see Teutonic Knights marching toward you, and they're tough. Do not let them get too close! Fire on the Teutonic Knights and their Archers, but keep retreating up the hill along the path as the enemy advances (as shown in Figure 16-35). With help from the Guard Towers, you should be able to wipe out the first column of enemy units.

Move your troops north of the gauntlet of Guard Towers, and let the enemy horsemen attack; then swoop back in to pick off one unit at a time. Keep your eyes peeled for forces trying to move around behind you, and be on the lookout for the coming of the siege engines. The Scorpions are especially deadly, and they can destroy your army in no time.

By using delaying tactics with your Mangudai, you should be able to take on any single unit, but even a few Teutonic Knights or Cavaliers are a serious threat. If you are in doubt, use your speed to disengage and find a way to

> **Tip:** *Use the Guard Towers to your advantage at every opportunity. You have a speed advantage, so loop around the Guard Towers and lure pursuers back into a hail of arrows.*

even the odds. Keep moving, making hit-and-run attacks. When you hear the enemy's Trebuchets opening up, circle back down toward the river and see if you can eradicate one or two of them.

When the enemy is bearing down on your Castle, it's time to decide whether you're going to fight to the last man or get out while the getting is good. This is a make-or-break moment; you must not allow your forces to be overrun or your Villagers to be wiped out. If you think you can't stop the Teuton advance, move your Villagers and other units north, and then southeast along the northeast side of the map. Send everyone to the eastern corner of the map, and make sure Teutonic scouts do not sneak in for an attack on your retreating troops.

Figure 16-35 *Stay out of their reach and it's the end of the road for these Teutonic Knights.*

> **Tip:** *If you want to hold the town, you must find and destroy the Trebuchets. If they remain unopposed they will level your buildings in minutes.*

If you save your city: A small number of units at your end of the bridge will stop enemy Villagers from poaching on your land, and you can safely spend the rest of the time waiting for Subotai's arrival by rebuilding your resources. When Subotai arrives, do not rush the bridge and try to attack the Hungarian city head-on. The other side of the bridge is a killing field.

If you do not save your city: As your fleeing forces move through various pinch-points of the map, have a Villager erect a Stone Wall—but only if no enemy units are in the area. Your goal from here on out is to make sure that the Teuton forces are delayed and distracted from attacking your Villagers until Subotai arrives.

The eastern corner of the map is defensible if you get Walls up quickly and if you've dealt with several of the Trebuchets. Try to secure the Gold on the small plateau, and the woods nearby. If you close off access from the north and west, the southwest can be defended for some time by your Mangudai and Cavalry. If necessary, you can close off access from the river as well, but do this only as a last resort.

Until Subotai arrives, you need to rebuild your forces, and at the same time defend yourself. Put up multiple Walls at any point where you expect trouble, and throw in a Guard Tower where it can do some damage. For now, you must survive!

> **Tip:** *A well-placed Guard Tower is worth its weight in Gold. Enemy units will fixate on it instead of hunting you and that will give you an opportunity to strike back while they're immobile. (This tactic is especially effective against enemy Trebuchets.) For extra protection, sandwich a Guard Tower between two Walls.*

When you're sure your defenses are solid and Subotai is ten minutes away, use your 100 Wood in reserve and build a Lumber Camp, harvesting all the Wood you can. When you have enough to build a Mining Camp, do so near the Gold, and start stockpiling it as well.

The Mongols' Revenge When Subotai arrives, the Teutons are going to cower in fear, and that means you're going to have to cross the river and dig them out of their fortress. To do the job, you need a Town Center, and enough Villagers to produce Food, Wood, and Gold for a Siege Workshop to produce upgrades and expensive units. A Castle on the high ground above the south end of the river wouldn't hurt either.

While you're waiting for your resources to pile up, take a ride down to the river if you haven't already. You'll notice that the ice is solid in some places, and at the south end of the river, there is a patch where troops can cross. Directly across the river on the Hungarian side, you will find a clearing surrounded by trees. That's the entrance you'll be using, but you need to upgrade to Siege Onagers to clear the way.

> **Tip:** *Subotai's dogs slow the rest of the horde down a great deal. Leave them with a bone to gnaw on while you strike a blow for Genghis Khan.*

When you're ready, crash through the trees and let loose the destructive might of your Mongolian hordes. But don't underestimate the bite left in the Hungarian dogs, especially when you attack their prized creations. (See Figure 16-36.) Build your own Trebuchets, but be careful where you place them lest

Figure 16-36 *Attacking these wondrous spires will loose yet another Teutonic attack.*

the plentiful Guard Towers do them in. Likewise, use your Mangudai to attack the enemy's Trebuchets and Rams, but keep them out of reach of the Scorpions if you can.

You have control now, and the Hungarians are cowering at the sound of your hoofbeats! Lead your horde to victory for Genghis Khan!

Saladin's Campaign

Outraged that the Holy Land is ruled by Saracens, Knights from Europe have descended on the Middle East in a series of crusades. Now four European kingdoms have sprung up in the desert. The Saracen king, Saladin, rallies his troops in an attempt to drive back the invaders. In response to the European crusades, the Saracens have organized a Jihad. In response to European vileness, the once cultured Saracens have become treacherous. But will it be enough to save their homeland?

Mission One: An Arabian Knight

Objectives:

- Defeat the Franks west of Cairo by destroying their Town Center.
- Get your soldiers to the Mosque in Cairo.
- Defeat the Franks east of Cairo.

Hints:

- Use the line of sight of your Light Cavalry to avoid unwanted encounters.

Walkthrough:

Begin by placing your Saracens in sensible groups and assigning them hot keys. Make two groups of the Light Cavalry, one group of Camels, one of Men-at-Arms, one of Mamelukes, and finally a group consisting of four Men-at-Arms and the two Heavy Scorpions. Place all but the Heavy Scorpion group in Line Formation. Put the Heavy Scorpions in a Box Formation with the Men-at-Arms on the outside. Order everyone to take a Defensive Stance. You don't want them to chase Franks on this mission.

> **Tip:** *Detach one rider from your Light Cavalry to serve as both a scout and a decoy. You'll use him to range ahead and spot danger.*

The initial Frank assault is weak. Defeat the hapless French and march southwest. At the pyramids you'll find another smattering of French Cavalry. Hit them with the Camels and turn south. Here you find the first serious resistance of the mission. Just south of the low hills is a Frank encampment defended by Crossbowmen, Throwing Axemen, and Knights.

Form a battle line of Camels extending northeast from the pond. Put your Mamelukes behind them. The Camels should defend, and the Mamelukes should hold ground. Keep the Light Cavalry in reserve. Send the scout west of the pond until he spots the Frank tents. Roll up the Heavy Scorpion (protected by the Men-at-Arms), and begin firing.

This should stir up the bees' nest. The Knights will pour around the east side of the pond, supported by Crossbowmen. Fight the Knights first with the Camel, then with the Mamelukes, and ride down the Crossbowmen and Throwing Axemen with the Light Cavalry. Push south to the bridge, leading with the Camels. Destroy any wooden buildings, as shown in Figure 16-37, but ignore the tents.

Figure 16-37 *The attack on the French Village.*

The Egyptians will betray you, but don't worry. Form a barrier across the bridge with your Camels and Men-at-Arms. Back them up with the Mamelukes and Heavy Scorpions. If the Egyptians don't attack, bait them with the scout. Once they are defeated, sweep into the final Frank encampment. Take down the buildings and the Franks will fall.

With the Franks down, it's time to visit the Mosque. Direct the Cannon Galleon to destroy the two southernmost Guard Towers and open a hole in the Wall. Enter and wind your way north to the Mosque. Kill the Monk at the entrance and charge into the courtyard. The Egyptians will once again switch sides.

Note: *Use the Cannon Galleon to demolish the remaining Frank buildings. Its rate of fire is slow, but it deals tremendous damage.*

Take the offered reinforcements and organize your forces. Keep melee units in groups with similar units, and keep the Cavalry Archers separate. The Siege Ram should be in its own group. Head to the northern edge of the Frank encampment.

Send a scout ahead with your remaining Light Cavalry. When you find a Guard Tower, use the Siege Ram to destroy it. Continue to move south, stopping just before the northern Frank camp, ready to place your soldiers in formation. Once again, put the melee units in front and back them up with missile units such as Cavalry Archers and Mamelukes. Keep the Light Cavalry in reserve. Slowly advance on the camp, and engage the bulk of the Franks with your Camels and Cavalry Archers. Use your Light Cavalry to sweep in on the Frank Crossbowmen. Once the Franks are defeated, you can march south to their Town Center. Destroy it and victory is yours.

Tip: *Sometimes the Franks may enter Cairo's east gate and commence pillaging. This isn't a big force, so you can take them out. Be careful, however; if you lose too many people here, you might not have enough for the final battle.*

Mission Two: Lord of Arabia

Objectives:

- Defeat Reynald's pirates.
- Defeat Reynald's raiders.
- Do not allow your allies of Aqaba and Medina to be defeated.

Hints:

- The Saracen capital can spare little to get you started. You must develop your own base and army.
- Research Cartography in order to see where your allies need help.
- Keep your allies' trade routes open and they will reward you.
- Assign units to guard allied Trade Carts.

Walkthrough:

The path to victory can be clouded with misperceptions. You enter the mission allied with Medina in the map's east corner and at war with both the pirates in the west and Reynald's raiders in the northeast. Reynald will constantly drip Archers into your village, but don't build your defenses. The key to this game is to attack, attack, and attack.

Begin your mission conquest by creating ten or twelve Villagers, and set them to work mining Gold and harvesting Food. Have one Villager erect a Watch Tower near the Town Center. Recall your Light Cavalry to your Town Center, and use them to slay any Archers that wander through your town.

Tip: *Don't forget to buy all the Villager production-related upgrades that you can. A thriving economy is the most important aspect of the early game.*

Once the economy is strong, create a Barracks northeast of your original village. Generate 15 Men-at-Arms and have them escort three Villagers to the break in the Palm trees northeast of your camp. Build a Watch Tower there.

Reynald may try to take the Tower down, but your Men-at-Arms will usually be enough to prevent him from succeeding. Once Reynald's initial attack is quashed, construct one or two Watch Towers (as shown in Figure 16-38) closer to the gates of Reynald's fortress, near the east edge of the map.

Figure 16-38 *Placing Watch Towers between the ponds is your first step to defeating Reynald.*

Continue to research new technologies, and produce a good mix of Men-at-Arms, Cavalry, and Archers as you continue erecting a string of Towers for offensive purposes. Specifically aim your improvements at entering the Castle Age. Finally, you arrive at Reynald's gates. Some of his men approach the gate to meet you. Try to sweep your entourage through the open gate. Once you're inside the fortress, attack buildings that limit your exposure to the enemy Watch Towers. Weaken Reynald's economy, and, if possible, bring down his fortress.

Unfortunately your raiding party will eventually be killed. They just don't have the power it takes to bring down a Guard Tower. But don't worry—the damage they have inflicted will significantly impede Reynald's economic progress.

Note: *You can search the area for Reynald's raiders before you eliminate their fortress. Once you have his troops contained in the fortress, you can clear the trade corridor of enemies and press on with your trades.*

By now you should be in the Castle Age. Build a Siege Workshop and a Battering Ram or two, and accompany them with a handful of Long Swordsmen, Crossbowmen, and Camels. Break down the gate and attack Reynald's Guard Towers. With the Towers down, you can demolish the rest of the camp.

With Reynald's raiders gone, it's a good idea to sweep the area between your camp and Aqaba. Exterminate the bandits and you'll have a clear trade route to Aqaba. Make sure you have a constant stream of Trade Carts churning the trail between your towns.

Build two Docks southwest of your camp. Build four Transport Ships and six War Galleys or Galleons (depending on your technology level) to guard them. Load the Transport Ships with six Villagers and a solid mix of ten fighters. Sail to the southwest edge of the map, and then follow the map edge north until you hit land. Unload the ships, but don't advance. You don't want to alert the pirates. Build two Guard Towers, a Barracks, and an Archery Range (as shown in Figure 16-39). Crank out 15 Long Swordsmen and ten Archers, and begin your push north. Support the troops with your warships and keep a semi-constant supply of vessels inbound from your Docks. Continue to make your way up the coast.

Once you have a little breathing room, erect a Siege Workshop and generate a couple of Battering Rams. Lead the Battering Rams up the coast with your troops, and use the Rams to take down the tough buildings. Keep pushing until the pirates are defeated.

Order your initial camp to produce a mix of Camels and Light Cavalry. Use them to hunt down and kill the Bandits. The enemy's main camp is located on a plateau just northeast of the Pirates' camp. Eliminate the Bandits and victory is yours.

Figure 16-39 *These buildings are your first toehold on the pirates' soil.*

Mission Three: The Horns of Hattin

Objectives:

- Capture the Piece of the True Cross.
- Return the Piece to the Horns of Hattin.

Hints:

- There is precious little Stone in the desert. You will have to rely on the strength of the troops to defend you, as you can't build Walls or Towers.
- In this case, the best defense is a good offense.
- There are not many fish in Lake Tiberias. Support your economy with Farms.
- As with any Relic, your enemy may garrison the Piece of the True Cross in a Monastery.
- Beware of the Templars and Hospitallers. They are your most dangerous opponents.

Walkthrough:

Split your northern Villagers evenly between Food and Wood production. Most Food producers should be herding the nearby Sheep, but a couple need to till the soil. Research both the Wheelbarrow and Horse Collar to increase your productivity. Gather all your Spearmen, Cavalry Archers, and the Mangonel, and send them to the northwest corner of your encampment.

> **Tip:** *Place the Spearmen and Cavalry Archers in one group. Choose the Line Formation. This will keep the Spearmen in front and the Archers in support. That's a bad combination for your mounted enemies.*

Meanwhile, back on the southern ranch, order the southern Villagers to mine Gold. As soon as feasible, build six to eight Spearmen, and send them and the Cavalry Archers to the western fence.

Knock a hole in your western Palisade Wall (remember, I'm talking about the southern camp). Take your group of Spearmen and Cavalry Archers through it. You'll be accosted by a troop of Cavaliers, but don't panic; horses hate Spearmen and your formation should soon make mincemeat of the Byzantines (as shown in Figure 16-40). If necessary, reinforce your troops with additional Spearmen and Archers from your southern Archery Range.

Figure 16-40 *The Spearmen fight the hapless Cavaliers.*

> **Tip:** *You may need to create a couple more Archers to hasten the Town Center's demise. Remember Saracen Archers get a bonus when attacking buildings. Be frugal, however, as you need to save Food and Gold in order to advance to the Castle Age.*

Once Jerusalem's horsemen have been slain, march your troops to the enemy's Town Center and destroy it. Kill any passing enemy Villagers. With both the Town Center and supporting Villagers obliterated, the Byzantines will cease to be a problem.

Now save all the Food and Gold that you can. As soon as you can, advance to the Castle Age. Build a Monastery in your northern camp, and research Sanctity—you'll need the extra hit points.

Produce three Monks and use four Spearmen to guard them in a Box Formation. Group your remaining Cavalry Archers and Spearmen (again, I'm discussing the northern forces), and form a separate group for the Mangonel. Head west along the northern edge of the map.

> **Note:** *Don't forget your Market. It's silly to wait on Food to join the Castle Age, when you can use the Gold generated by your southern miners to buy the sustenance you need. Your enemies won't wait forever.*

While the northern group marches west, take the southern group (the folks that took down the Byzantines) and head north. The Piece of the True Cross is in the west section of the map. The Hospitallers guard it with a combination of Monks and the very dangerous Teutonic Knights. Use your southern group to take on the Teutonic Knights. Once the southern group has drawn the Teutonic Knights away from the Relic, use the Mangonel to knock down the northern wall of the compound housing the Relic.

Once said hole is made in both Palisade Walls, stream the northern group, supported by any remnants of the southern group, into the compound. Kill the Monks, seize the Piece of the True Cross, and hurry home to the northern camp (as shown in Figure 16-41). Place the Relic by your large tent marked with the flags and you win.

Figure 16-41 *The Monks return with the Relic.*

Mission Four: The Siege of Jerusalem

Objectives:

- Do not allow any Jerusalem Monastery or the Dome of the Rock to be destroyed.
- Destroy the five Towers defending Jerusalem so that Saladin's army can occupy the city.

Hints:

- Cut off Jerusalem's food supply by raiding outlying Farms.
- The two Orders of Knighthood have bases nearby that should be destroyed before assaulting the city.
- Trebuchets can make short work of Towers from a distance.

Walkthrough:

Build a Mining Camp and a Lumber Camp adjacent to the Gold and forest that abut your starting position. Assign a couple of Villagers to gather Wood and one to mine Gold. Direct everyone else to move southwest.

Tip: *Assemble your mounted warriors into a Line Formation. This will place the Heavy Camels in front and the Mamelukes in the second line. Kill anyone you spot—especially enemy Villagers. Remember that a dead Villager can carry no Food.*

Lead with the Light Cavalry, as they have the best sighting range. Trot the Light Cavalry southwest until you spot Jerusalem's walls. Halfway between your camp and Jerusalem's walls is a non-mineable rock pile. Build your Town Center next to the rock pile. Crank out five Villagers. Have four farm while the fifth Villager heads northeast in search of game. Leave the Archers to protect your fledgling village while all your mounted warriors escort the Hunter.

In the north corner of the map, you'll find a herd of Deer. Build a Mill, and then slaughter the Deer. Move your mounted warriors southwest along the edge of the map. You'll run into a camp of your old nemesis, the Hospitallers. Bait their mounted units, drawing them away from the Teutonic Knights and Scorpions. Turn and destroy their mounted units, and then lead the Teutonic Knights and Scorpions south. Line your Archers on the northern side of your camp. Lead the Hospitallers into their waiting arms, and then crush them with the joint might of your forces.

Once the Hospitallers are destroyed, sweep your Heavy Camels, Mamelukes, and Light Cavalry north, destroying enemy Villagers and the Hospitallers' Town Center. Finally—in the west corner of the map—destroy Jerusalem's Lumber Camp and its attendant Villagers. Continue to ravage the countryside with your mounted units, but stay clear of the southeast corner of the map. The Knights Templar await you there, and there is really no reason to fight them if you don't have to.

> **Note:** *It doesn't hurt to have a Barracks producing a few Long Swordsmen to reinforce your troops. Nor would a couple more Archers be unwelcome additions to your ranks.*

Build a Castle if you haven't already (as shown in Figure 16-42), a Siege Workshop, and a University. You'll also need about five Trebuchets. Recall your mounted units, refit them in the Castle, and create about ten Two-Handed Swordsmen and an equal number of Crossbowmen.

Figure 16-42 *Building a Castle is critical to winning mission four.*

Put the Two-Handed Swordsmen and Crossbowmen in Line Formation, and place them in front of one Trebuchet, as shown in Figure 16-43. Keep the others well to the rear. Order the Trebuchet to attack the westernmost of Jerusalem's Guard Towers.

> **Tip:** *Often the Trebuchet's attack will "stir the ants" and trigger a counterattack. Fend off the enemy units with your Two-Handed Swordsmen and Crossbowmen formation, and then counter-attack the counterattacks with your mounted units.*

Continue counterclockwise around the city, destroying the Bombard and Guard Towers. You'll need to frequently reinforce the troops guarding the Trebuchet. There are four Towers on the city's perimeter and one in the center.

Knock a hole in Jerusalem's east wall, and pour your troops through it. Remember, you don't have to take the entire city. In fact, you do not want to destroy any Monasteries; you only need to eliminate the final Tower.

Figure 16-43 *Guard it well—the Trebuchet is the key to mission victory.*

Use your troops to screen your Trebuchet from enemy counterattacks. Have the Trebuchet destroy the final Tower and victory is yours.

Mission Five: Jihad!

Objectives:

- Defeat any two of the three Crusader cities: Tiberias, Tyre, and Ascalon.

Hints:

- Remember, you only need to defeat two enemy cities.
- You can trade with the village of Hebron, as long as it survives.

Walkthrough:

This mission is long but not complicated. There are many roads to victory, but the following is my favorite. The strategy is straightforward: clear the route to Hebron and commence trading. Attack and eliminate Tyre, and then do the same to Tiberias. Stay away from Ascalon in the south corner of the map; they are too big and too bad (as shown in Figure 16-44).

Note: *As always, research any technology that will make your Villagers more efficient. In this case it's the Hand Cart and Heavy Plow.*

When the mission begins, send your Fishing Ships out for Food. Create eight Villagers and build a Lumber Camp adjacent to the Palm Forest that lies east of your Walls. Direct several Villagers to cut Wood, several to mine the Gold inside your Walls, and three to start Farms.

Figure 16-44 *Ascalon is to be avoided at all costs.*

Have the Stable generate four Knights and four Heavy Camels. Group them together and ride northeast of your gate. They'll meet and subsequently defeat a detachment of Tripoli Guards. Now build a couple of Trade Carts and establish a trade route with Hebron.

Use your mounted detachment to patrol the area in front of your camp, killing any enemy Villagers they spot. It's good for crowd control and hurts your opponent's economy.

> **Note:** *There's a definite method to the madness. We want to get to the Imperial Age in order to build Elite Cannon Galleons. The Cannon Galleons that precede them require a University to research Chemistry.*

Construct a Monastery and a University. Both will come in handy later. Use all of your buildings to research technologies that improve your ballistic capabilities. Upgrade to the Imperial Age as soon as possible.

> **Note:** *You'll need quite a bit of resources to support this high-level weaponry. You should at least have another Lumber Camp operating at the woods south of your city's main entrance and a total of 20 to 30 Villagers at work on different production tasks. There is a stash of Gold on the island northwest of your starting position. Level its defenses with your warships, transport Villagers to its shores, build a mine, and reap your rewards.*

At the Dock, upgrade to the Elite Cannon Galleon and manufacture three of them immediately. Send them to Tyre and bring down all the Tyre Keeps and Bombard Towers. You may need to escort the Elite Cannon Galleons with Fire Ships and Demolition Ships to keep the Tyre navy off of their backs. Once the island's defenses have been leveled, load some

Figure 16-45 *The Castle isn't so tough when you have the right troops.*

ballistic units—for example, Arbalests or whatever else you have available—into a couple of Transport Ships and destroy the rest of the island.

Put together a significant army of Two-Handed Swordsmen, Hand Cannoneers, and Trebuchets (if available—use the Bombard Cannon if not), and head southeast to Tiberias. Take out the Guard Towers from afar with your siege weapons; make sure you protect these weapons with your other troops. Once the Guard Towers are down, sweep into the city and destroy everything in sight, hence winning the mission (as shown in Figure 16-45).

Mission Six: The Lion and the Demon

Objectives:

- Construct a Wonder and defend it.

Hints:

- Managing a large city can be confusing. It might prove helpful to rebuild military buildings where you can easily find them.
- When you are ready to build the Wonder, you can delete some of your houses to make room for it.
- Attacking one of your enemies early can benefit you later on, but be careful venturing outside Acre's walls.

Tip: *It is not a bad idea to send your Mangonels with the Lumberjacks. Frequently, the Mangonels can take out several Briton buildings before they are destroyed.*

Walkthrough:

Don't let the mission objective fool you. You must accomplish it, but a passive Defensive Stance will not get you there from here. Attacking is the easiest way to win. Make no mistake, you cannot destroy your opponents, but the longer you harass them with spoiling attacks, the longer it will take them to mount their inevitable assault.

Summon five additional Villagers and assign all their chores. Most should farm, but four should mine Gold and Stone in the western section of Acre, two should trundle to the forest northeast of Acre, and two should take a Transport to a Gold-encrusted island that you'll find west of your city.

Build a Lumber Camp with those hiking to the northeast forest, and commence chopping. Erect a Mining Camp with the pair headed to the island, and commence digging.

Research Chemistry at the University and Conscription at the Castle, and Bombard Cannons at the Siege Workshop. Create a few of the Bombard Cannons at the Workshop; otherwise, save money for the Wonder (as shown in Figure 16-46). Once you start its construction, then you may begin raising an army.

Tip: *Escort the Transport Ship with at least a pair of Galleons. The Genoese have a significant navy patrolling the unfriendly seas, and you need to keep them away from your miners.*

Note: *Escort the Lumberjacks with your Mamelukes and Cavalry Archers. The Lumber Camp and attendant Villagers are crucial to your early Wood production. Eventually they will be destroyed, but if the Europeans are busy destroying your Lumber Camp they won't be destroying your Wonder.*

Figure 16-46 *The Wonder is obviously the key to the mission.*

Tip: *Direct several Villagers to erect the Wonder. The more Villagers on the job, the quicker the Wonder will be built.*

Tip: *Build the Wonder in the center of Acre. You'll have to knock down some houses, but doing so will keep the Wonder safe longer.*

Tip: *The computer is no dummy. Often it will send Pikemen to counterattack your mounted charges (horses hate Pikemen). You can mitigate the enemy Pikemen's effectiveness by including several Archer-types (but not Cavalry Archers) in your mounted formations.*

Note: *Villagers also have their place in the battle. More often than not the computer-led opponents will chop their way through each building before moving on. You can slow their onslaught by repairing a building as the bad guys attempt to destroy it. Place the Villagers on the opposite side of the building from the attackers (as shown in Figure 16-47).*

You'll need a serious army to fend off the hordes attacking Acre. One or two Bombard Towers on each of the landward walls will help defend against the lesser siege units. Your primary combatants for most of the mission will be combined task forces of Knights, Heavy Camels, and Cavalry Archers. These groups, set in Line Formation, are ideal for eliminating the waves of Bombard Cannons, Mangonels, and Trebuchets the Europeans will send after your walls. Routinely sweep the outside of your walls with these groups (and the Persian Elite War Elephants when they arrive). The theory is simple: your Bombard Towers can't keep everyone off your back, so it'll take several excursions by the mounted units to knock back the siege-type weapons.

Eventually, it'll turn into a slugfest for the walls. The Europeans will breach them and Two-Handed Swordsmen, Hand Cannoneers, and Crossbowmen will become the defense du jour. Nevertheless, try to keep a mounted reserve to continually harass the siege engines behind the enemy lines.

Delay the Europeans, fighting for every inch of ground. If you do, your Wonder will stand, and you will win.

Figure 16-47 *The Villagers aid in repair.*

Chapter Seventeen

Alternate Empires

You've helped Joan of Arc in the Hundred Years War and Saladin in the Crusades. Congratulations, you are now a veteran of medieval combat. But your *Microsoft Age of Empires II* experience is far from over. With a multitude of random maps and victory conditions at your fingertips, you can now take the first steps to becoming a famous conqueror yourself.

In the campaigns, you were restricted to a limited number of civilizations. However, in the non-campaign scenarios, all 13 civilizations are available. On top of that, *Age of Empires II* offers a number of new parameter options. Rich in variety and strategy, the Random Map, Regicide, and Death Match contests provide many more hours of enticing gameplay. In this chapter, you'll find some general tips and walk-throughs for these contests. And you thought your military training was over!

Maps Available in Non-Campaign Empires

There is a plethora of single-player non-campaign contests. They range from Middle Eastern deserts and islands to lush forests and lakes. Obviously, this divergence of terrain will affect your strategy. For example, if there are any large bodies of water present, building a navy is almost mandatory to keep up with the technology of your enemies. Resource availability is also important. Many situations in lands with little Gold or Stone force you to be efficient in your deployment of offensive and defensive units.

Another important strategic aspect involves the size of the terrain. Larger maps give you the chance to build more defenses and develop your army, while smaller maps force opponents into numerous offensive battles. All terrain types are available in six different sizes. These sizes are as follows:

- Small (2-3 players)
- Medium (4 players)
- Large (6 players)
- Huge (8 players)
- Extended Game (8 players)
- Long Game (8 players)

The diversity in size, terrain, and resource amounts makes for some interesting battles. You have an assortment of variables to master in each map. Here's an overview of all thirteen single-player, non-campaign maps.

Arabia

This map consists primarily of a flat, sandy area with a few spots of water. Despite being a desert, quite a number of resources can be extracted there. Deer, Sheep, and Wild Boar populate the region. There are usually few evergreen trees, but Palm Tree forests can often be cut down for wood, as shown in Figure 17-1.

Figure 17-1 *The Arabian Desert is full of Palm Tree forests.*

Archipelago

Archipelagos exist in several varieties. Usually, several islands dot the map. Sometimes, though, the kingdoms have to battle things out on one large island. One of the more popular versions of the Archipelago map consists of two large islands sandwiching two smaller ones.

Baltic

The Baltic map features a good mix of land and water. Usually a large lake is spread about the middle of the region, which also contains splotches of forest. The Baltic has a good supply of Fish and Deer. Because of the large lake, the raising of Docks and ships is often necessary for victory, as shown in Figure 17-2.

Black Forest

Half of every Black Forest region is usually covered in trees. Although these maps contain Deer, Sheep, and Wild Boar, they also have a heavy Wolf population. A lake often accompanies each settlement. Most resources on the map are accessible within the open areas of the Black Forest.

Figure 17-2 *Construct Docks and Fishing Ships on the Baltic map.*

> **Tip:** *When playing on the Black Forest map, you can use the forest as a Wall, placing Watch Towers near the entrance of your area. Although enemy Lumberjacks can cut down the timber, I wouldn't worry about them thinning out this forest.*

Coastal

This map is ideal for seafaring civilizations. A large coastline constitutes much of the land. Often it is necessary to set up multiple encampments using Transport Ships in order to collect scattered resources. Spreading forces around (both on land and sea) for compound attacks is also a good idea.

Continental

In this scenario, civilizations are strewn along a large island or two. Allying is often critical for victory when playing on the Continental map. Be sure to scour all resources, including the heavy supply of Fish. Needless to say, a strong navy is a necessity here.

Fortress

Tip: *The University is a major key to winning here. Defensive technologies, such as Masonry, Murder Holes, and Fortified Walls keep the enemy outside your gates longer. Meanwhile, Ballistics, Chemistry, and Siege Engineers technologies provide you with an advantage in offensive tactics.*

Each civilization begins the match enclosed by a stone fortress. Outside the encampments lies an open area with scattered forests and small lakes. This scenario demands a full army of Cavalry, Archers, and siege weapons. The Trebuchet's long range and power, in particular, are excellent for taking down fortress walls. Be sure to upgrade your defenses in each Age, and place new Towers near your encampment.

Gold Rush

At first glance, this scenario looks simpler than it really is. There are lots of resources, particularly the hordes of Gold in the center of the map. But don't jump too quickly; several Wolf packs patrol this area. If you're not careful, your Villagers won't mine much Gold before becoming dinner. So make sure you have enough troops before trying to build Mining Camps in the center of the map, as shown in Figure 17-3.

Figure 17-3 *The center of this map is full of Gold...and Wolves.*

Highland

A large river divides the Highland map in two. However, shallows connect both regions. Building Towers near these shallows is an excellent way of preventing enemy forces from infiltrating your settlement. Although there is a restricted amount of water, investing in naval warfare is still an excellent way of keeping the enemy at bay.

Islands

Civilizations must extend the battlefield across the sea, for a strong navy is essential to winning with these maps. Often, surrounding an enemy island with Cannon Galleons is the final stage in putting your opponents to rest. And don't worry about resources. A substantial amount of Sheep and Deer populate the islands, and when your Villagers run out, they have tons of Fish to net.

Mediterranean

The Mediterranean map is reminiscent of the Baltic map in that it features a large lake surrounded by land. One of the best ways to disrupt the enemy is by using Transport Ships to haul infantry onto their territory and sending another horde of troops by land at the same time. This one-two punch will put a strain on the bad guys fast.

Tip: *Always defend your Docks with offensive vessels like War Galleys and Demolition Ships. Guard Towers are fodder for enemy Galleys and Galleons due to their limited range (as compared with the range of some ships).*

Rivers

In this scenario, land is often divided by one large winding river. Because there are few or no shallows, the building of Docks and Transport Ships is necessary for battling enemies posted behind the river, as shown in Figure 17-4.

Figure 17-4 *"Shipping" troops via Transport Ships.*

Team Islands

Team Islands are very similar in layout to the Archipelago and Islands maps. As with those maps, a strong navy is crucial for victory. In fact, you should invest in naval vessels for both offensive and defensive purposes.

Strategies for Random Map Games

Random Maps offer lots of fun for gamers; you can win in several different ways—depending on the parameters set. Standard contests, for example, allow players three distinct methods for victory. Victory conditions in other instances can be based strictly on points. And for those with aspirations of ruling the world, Conquest is always an option.

Standard and Conquest Victory Conditions

You can win Standard victory contests in one of three ways:

- By destroying all enemy units—the only parameter set for Conquest victory conditions
- By maintaining control of all Relics within a given time period
- By building a Wonder and protecting it for a specific amount of time

Because of the variety of conditions, each civilization might go into battle with a different game plan. Other variables that dictate play include the given map or civilization at your disposal.

There are several keys to conquering your opponents in Standard victory mode. The most important, though, is efficiency. Your primary goal throughout most of these battles is to progress as quickly as possible into the next Age in order to gain the advanced weaponry and technologies available (such as the Siege Workshop, shown in Figure 17-5). These are crucial for getting a leg up on the enemy. Meanwhile, you also want to halt your rival's progress. The more advanced offensive and defensive weapons you have, the more likely that your victory is in the bag.

Figure 17-5 *The Siege Workshop is a necessity in most Random Map games.*

Dark Age

In the beginning of this Age, you have two primary objectives. First, explore the map so that you know the lay of the land and where enemy forces are stationed. Next, gather enough resources to enable you to produce the appropriate forces and research Feudal Age technology. These are a must in all Random Map scenarios, but are especially necessary when you are in Conquest and Standard victory contests.

Note: *It's possible to win big early. Building numerous low-tech units such as Militia and Archers is cheap. A 30-man Militia/Archer unit can often take a fledgling empire right out of the game.*

Tip: *Immediately research the Wheelbarrow and Horse Collar. The basis of a strong military is a thriving economy. The more efficient your Villagers are, the more productive your economy will be.*

Direct your Villagers to gather Wood and Food. Then, have the Town Center create 15 to 20 more Villagers. Because every person needs housing, order the first few Villagers to build Houses, as shown in Figure 17-6. Have the others gather resources. After the Builders finish with the Houses, have them build the appropriate structures for advancing to the next Age (usually a Mill and Barracks—and later Farms).

Figure 17-6 *Have your Villagers build Houses.*

As you research the Feudal Age, generate a few Militia (if you haven't already) and explore the surrounding area with your Scout Cavalry.

Note: *All civilizations begin with three Villagers, one Scout Cavalry, and a Town Center. Some exceptions include the Chinese, who are given three extra Villagers at the expense of having less stockpiled Food.*

Feudal Age

Once you know where the enemy is, upgrade your Militia to Men-at-Arms. Next, send about 10 of the troops to disrupt

Tip: *In certain maps, it is imperative to develop a navy in the early stages of the game (for example, Baltic, Coastal, and Islands). If you are on a map with plenty of rivers or seas, make sure that you've built several Docks by this time. Use Fishing Ships and Fish Traps to net some catches. Also build a couple of Galleys for the fishermen's protection.*

Tip: *Sprinkle a few Watch Towers near local Gold and Stone sites (as shown in Figure 17-7). This will prevent enemy Villagers from stealing your resources, building enemy structures nearby, or both.*

your rival's encampment. To halt the enemy's progress, aim for a critical building like the Archery Range or Stable (if they're already in the Feudal Age) or the Barracks (if they're still in the Dark Age). This will hurt their offense and their chances of progressing to the next Age.

Meanwhile, continue tending to your settlement's resources and technology. To increase the gathering efficiency of your Villagers, research the Wheelbarrow at the Town Center. Order some of your Villagers to collect Gold and Stone from local mines. Next, erect Mining and Lumber Camps near the sites. This will enable your people to place the goods there rather than waste time walking back to the Town Center. Also, create 10 or so additional Villagers (and three Houses for them) to help with resource management.

Figure 17-7 *Place Watch Towers at resource sites.*

With supplies under control, focus on erecting the two major Feudal Age buildings necessary for advancing to the next Age. Usually the Archery Range and Blacksmith are your best bets. Because the Stable can only produce Scout Cavalry at this stage of the game, it's better to invest in more effective offensive forces and technologies while you have the chance. Meanwhile, order some more Men-at-Arms and Spearmen to harass the enemy villages. Now you're ready to advance to the Castle Age.

Castle Age

If you've established an efficient economy, you shouldn't be left micro-managing resources. In fact, with the use of technologies like the Wheelbarrow, the Hand Cart, and the Horse Collar, things should be going fairly well. Instead of worrying about the Food and supply stockpiles, shift your focus to combat.

Tip: *If you are in a seafaring scenario, use your Transport Ships to carry infantry to enemy territory. War Galleys are ideal for taking down enemy Docks and Fishing Ships.*

First things first: Erect a Stable (shown in Figure 17-8) and have it generate several rounds of Knights. Order the Archery Range to produce a couple of Crossbowmen. Send this combination into the enemy settlement. Here you can try two tactics. The first involves destroying their primary defenses (for example, a Watch Tower) and offensive training sites (such as a Stable and Archery Range). If you don't want to focus on the enemy's military, take down chief economic units like the Villagers and Town Center. Damage to the latter will drastically slow down the enemy's production rate.

Figure 17-8 *Train Knights at the Stable during the Castle Age.*

In this Age, you need to decide which of three methods you will employ for victory. Your choice will determine which two Castle Age buildings are best for you. For example, if you choose to pursue the Relics, you will need to construct a Monastery (to obtain the Relics with Monks) and a Castle (for extra defenses. Perhaps you want to build a Wonder instead. If so, the monument's protection will depend on heavy fortifications, so you'll need Walls, Towers, and plenty of ballistic equipment. Conquering your enemy, on the other hand, requires lots of brute force. If this is the route you want to take, you'll need University and Siege Workshop technology to put you over the top.

Tip: *I highly recommend against building a Wonder. Although they are tough to destroy, they still require a ton of resources for construction. You also have to defend your Wonder against enemy attacks for 300 years. Consequently, only choose this route when you are equipped with plenty of defensive barriers (such as you'll find in the Fortress, Black Forest, and Islands maps). Other situations conducive to building a Wonder are contests that begin in the Castle or Imperial Age and feature large maps and few players.*

In all cases, the University and Castle are good investments. I highly recommend both. The University offers plenty of offensive technologies, such as Ballistics in the Castle Age and Siege Engineers and Chemistry in the Imperial Age. Chemistry is a necessity for all gunpowder units, including the Hand Cannoneer, Bombard Cannon, and Cannon Galleon. Needless to say, these units provide considerably more attack points than the standard Ballistics fare. The University also offers defensive technologies such as Murder Holes and Guard Towers.

Figure 17-9 *Castles can create unique units, such as the Persians' War Elephant.*

The Castle is essential for producing each civilization's unique units, as shown in Figure 17-9. It also has strong defenses. If you are trying to rescue the Relics, you'll need to place plenty of Towers and a Castle near the Monastery for protection. The same strategy applies if you are building a Wonder. But don't forget to beef up your infantry and Cavalry. Although you're planning a defensive game, remember this all-important truth: the best defense is always a good offense.

Imperial Age

There are very few additional structures provided in this Age. Most of the advances lie in upgrades—necessary enhancements for hard-nosed battles against several foes. Important units for attacking the enemy or defending your Won-

der or Monastery include the Galleon, Siege Onager, Paladin, Trebuchet, Hand Cannoneer, and Keep. The Cannon Galleon is the best weapon for bringing your enemy down quickly. (See Figure 17-10.) Unfortunately, it can only be used in seafaring campaigns.

Tip: *Control the sea and lake with Cannon Galleons, taking out all enemy Docks and ships. Surround enemy territory with at least 10 of the Cannon Galleons, and then bombard the enemy structures. Even Castles and Keeps are no match for the Cannon Galleon.*

Time and Score Victory Conditions

Figure 17-10 *Cannon Galleons bombard a Castle.*

Time and score victory conditions are very similar in that both depend on the victor's accumulation of points. The only difference lies in the parameters. With time-oriented games, play is governed by a time limit. The civilization with the highest score wins when time runs out. (You can check your standings on the Achievements page, as shown in Figure 17-11.) With score-oriented games, time is not an issue. A game can last one hour or ten. The match ends only when one of the following three things happens:

- Your enemies are destroyed.
- You are destroyed.
- Your civilization or one of the rival civilizations reaches the designated point total.

Score Victory Conditions

Playing to reach a certain score can be tense. Score conditions can be set from 4000 to 14000, in 1000-point increments. To give you an idea of how far you

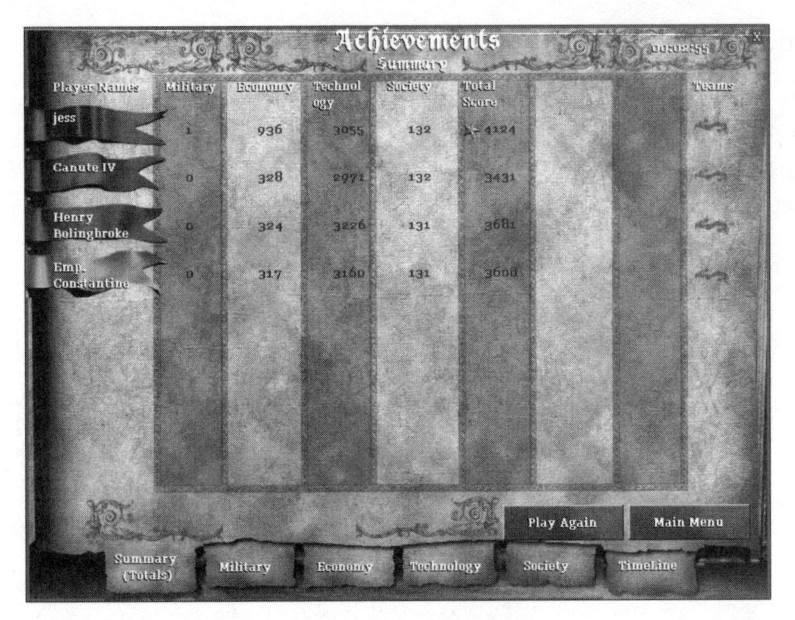

Figure 17-11 *Turn to the Achievements page periodically for a look at the point standings.*

want to go, you should keep in mind that you begin each mission with around 1300 points. The score is calculated as follows:

- Resources are worth one-tenth of their stockpile value. Therefore, 20 Wood is worth only 2 game points, and 400 Food is worth 40 game points.
- Researching technologies, constructing buildings, and creating units doubles the game point value of the resources used. For example, a structure that requires 100 Stone and 50 Wood (150 total points) is worth 30 game points. The 15 game points for the Wood and Stone used have doubled.
- Killing or converting an enemy unit subtracts the unit's game points from the rival civilization, placing them under your column.
- Each percentage of explored territory provides 10 points. Therefore, exploring 40 percent of the map results in 400 game points.
- As always, efficiency and speed are integral parts of winning these scenarios. Progressing to each Age before your enemy has a chance to do so is important as in other matches. Economic wealth and military strength are also major factors. You want to keep your Villagers busy, and you don't want to have too many casualties. Here are more keys to racking up points:

> **Note:** *What are two of the easiest ways to gain points quickly in the first few minutes of play? First, send Hunters after the Wild Boars; they are worth more points than Deer or Sheep. Second, direct your Scout Cavalry and several Villagers to explore the territory. You'll have several hundred points before you know it.*

- Obtain as many resources as you can. Create lots of Villagers early in the game. They are essential for gathering and producing goods. Gather all available resources (especially Wood, Fish, Deer, Sheep, and Wild Boars).
- Invest in technologies (such as those from the Mill, Town Center, Mining Camp, and Lumber Camp) that improve gathering and production efficiency. Remember: researching technologies doubles the point value of resources.
- Create both costly and effective units. Cavalry units, siege weapons, and ships (especially the Cannon Galleon) are useful and worth quite a bit in points.
- Avoid sending tributes to enemy civilizations unless absolutely necessary. If you must send them to keep an enemy from attacking, be sure to research technologies that reduce fees (for example, Coinage).
- When attacking your opponent, aim for structures that have the most worth in points. Buildings and Towers, in particular, are good targets.

Time Victory Conditions

In time victory games, you try to attain as many points as you can before the clock runs out. Keep your eye on the time listings in the upper-right corner of your screen, shown in Figure 17-12; they are extremely critical. Players can choose from an assortment of time limit parameters. The following are some of the available options:

> **Tip:** *Buildings are an excellent investment of your resources because they double a large amount of resource game points in a relatively short time. The Castle and Wonder are by far the best; the former converts 65 game points into 130, while the latter inflates 300 game points to 600.*

- 1,500 years (2 hours)
- 1,300 years (1 hour, 45 minutes)
- 1,100 years (1 hour, 30 minutes)
- 900 years (1 hour, 15 minutes)
- 700 years (1 hour)
- 500 years (40 minutes)
- 300 years (25 minutes)

Figure 17-12 *The time remaining is shown in the upper-right corner of the screen.*

With timed victory conditions, you can win by either Conquest or points. The longer the time limit, though, the tougher it will be to win solely by points. In fact, when playing past the 900-year mark, it's best to just use a strategy similar to the ones mentioned in the section "Standard and Conquest Victory Conditions" earlier in this chapter. Of course, a large map with few opponents is often conducive to point accumulation, even in long games.

There are several general tactics that you will want to consider when trying to win by points in a Time Limit game, many of which are similar to tactics used in Score victory games. These are as follows:

- Obtain as many resources as you can. To do this, you must create plenty of Villagers to gather and produce goods, as shown in Figure 17-13.

Figure 17-13 *Create plenty of Villagers and Farms.*

- Invest in technologies (such as those from the Mill, Town Center, Mining Camp, and Lumber Camp) that improve gathering and production efficiency.
- Create both costly and effective units. Cavalry units, siege weapons, and ships (especially the Cannon Galleon) are useful and worth a lot of points.
- In the last 50 years, invest heavily in unit production. Turning your resources into units and structures doubles the points. In other words, don't end the game with a large stockpile of resources; double your points by creating units and buildings.

While doing all this, remember that the enemy units you vanquish or convert add points to your column and are subtracted from your enemy's score. However, don't forget to build some defensive units for protection. Overall, focus more on defenses, units, and resources. Offensive tactics are necessary, but less instrumental in your success with these scenarios. Unlike the Standard, Conquest, and Score contest conditions, the Time Limit matches require a healthy defensive slant. In the other contests, you are just fighting against enemy forces. Here you are also racing against the clock.

Strategies for Regicide Games

Long live your King! In Regicide matches, the game hinges on the survival of this royal figure, shown in Figure 17-14. These scenarios are very similar in nature to chess in that the goal is to "checkmate" your opponent's King. Therefore, Regicide contests require both offensive and defensive tactics. You must defend your monarch while putting the enemies' monarchs to rest.

Figure 17-14 *A Teutonic King stands outside his Castle.*

Although you do not have to destroy all enemy units, you probably will—or you'll be close. In short, this game is not going to be any easier than the Conquest victory scenarios. The opponents' Kings are typically stationed in Castles, which are usually well protected by troops and structures. To take down the rival Kings, you will have to walk over a number of dead bodies.

Starting Out

Regardless of the Age in which you start, you will probably begin with the same units and buildings: one King, one Castle, one Town Center, one Scout Cavalry, and ten Villagers. Place the monarch in the safest building, the Castle. Direct the Scout Cavalry to explore the map as the Villagers gather Wood and Food. Meanwhile have the Town Center create a few more Villagers for building offensive structures, such as the Barracks, Stable, and Archery Range. Once you have the necessary resources and structures in place, upgrade to the next Age.

> **Note:** *The Franks only need to build a Mill to have access to all farming technologies that their current Age allows. Other civilizations need to research technologies like the Horse Collar and the Heavy Plow to improve efficiency.*

Send a couple of Villagers to erect Watch Towers over distant Gold and Stone Mines. This should keep the enemy from gaining extra resources. Place a Mining Camp nearby for the sake of efficiency. Dispatch your troops inside the rival village. Hack down economic structures such as Lumber Camps and Mills, as shown in Figure 17-15. If you can take down the Town Center, all the better. The goal is not to lay siege on the Castle, just to put an economic strain on the enemy—which, as a result, hampers their military activities.

Figure 17-15 *Soldiers destroy a Lumber Camp.*

The Middle Stages

Before making one mad rush into enemy territory, you need to build sufficient offensive forces. The University is necessary for effective upgrades. Certain studies improve your siege weapons, Towers, and Galleons. Furthermore, gunpowder units such as the Hand Cannoneer and Bombard Cannon offer you more diversity and power within your arsenal. In almost all Regicide cases, the University and Siege Workshop are necessities.

> **Note:** *Researching Gold Shaft Mining and Stone Shaft Mining increases your digging speed by 15 percent. This is beneficial against a civilization such as the Japanese, who lack both technologies.*

Meanwhile, to prevent the enemy from getting into your Castle, order some Villagers to build a Wall some distance around it, as shown in Figure 17-16. The goal is to keep enemy forces far enough away so that the Castle's spears and arrows can take them out before they get too close. Erect a Guard Tower or two inside the fortress for additional support. If you want, produce some of your special units for an upcoming attack. Continue with the Age upgrades and research.

Figure 17-16 *Build a Wall around your Castle.*

The Knockout Punch

Before sending in your troops, find out where the enemy monarch is stationed. Do this by clicking the Treason button offered at the Castle. For the price of 400 Gold, the minimap will then reveal the King's location for a few seconds. Usually he hides in the enemy's original Castle; however, he could be garrisoned elsewhere—especially if you've let his kingdom build more than one Castle. That's why Treason is worth the price. You'll lose much more if you attack the wrong place.

When attempting a siege, strew a couple of Guard Towers or Keeps around the enemy's compound. Build as closely around the compound as possible without entering a battle. Use Knights and Crossbowmen to protect the Builders. Once the Towers are constructed, your soldiers will have backup. This way, if your men get into too much trouble inside the compound, they can head back to the Towers and use them for support.

Tip: *When the enemy kingdom is located on an island, you should corral several Cannon Galleons for an attack on their base. Have them take out all enemy Docks and ships first. Then take out the opponent's soldiers and military structures.*

Send your soldiers to take down the minor buildings—Lumber Camps, Mining Camps, Markets, and so forth. If you are unheeded by enemy forces, continue moving inside to hack away at military structures like the Stable, Archery Range, and Barracks. These areas usually offer less resistance than the Castle does. Also, by dismantling the kingdom's military and economic structures, it will be much easier to defeat the kingdom in another attack—if you happen to be unsuccessful this time.

Tip: *When playing in a scenario with lots of Walls, such as a Fortress, use the siege weapons to crush Towers and enemy soldiers first. Next, aim for the military facilities. Once they are down, bombard the Gate, moving troops in to destroy any enemy Villagers or buildings. Use the Siege Onager or Trebuchet to rain destruction down upon the Castle.*

Bring in siege weapons like the Mangonel and Onager to help the soldiers with enemy buildings. The weapons will especially come in handy against the Castle. Be sure to protect them with several melee units. Due to the instruments' delicate nature, I prefer to post about six Knights around each one. When attacking the Castle, use everything you have. Use the Treason button again to make sure your target is still resting inside.

Strategies for Death Match Games

Note: *The Chinese begin with a slightly different configuration in Death Match contests. They have an additional three Villagers at the expense of less Food units.*

Have you ever longed to just build some military facilities, generate some troops, and attack the enemy—without a single concern for economic conditions? Well, if that's your wish, you'll love the Death Match scenarios. Although you're not entitled to unlimited resources, your civiliza-

tion still harbors a hefty stockpile of supplies. In fact, you'll begin with 20,000 Wood, 20,000 Food, 10,000 Gold, and 5,000 Stone. However, your village is only composed of one Town Center, one Scout Cavalry, and three Villagers. That's not a lot, but with your load of resources that will change quickly.

You also have a variety of parameters at your disposal. Death Matches can be set according to Standard, Conquest, Score, or Time Limit conditions. You can also begin in the Age of your choice. The primary difference in using Death Match scenarios is that you do not have to worry about building up resources. Forget the Mill and Farms, and concentrate on military forces. After all, these contests are specifically set up as slugfests. (See Figure 17-17.)

Figure 17-17 *A classic Death Match clash between two civilizations.*

Basic Strategies for Each of the Parameters

Before discussing how each parameter changes particular elements of your strategy, I'd first like to mention those elements that apply to Death Matches regardless of the Age, map, civilization, or conditions. If any *Age of Empires II* game tests your building efficiency and strategic planning, it has to be the Death Match. Everything is at your disposal; you just have to know what to do with it. Efficiency and smarts are the name of the game. Like many things, military strategy is an art form, and these are some common approaches to this art of war:

- In Death Match contests, you need to research warfare technology, churn out tons of offensive units, and install defenses.

- At each Age, quickly build the necessary buildings to advance to the next Age. For instance, in a landlocked battle during the Feudal Age, construct an Archery Range, a Blacksmith, and a Stable. Be sure to build them as your Town Center researches the Castle Age and the Blacksmith researches combat technology.
- Build more than one Stable, Archery Range, or Barracks in these games. This will help you create at least twice as many soldiers as usual. Believe me, you'll need them.

There are four different criteria that determine who wins a Death Match. Although you will usually fight an Armageddonlike battle, the variety of parameters can shift portions of your strategy. For instance, an attempt at controlling all Relics in a Standard contest demands a Monastery fortified with lots of defenses. Playing by Score or Time Limit emphasizes the building of multiple Castles and the conversion of most of your resources into structures. Here is a quick look at some basic strategies for each scenario.

Standard and Conquest Victory Conditions

For the most part, it is easiest to destroy an opponent by conquering them. However, there are times when winning by controlling the Relics or building a Wonder is fun. In fact, if there is any time you should try to build a Wonder, it's in a Death Match. You have enough resources from the start to put one in place—and build defenses to protect it. The same applies to maintaining the Relics within your Monastery. Here are some simple pointers to keep in mind regarding these three strategies.

Conquest Victory

- Try to progress to the next Age as quickly as possible.
- For the most part, forget about the economy. The only resource you'll most likely need is more Gold. (See Figure 17-18.) Often there is not enough Gold stockpiled at the beginning of the game to build enough troops for a long battle.
- Scout the map, placing Towers and military structures near the enemy compound. If you are in the Castle Age, build a Castle nearby.
- Use the Blacksmith and University to research combat upgrades.
- Send in an army of infantry and Cavalry to destroy any military structures the enemy has. Continue to create soldiers—*never* stop.
- Use siege weapons with your next army to crush more buildings and, ultimately, bring the enemy down.

Wonder Victory

Figure 17-18 *You will probably need more Gold in Death Match contests.*

- Create several more Villagers at the Town Center. Have the other Villagers erect houses and a large Wall enclosing the Town Center. You want to leave enough space to build essential structures like the Barracks, Stables, University, and, of course, the Wonder.
- Have Builders construct Towers near the site where your Wonder will stand.
- Build a Siege Workshop and churn out several Mangonels and Onagers. Place them strategically inside the fortress.
- Create any other buildings necessary for upgrades and research. Once you've advanced to the Imperial Age, direct 10 Builders to construct a Wonder, shown in Figure 17-19.

Figure 17-19 *The Byzantine Wonder in all its glory and splendor.*

Relics Victory

- Protect your base with Walls and Towers until you're able to build a Monastery.
- Produce at least as many Monks as there are Relics. Flank each Monk with several Knights and Crossbowmen. Navigate each of these groups to a Relic. Pick a Relic up and head back to the Monastery.
- Build a Wall directly around the Monastery, as shown in Figure 17-20. Place some Guard Towers and Trebuchets nearby for additional protection.

Score and Time Victory Conditions

These scenarios are similar to the ones in the Random Map games, except this time you have the winning lottery ticket on your side—unfortunately, your enemy has hit the jackpot, too. One of the primary keys to winning these contests, other than just conquering the enemy, involves converting as many resources as you can into units. This doubles your game points. Therefore, building Castles and Wonders is great for score-oriented Death Matches.

Figure 17-20 *Erect a Wall around your Monastery to protect the Relics.*

Here are some basic strategies to keep in mind when playing Death Match scenarios governed by time and score:

- Order the Town Center to produce between 10 and 20 more Villagers. Have them build Houses and gather resources.
- Place Towers near all Gold and Stone Mines. This will thwart any plans the enemy has of digging there.
- Progress to each Age as quickly as possible. Keep in mind that you want to build a Wonder, so you'll need to reach the Imperial Age.

- Construct plenty of buildings. Duplicating ones like the Castle, Stables, and Archery Range is a good idea.
- Create lots of Cavalry and siege weapons. Mount hit-and-run attacks on the enemy.

Tip: *A favorite trick of mine is to send some troops onto an enemy island on a Transport Ship. Have them attack buildings and soldiers until the attackers are almost dead. At this point, load them onto the Transport Ship and send them back to your island to be healed by Monks.*

March On

As I said, the non-campaign scenarios are loaded with all kinds of features. Such variety makes these games a pleasure to play. It will take some time before you've perfected your play on all the battlefields. However, once you do, you'll have the advantage when it comes to multiplayer duels with your friends.

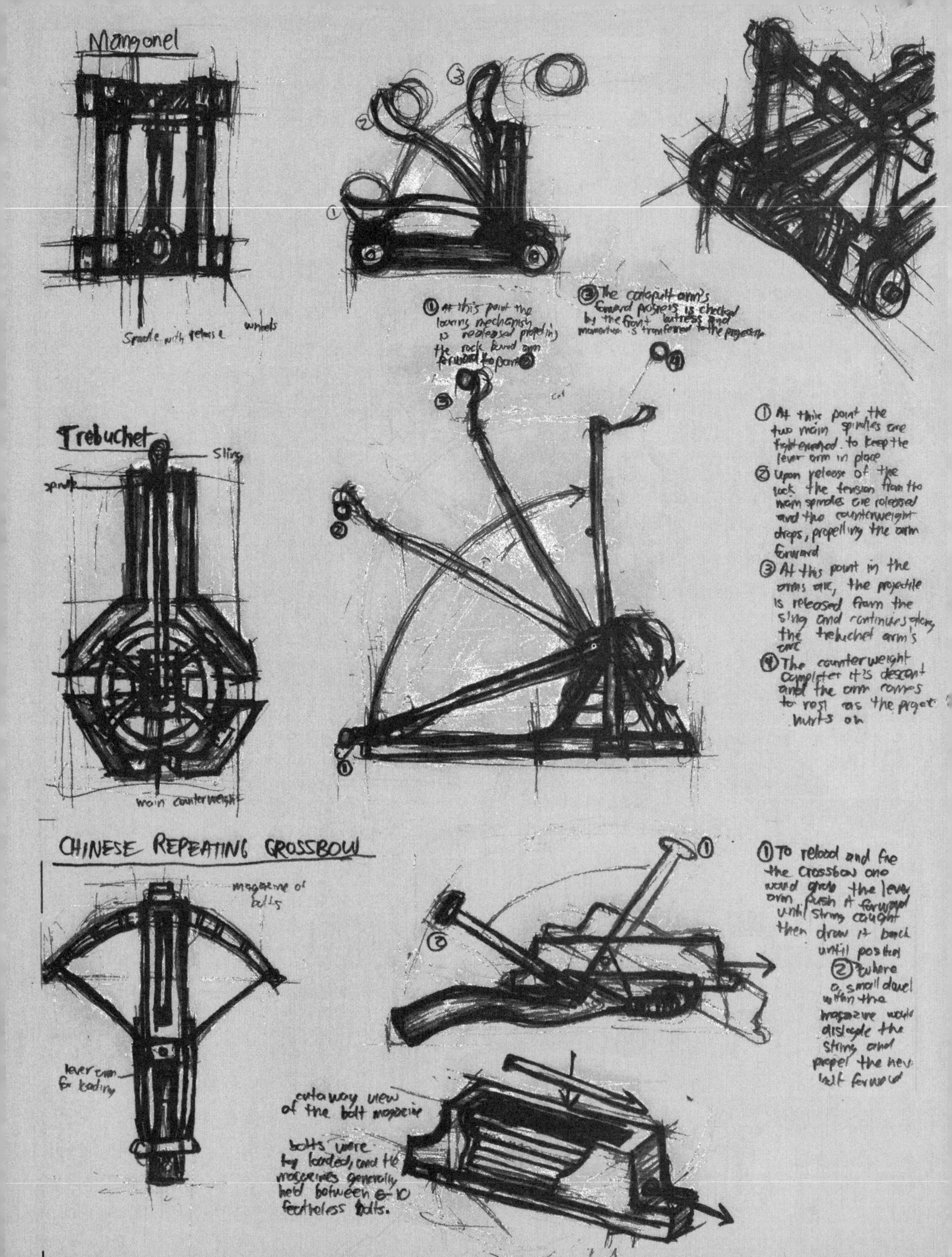
Mangonel
Spindle with release
wheels
At this point the locking mechanism is released propelling the rock laund arm forward to point
The catapult arm's forward progress is checked by the front buttress and momentum is transferred to the projectile
Trebuchet
Sling
spindle
main counterweight
At this point the two main spindles are tightened. to keep the lever arm in place
Upon release of the lock the tension from the main spindles are released and the counterweight drops, propelling the arm forward
At this point in the arms arc, the projectile is released from the sling and continues along the trebuchet arm's arc
The counterweight completes it's descent and the arm comes to rest as the project hurts on
CHINESE REPEATING CROSSBOW
magazine of bolts
lever arm for loading
To reload and fire the crossbow one would grab the lever arm push it forward until string caught then draw it back until position
where a small dowel within the magazine would dislodge the string and propel the new bolt forward
cutaway view of the bolt magazine
bolts were loaded, and the magazines generally held between 6-10 featherless bolts.

Chapter Eighteen

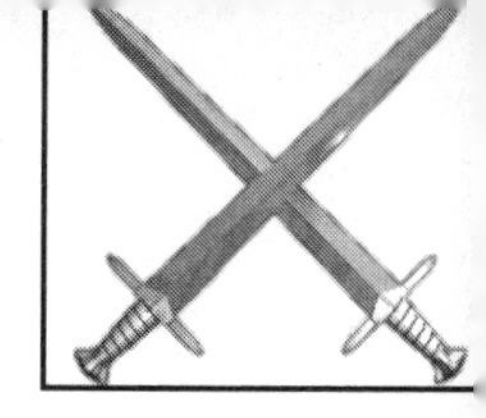

Multiplayer Empires

Playing games on the computer is great fun, and *Microsoft Age of Empires II: The Age of Kings* throws a sophisticated artificial intelligence at gamers that is hard to beat. But beat it you will—at least with the help of this book. No doubt, once you have mastered the motherboard, you will want tougher prey to feed on. That prey waits at the other end of your phone line or the far side of your LAN connection. Follow along as we explore how to bash your fellow man (or woman) in *Age of Empires II: The Age of Kings*.

Choose Your Connection

There are several ways to play multiplayer games in *Age of Empires II: The Age of Kings,* from direct connect null modem cables to Microsoft's own MSN Gaming Zone. Each has its strong and not-so-strong points.

Local Area Network

If you are part of a local area network (LAN) that includes other *Age of Empires II* gamers, you are in for a treat. LAN games are the best multiplayer games, hands down. These games are virtually lag free, easy to set up (you can walk over to your friend's desk and invite her to a game), and there's nothing better than savoring your victory over the office worker next door when you take down his or her civilization (as shown in Figure 18-1). Try that over an Internet connection to Germany.

On the downside, not everyone has access to a LAN, let alone a LAN with *Age of Empires II* installed. Hence finding a place to play can be a pain.

Serial Connection

The serial, or direct, connection is similar to a LAN. In this instance a cable —called a null modem cable—connects two computers' COM ports (the place where you normally plug in the printer or scanner). There is no lag, and you have the same type of proximity convenience common to LAN games. Unfortunately only two can play, and although the technology is simpler than that employed on a LAN, null modem connections are more rare.

Figure 18-1 *Victory is much sweeter when the vanquished is your friend.*

Modem Connection

With a modem connection, you dial your buddy's phone number, his modem answers, the two modems connect, and you're playing *Age of Empires II*. Lag is not as good (in other words, not as low) as a LAN or serial connection, but it is nonetheless better than Internet games.

Of course there may be a problem finding opponents. With a modem connection, you need to find someone in your own area code to compete against (unless you want to pay long distance charges).

Note: *So what is lag? Lag, or latency, is a measure of how quickly information travels from your computer across the connection (whatever the connection may be) to the other folks in the game. The latency is measured in milliseconds. If your latency is below 100 (which means 100 milliseconds) you're cooking with gas (well, actually electrons). If it's below 300, you can play; if it's above 300, you need to disconnect and try again.*

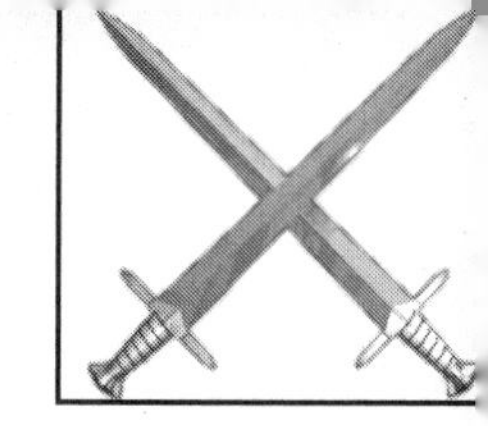

TCP/IP Internet and the MSN Gaming Zone

The Internet—and specifically Microsoft's MSN Gaming Zone—is where the action is. Playing *Age of Empires II* is free on the MSN Gaming Zone, and there are usually hundreds of wanna-be kings waiting to play. But there are still disadvantages. Certainly there are tons of opponents, waiting to play at just about every hour of the day, but occasionally the lag will be too slow for enjoyable games. Nevertheless, infrequent lag problems aside, the MSN Gaming Zone is a very good place to play *Age of Empires II: The Age of Kings*.

Choose Your Game

Multiplayer *Age of Empires II* is more than a bashfest; there are several different games to play. The game you choose often depends on your personal gaming preferences. Nevertheless, each game requires a closer look to understand the victory conditions and how to reach them.

Random Map

In reality this is a bit of a misnomer. The maps are usually not random, but rather chosen by the host—although she may select Random as the map type. There are four types of victory conditions for Random Map games: Standard, Conquest, Time Limit, and Score.

Standard Victory

You can win Standard victory games in one of three ways: conquer your opponents, build a Wonder, or control all the Relics. These can be very long or very short games. Games on a small map with many opponents will be short, brutal affairs as civilizations destroy each other—often before they have advanced beyond the Feudal Age. In contrast, two-player contests on large maps can last a couple of hours or longer.

Note: *To win you must explore, but human players are meaner than the computer. Be careful on your quests for geographical knowledge and stand ready to pull back your Scout Cavalry as soon as it discovers any trouble.*

> **Tip:** *Use your Militia to destroy your opponent's Town Center and your lone Scout Cavalry to hunt down his Villagers, as shown in Figure 18-2. The Scout Cavalry is quick enough to keep pace with the Villagers, constantly whacking them in the head.*

Aggressive strategies work best in games with one or two opponents. Immediately attacking your adversary with whatever Militia you can scrounge will frequently sink his ship.

If there are a lot of players, it's best to sit back. In these situations, you should strive to advance rapidly through the Ages and let the other gamers take each other out. Look for opportunities later in the game.

Figure 18-2 *Scout Cavalry are poison to Villagers.*

If your civilization is still unmolested, perhaps it would be best to build a Wonder. If the situation has become a one-on-one fight with another civilization, total conquest might be the best way to go.

> **Note:** *Don't forget the human element. Unless the teams are locked, you can try to bribe, cajole, or threaten whomever you want. You don't even need a Market to do so—although it would be nice to generate trade money with your rivals.*

> **Tip:** *Relic wins are tough, but they are most likely in the early Castle Age. Use your Light Cavalry and Cavalry Archers to find the Relics and conduct raids to thin out the Relic's defenders.*

Conquest Conquest strategies are often personality things. Aggressive folks tend to play aggressively, and those who don't have aggressive personalities tend to hang back a bit. Aggressive types should commit to producing no more than six Villagers, get them gathering and chopping, build a Barracks, and crank out as many Militia as you can. Send the Scout

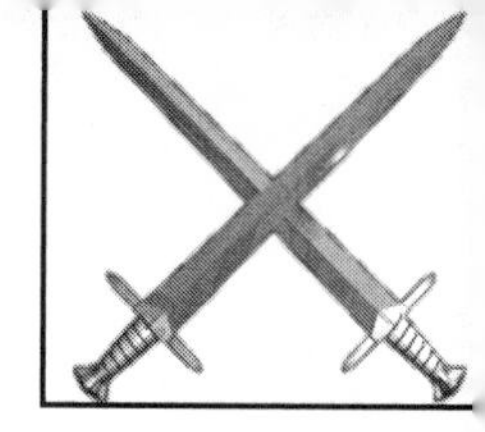

> **Tip:** *If the enemy fails to garrison a Villager in the Town Center, you can take down the Town Center itself. Remember, however, that even with one Villager inside of it, the Town Center can fire some serious arrows.*

Cavalry on a sweeping circle through the map. As soon as you locate the enemy, send the Militia in for the kill. Destroy production centers, such as the Mills and Lumber Camps, first. Continue to build Militia, setting their gather point near the enemy camp. This persistent—albeit weak—attack might often be enough to eliminate a civilization.

Conservative types should concentrate on building a strong economic base and defensive fortifications, and harassing the enemy with raids aimed at Villagers. Try to build strong defenses and then lure the enemy into them.

Wonder Grab a snack and a six-pack of soda if you're intent on building a Wonder; these games can take awhile. Economics is the name of the game here. You must reach the Imperial Age, build a Wonder (as shown in Figure 18-3), and defend it for 300 years.

Figure 18-3 *These Wonders are tough to build and tough to destroy.*

Obviously your emphasis must be on Villagers, their gathering process, and anything that enhances it. But don't forget your military. Raid the enemy camp frequently. Aim for the economic facilities, but keep in mind that the opponent hopes to inflict the same type of

> **Tip:** *Remember that these are humans you're playing against. Whereas the computer can be easily lured into a false attack, humans are not usually so naïve. More often than not, you'll have to bully your way into an opponent's base, take the Relic, and then retreat.*

setbacks upon you. You should also not fixate on the construction of a Wonder to the exclusion of all else. If you wipe out the bad guys, you still win. So don't forget to mix it up. Play one game straight up—striving to build and protect a Wonder—and then try to swamp the same opponent with Militia at the start of your next Wonder contest.

Relics Controlling the Relics is a unique way to win the game. It requires a combination of economic prowess, cunning, and military strategy. Unless you begin in the Castle Age you must flex your economic muscles in a race to reach that Age of Monasteries. Then once you arrive, you must concoct a strategy of military might and cunning that allows you to snatch each of your opponent's Relics and then hold on to them for 300 years.

Conquest Victory

The Conquest victory is just a subset of the Standard victory. The strategy for this type of victory is the same as that given in the "Conquest" section earlier in this chapter.

Time Limit Victory

Time Limit victories are a mixed breed. Stretch the time constraints and the game plays very much like a straight Standard Random Map game. In other words, you don't need to worry about the score. After all, if you wipe out a civilization it won't score any more points.

On the other hand, short matches are a Cavalry of a different color. The point in these is to build a healthy economy and prevent your neighbor from doing so. Build and advance as quickly as possible, explore the map, research technologies. All will contribute to an eventual victory. Send small raiding parties (as shown in Figure 18-4) into the enemy camp; disrupting the flow of raw goods can give you the lead in the economic race you are running.

Score Victory

Figure 18-4 *Even small parties of Militia can disrupt the enemy's economy.*

No doubt you can win these games with military might (if you attack quickly), but the occurrences will be rare. Yes, you receive as many points by eliminating an enemy's Mill as you receive by erecting your own, but it is so much less painful to build rather than to destroy. Unless you are attempting to eliminate the opposition, focus on economics and give the military a bit of the back seat.

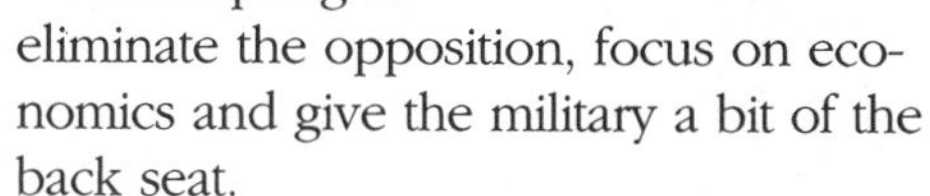

Tip: *Now this doesn't mean you should ignore your troops. As always, they can be very useful in disrupting the enemy economy. Using your troops in this manner provides two benefits: you receive points for every Villager or building destroyed, and every enemy Villager destroyed is one less resource-gatherer that the opponent can use to gather points.*

Regicide

If ever there was a multiplayer game that was ripe for diplomatic maneuvering, it is the Regicide game. You start with a Castle regardless of what Age the game begins in. It may take quite a while to amass an army capable of destroying the enemy Castle. So in the meantime, you can negotiate, hoping to trade an ally now for a better position in the end.

In addition, the King is not confined to the Castle. He may hide anywhere —either in the open or garrisoned in a building. Despite all the diplomacy, these contests eventually turn into bloodbaths as one civilization wades into another.

> **Tip:** *You don't need to resign yourself to a prolonged battle. Kings (as shown in Figure 18-5) have only 75 hit points and cannot attack. If your opponent fails to garrison his King, a quick Cavalry raid can often sanction the monarch.*

Death Match

Ah, this is a warrior's dream. You begin with plentiful resources in your coffers, and all you must do is build an army and attack your enemies. Make no mistake, you'll need to build and you'll need to gather resources, but the amount of resources you start out with will accelerate the game's pace.

Figure 18-5 *Kings stand no chance against Scout Cavalry.*

Send your Scout Cavalry out, build four houses, and then have the Villagers erect a Barracks and a Mill. Once they are complete, advance an Age while producing 10 Militia.

As soon as you find the enemy, strike his camp. Keep attacking, even as you build an Archery Range and a Stable. The key to a Death Match is to keep the pressure high. Death Matches may be resolved by Relics or Wonders, but they rarely are. This is a pure and simple Conquest game, and the best way to win is to get there first with the most and keep attacking until the enemy is defeated.

> **Note:** *Kings are fast—faster than most infantry. You can use that speed to lead infantry on a merry chase about your Castle while the Castle's arrows kill the enemy one by one.*

> **Tip:** *It's a good idea to create the Militia before you advance to the next Age. Upgrading them to Men-at-Arms is cheaper than buying 10 new Men-at-Arms.*

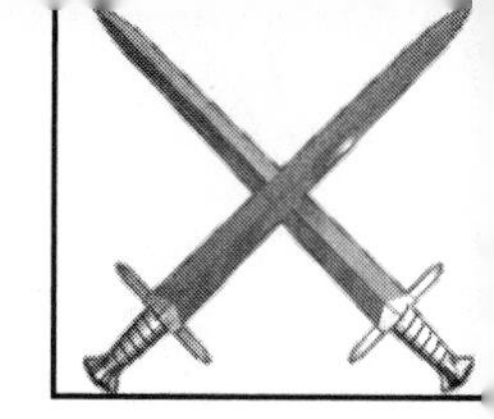

Note: *Death Matches are fast-paced games. Not only must you keep the pressure on the enemy camp, but you must also continue to research technologies and expand your own village. Nothing will stop a group of Dark Age Militia more quickly than a Castle Age special such as a Teutonic Knight. You can afford to lose neither the war in the field nor the war in the laboratory.*

The Final Game

Age of Empires II: The Age of Kings is an excellent multiplayer game. Nothing, however, is fun if you are losing. I hope this chapter will send you on your way to multiplayer wisdom and dump the thrill of victory in your lap.

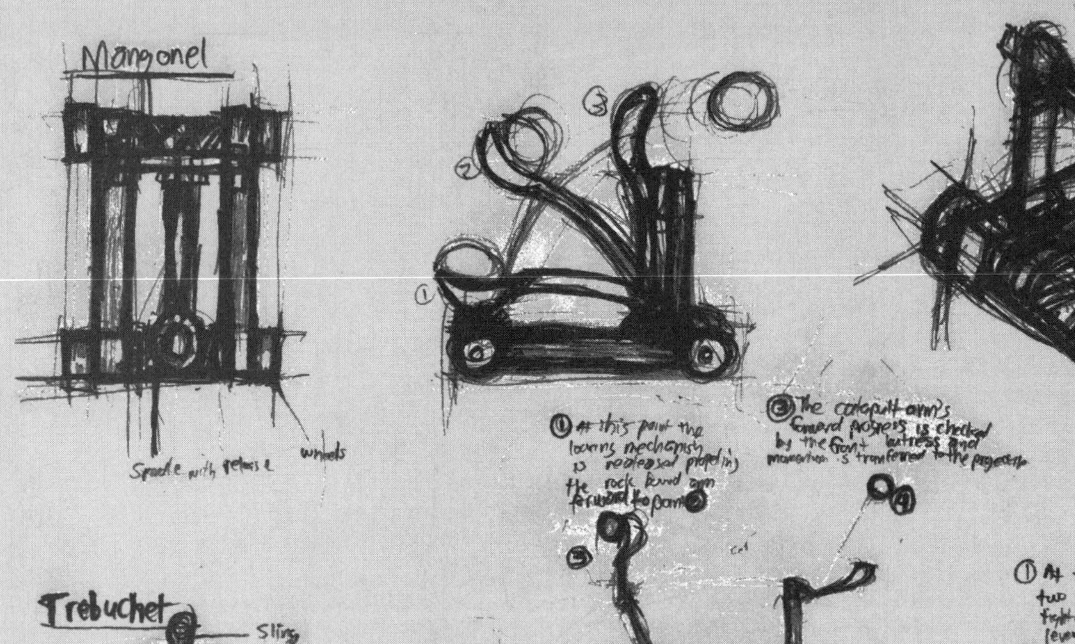

Trebuchet

sling
spindle
main counterweight

① At this point the two main spindles are tightened to keep the lever arm in place
② Upon release of the lock the tension from the main spindles are released and the counterweight drops, propelling the arm forward
③ At this point in the arms arc, the projectile is released from the sling and continues along the trebuchet arm's arc
④ The counterweight completes it's descent and the arm comes to rest as the projectile hurts on

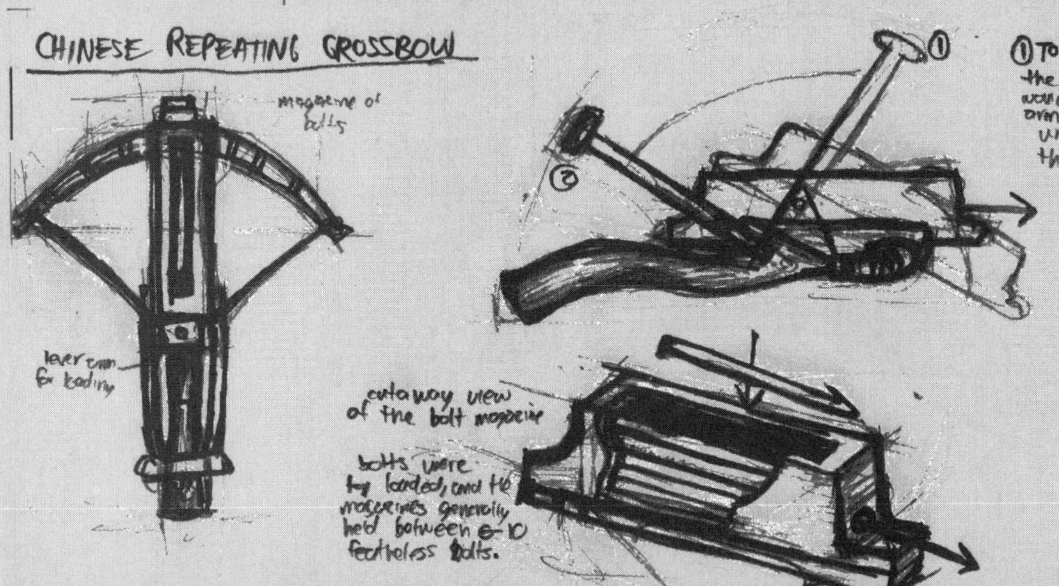

① To reload and fire the crossbow one would grab the lever arm push it forward until string caught then draw it back until position ② where a small dowel within the magazine would dislodge the string and propel the new bolt forward

Index

Italicized page references indicate figures or tables.

C

Mark H. Walker

Mark H. Walker is a former officer in the U.S. navy and a veteran electronic entertainment journalist. He is perhaps the most prolific writer in that industry and has authored or contributed to 20 books, including game user manuals, industry analysis texts, general computer books, and strategy guides. Additionally, he has written hundreds of computer–gaming related articles for magazines such as *Playboy, Alaska Airlines Magazine, Autoweek, Computer Games Strategy Plus* and for several Web sites, including the Science Fiction Channel, CNET's Gamecenter, and CMP's GamePower. He lives in rural Virginia where—when he isn't embroiled in his latest writing project—he races his Lola T-342 Formula Ford. Visit his Web site at *http://www.markhwalker.com* and read the "Random Rant"—Mark's series of editorials on the computer gaming industry.

The manuscript for this book was prepared and submitted to Microsoft Press in electronic form. Text files were prepared using Microsoft Word 2000. Pages were composed by Microsoft Press using Adobe PageMaker 6.52 for Windows, with text in Garamond and display type in Ultra Condensed Sans One and Helvetica Condensed Black. Composed pages were delivered to the printer as electronic prepress files.

Cover Graphic Designer

Tom Draper Design

Interior Graphic Artist

Rob Nance

Principal Compositor

Dan Latimer

Indexer

Bill Meyers